P9-DDX-334

# Serving
## with the
# Urban Poor

# Serving
# with the
# Urban Poor

Tetsunao Yamamori, Bryant L. Myers and Kenneth L. Luscombe,
editors

A division of World Vision
800 West Chestnut Avenue, Monrovia, California 91016-3198 USA

*Other books in this series:*
Serving with the Poor in Asia
Serving with the Poor in Africa
Serving with the Poor in Latin America

Serving with the Urban Poor
Tetsunao Yamamori, Bryant L. Myers and Kenneth L. Luscombe, editors

ISBN 1–887983–10–4

MARC books are published by World Vision, 800 West Chestnut Avenue, Monrovia, California 91016–3198, U.S.A.

Printed in the United States of America. Editor and typesetter: Joan Weber Laflamme. Cover design: Richard Sears. Cover photo: Sanjay Sojwal, World Vision.

# Contents

97275

## Part three
## Conclusion

## Appendices

# Editors and contributors

**Benigno P. Beltran** is parish priest of the Church of the Risen Christ, in the area known as Smokey Mountain. Smokey Mountain is the name of the garbage dump in Manila, Philippines, where 25,000 garbage scavengers have lived and labored. Fr. Beltran's work among the people of Smokey Mountain began in 1978, when he was a seminary student, and continues to this day. He is a member of the Society of the Divine Word Order (S.V.D.); has degrees from the University of Santo Tomas, Philippines, and Gregorian University, Rome; and is a recipient of several awards, including the Robert W. Pierce Award for Christian Service.

**Grace Roberts Dyrness** is associate director of the Center for Religion and Civic Culture at the University of Southern California, U.S.A. She holds a master's degree in urban anthropology from Ateneo de Manila University in Manila, Philippines.

**Franklin Joseph** was born in a small village in Tamil Nadu, India. After graduating from the university, he went to a theological college and earned his degree in 1977. After working at the theological college, he spent much of his time serving with the poor. He has been involved in community organizing through training and workshops in Madras and in eight other cities in India.

**Robert C. Linthicum** is executive director of Partners in Urban Transformation, a company involved in contributing to the empowering of the urban poor, the urban church and urban people's organizations. Dr. Linthicum served for 10 years as director of Urban Advance, World Vision International, and is the author of *City of God, City of Satan* and other books on the church's urban mission. He holds the D.Min. from San Francisco Theological Seminary, U.S.A.

**Kenneth L. Luscombe** is president and CEO of DGL International, a company involved in amplifying emerging voices through leadership development and urban transformational strategies. He was formerly director of Urban Advance, World Vision International, and has had many years of experience in urban mission throughout the world as a pastor, teacher and community organizer. An ordained

Baptist minister from Australia, Ken has studied theology in Melbourne, Zurich and San Francisco.

**Colin Marchant** is widely recognized as one of the leading senior figures in urban mission. Before his retirement from active ministry, Dr. Marchant served as a Baptist pastor and City Mission director in East Ham, U.K., for the better part of his working life. He has served as president of the Baptist Union of Great Britain and Ireland, teaches at Spurgeon's College in London, and is in demand as a speaker and writer. He is the author of several works, including the book *Signs in the City*. Dr. Marchant has the doctorate in sociology from London University.

**Toniel Marimba** was born in Zimbabwe. He is an ordained minister and affiliated with Apostolic Faith Mission in Zimbabwe. For 15 years he was general secretary of an indigenous organization caring for the aged. For the past seven years he has worked with World Vision's Urban Advance project in Zimbabwe.

**Donald E. Miller**, Ph.D., is professor of religion at the University of Southern California, U.S.A. He is also director of the Center for Religion and Civic Culture at the University of Southern California. Dr. Miller has written on topics ranging from genocide to homelessness. His latest book is *Reinventing American Protestantism: Christianity in the New Millennium* (University of California Press, 1997).

**Bryant L. Myers**, Ph.D., is vice president of ministry at World Vision International and executive director of MARC (Mission Advanced Research and Communication Center). Dr. Myers is the author of *The New Context of World Mission* and *The Changing Shape of World Mission*.

**Grant Power** was policy and planning director of West Angeles Community Development Corporation, a non-government organization developing low-income housing and neighborhood businesses in Los Angeles, U.S.A. The corporation is based in West Angeles Church of God in Christ, a large African-American congregation in South Los Angeles. Currently he is regional program director for DGL International.

**Nancy Power** is an agriculturist specializing in extension work and research on ecological methods of vegetable and fruit cultivation. She has a graduate degree in agricultural sciences from California State Polytechnic University, Pomona, with a concentration in environmentally sustainable and community-based vegetable production. She has several years' experience in farm management. She is a member of Servants Among the Poor and InnerChange, a Christian order among the poor.

**Jayne Scott** is director of the Community Learning Network, Baptist College, Manchester, England. As a Baptist minister and adult educationalist, she specializes in group processes, non-formal education and integrative learning. She holds a bachelor's degree in theology from Durham University and a master's degree in education from Manchester. She is currently researching for her doctorate in adult education through the University of Manchester.

**Dan and Kathleen Sheffield** are Canadians living in South Africa. They have two children. Dan Sheffield is an ordained minister in the Free Methodist Church. He has a bachelor's degree in biblical studies and is currently enrolled in an MRE program at McMaster Divinity College, Hamilton, Canada. He also serves as an adjunct lecturer at The Evangelical Bible Seminary of Southern Africa. Kathleen Sheffield is a registered nurse who has worked in cardiac care units for many years. She has been involved in the process of developing resources for women affected by domestic violence. She is currently studying for a bachelor's degree in social sciences at the University of Natal, Pietermaritzburg.

**Althea Spencer-Miller** is a minister of the Methodist Church in the Caribbean and the Americas. She is a senior program officer with the Caribbean Conference of Churches (CCC). The CCC is a regional ecumenical organization offering a multidimensional ministry in the Caribbean and through Caribbean churches. As a minister of religion, much of her work has been with inner-city congregations.

**Tetsunao Yamamori** is president of Food for the Hungry International and serves as adjunct professor of sociology at Arizona State University. Previously he was director and professor of intercultural studies at Biola University. Dr. Yamamori holds the doctorate degree from Duke University. He is the author, co-author and editor of fifteen books, including *Penetrating Missions' Final Frontier* (InterVarsity Press, 1993) and *Exploring Religious Meaning* (Prentice-Hall, 1994).

# Introduction

*Tetsunao Yamamori*

In 1994, in the lobby of a Washington, D.C., hotel, Howard Ahmanson, Steve Ferguson (senior program officer at Fieldstead Institute) and I met to discuss the possibility of a series of consultations on holistic ministry. Our intention was to gather empirical data on various models of development work that had led to the formation of Christ groups. These consultation proceedings resulted in the publication of the books listed below.

> *Serving with the Poor in Asia* (MARC, 1995)
> *Serving with the Poor in Africa* (MARC, 1996)
> *Serving with the Poor in Latin America* (MARC, 1997)
> *Servir Con Los Pobres En America Latina* (Ediciones Kairos, 1997)—
> Spanish companion volume of *Serving with the Poor in Latin America*
> (MARC, 1997)
> *Serving with the Urban Poor* (MARC, 1998)

These books have been put to good use by a variety of readers. Professors in Christian colleges and seminaries use them as textbooks. Mission executives and denominational leaders have read them and pondered on the validity of holistic ministry in their strategic thinking. Some readers have simply enjoyed learning about what God is doing on the mission frontier. Those of us involved in this project are thrilled to hear that our ministry colleagues across the world are finding these volumes valuable.

The books are the products of teamwork. There are many people to thank. There would have been no consultations or books had it not been for those case writers and reflectors who gathered in Chiang Mai, Thailand (1994), Harare, Zimbabwe (1995), Quito, Ecuador (1996), and Manila, Philippines (1998). Their contributions came out of ministry

1

experiences and reflective abilities. Food for the Hungry International, Opportunity International, MAP and World Vision Development Foundation took turns making local arrangements for these consultations. MARC, under the leadership of Jack Kenyon and Edna Valdez, has produced these books on schedule. At the very beginning I organized a steering committee to guide us in the consultation series. The members of this committee are Steve Ferguson (Fieldstead Institute), Fred Gregory (President, World Concern), Bryant Myers (Vice President, World Vision International), David Bussau (President, Opportunity International) and Don Stephens (President, Mercy Ships). Don and Diana Schmierer of Fieldstead Institute were present in our consultations, helping us where needed, and were always a source of encouragement to us.

For the Manila consultation Ken Luscombe (consultation coordinator and co-editor of this book), Lisa May, Jo Ann St. Don (both from Fieldstead Institute) and Marie Demafelis (World Vision Development Foundation of the Philippines) worked tirelessly for the smooth execution of the fourth and final consultation. To all these, and others not mentioned by name, I wish to express my heartfelt gratitude.

During our Manila meeting Roy Lawson, president of Hope International University in Fullerton, California, served as chaplain to the group and did a remarkable job of inspiring and challenging us. Unfortunately, we could not include his devotional messages in this book. However, Dr. Lawson's presentation on Hope's MBA/International Development is appended (see Appendix C). The academic study of holistic ministry-based international development is now available through the Internet. It is my desire that practitioners of holistic ministry living anywhere in the world can have access to this program and benefit from it.

## Design of the book

In January 1998 the Holistic Ministry Consultation on the Urban Poor was held in Manila for one week. The previous three consultations were regional in nature, while the fourth was global in scope. Indeed, the topic of urbanization spans the globe and consequently requires a wide-ranging treatment. How is the church to address the plight of the urban poor in a meaningful and productive way?

As before, we studied actual cases of holistic ministry, this time in their urban context, and reflectors have analyzed these cases from their various perspectives. Case-study writers followed guidelines provided by the consultation (see Appendix B). Reflectors were asked to spell out their understanding of *urban* as a framework and to apply it to their analyses of the case studies. In Manila we considered the question of holism as it is being reflected in three of the four "streams" represented in the matrix provided by the consultation: urban mission, urban ministry and urban development (see Table 1).

| Urban Mission | Urban Ministry | Urban Development | Urban Institutions |
|---|---|---|---|
| *Missiologically focused work in cities* | *Denominational & congregational focused work in cities* | *Relief and development work in cities* | *Special issue-based agencies and institutions* |
| City missions | City center churches | Project-based development work | Welfare agencies |
| Industrial missions | Working-class suburban churches | Sectored urban development work | Special-interest agencies |
| Denominational urban missions | Parish-based urban ministry | Community-based development | Training institutions |
| Faith missions and mission communities based in cities | Denominational and ecumenical urban ministry networks | Mission-based development work in cities | Research and technical-support institutions |
| Urban mission networks and movements | | Urban relief and developement agency networks | Special-interest networks and events |

*Table 1: Urban Matrix*

The urban matrix was designed to introduce conceptual clarity to a complex field of action and reflection in cities. The underlying assumption is that by identifying distinctive interests, issues, context, focus, characters, competencies and development history represented in each of the "streams," the holistic intent of integration can be better achieved. The common element is engagement with the urban poor as the focus of Christian commitment.

*Urban mission* has a distinctive history of special concern for people whose lives have been adversely affected by the processes of urban social, political and economic change stemming largely from the impact of the Industrial Revolution. What distinguishes this stream, whether in the institutional form of city missions or the mission focus of intentional Christian communities living among the urban poor, is our focus on victims in the modern city. In this volume, for example, Colin Marchant provides us with an overview of urban mission efforts in the United Kingdom.

*Urban ministry* describes the city church actively involved in the lives of the urban poor, the entire congregation bringing its distinctive gifts and competencies to the task of transforming the city and incorporating and nurturing its poor in the name of Christ. Dan and Kathleen Sheffield present the case of a mission church in the inner city of Pietermaritzburg in post-apartheid South Africa. Robert Linthicum examines a solidarity "cluster" model, with a new set of guiding metaphors for struggling urban congregations based on his experience in the Hollywood-Wilshire district in Los Angeles.

*Urban development* refers to the efforts of Christian relief and development agencies and mission organizations as they respond to the physical and spiritual needs of the urban poor. In this book we offer two examples of community organizing efforts that have successfully fostered the spirit of empowerment and self-determination in slum and squatter settlements in the developing world. Franklin Joseph traces the transformation of several urban slums in Madras, India, through the efforts of a team of community organizers known as Organizing People for Progress. Toniel Marimba shows us the new life of the former street people of Harare, Zimbabwe, made possible through the efforts of World Vision's Urban Advance.

Fr. Ben Beltran, the leader of the Smokey Mountain community, reveals a unique model that powerfully integrates the interests of the three streams identified thus far. It is the story of a marginalized people's deliverance from their threatened existence in a noxious garbage dump in Manila to become an organized, self-determining, "whole" community. This model commends itself as an example of holistic integration in urban work.

The fourth stream locates special-interest agencies and institutions that provide the training and special skills needed to guide and sustain the efforts of change agents in the city. Although this stream is not discussed in the case studies, the reflectors chosen for this consultation bring competence, knowledge and experience to bear in lifting up the themes embodied in them. Don Miller investigates the process of modernization and the implications of societal change from rural to urban, noting population movement, value shifts and the emergence of an individual work ethic from the traditional one. He further delineates the role of the church as a mediating and catalytic agent for social change. Grace Dyrness addresses the issue of gender and the voice of women in urban mission. Jayne Scott, from the Community Learning Network in Manchester, England, raises the need for integral learning in all processes of urban action and reflection, including the consultation process itself. Grant and Nancy Power highlight the issue of integrity and coherence in institutional efforts to address the need for economic transformation in the interests of the victims of economic poverty. Althea Spencer-Miller, a Methodist minister and theologian, picks up the role of storytelling as a tool of transformation with special reference to the case studies. Ben Beltran reflects on the theological ramifications of the process of urbanization and its resultant paradigm shift from a static to a dynamic society. He then makes an observation of the cases from this dynamic-theological viewpoint.

Finally, Ken Luscombe provides an integration of themes and issues that emerged in the consultation process and offers some reflections on the way ahead.

## Focus on the urban poor

Interest in urban work has emerged only in recent years. Roger Greenway, founding editor of *Urban Mission*, reminisced about when he was trying to get his magazine underway in 1983. "Urban challenges were so unpopular," says Greenway, "that a friend of mine, editor of a leading Christian magazine, advised me against using the word *Urban* in the title."[1] Like it or not, we cannot ignore the magnitude of the impact of urbanization on the church and its mission. What is urbanization anyway? While the rural population remains stable, the urban population is growing at a staggering rate. The overwhelming percentage of these urbanites is unreached for Christ. And what do we see in the cities of the world? We see poverty and the inhumane conditions to which the urban poor are subjected. We see ethnic and cultural diversity. Doing ministry in the city requires an understanding of ethnicity and its interactive dynamics. The church has been slow to awaken to the complexity of these challenges—but that it is indeed awakening is the good news of this volume.

### Urbanization and population growth

Urbanization is the process of people congregating in cities that are essentially nonagricultural. Urban environments create a unique kind of social life called urbanism. How do we describe urbanism? How does social life in cities differ from social life in villages? Social life in cities espouses secondary group relations, anonymity, and a set of relationships with participants presenting only one specialized part of their social personalities (roles) to each other. Here the individual is free to choose, while in villages the individual is swallowed up in group life where the communal principle dominates social relationships and individual choice is stifled.

Urbanization implies a massive movement of people from rural areas to cities. Paul Hiebert describes the rapid rates of urbanization and population growth that have been occurring in the past two centuries.

> In 1800 about 97 percent of the world's population lived on farms or in villages with populations of less than five thousand. By the end of this century, more than 55 percent will live in larger towns and cities. In 1800 only one city, London, had more than one million people. By 1972 there were over a hundred cities with a population larger than that, thirteen larger than five million, and four larger than ten million.[2]

The projection for mega-cities continues:

> In 1950, only two cities, London and New York, were over ten million. As of 1980, ten cities had reached that size. By the end of this century, if the Lord tarries, there will be twenty-five cities like that—and five cities over twenty million.[3]

6

Alan Gilbert and Josef Gugler specify where such urbanization is taking place:

> The twentieth century may come to be seen as the age of urbanization. Urban settlements were first established more than five thousand years ago, but as recently as 1900 only one in eight people lived in urban areas. Before the end of this century half of the world's population will be urbanites, and of these three billion people two-thirds will live in the Third World.[4]

Urbanization is extensive and population growth is skyrocketing. This is the context of urban mission and ministry that our discussion on holistic ministry considered.

## Urban poverty

For a quick look at the size of the urban poor, let us turn to Bryant Myers, who says:

> By 2025, more than one-quarter of the world's population will be poor and living in the squatter settlements of the Two-Thirds World.
>
> There are over 1.3 billion urban poor, of which 520 million are slum dwellers; their numbers increase by 70 million a year.
>
> There are more than 100 million street children in today's world class cities—25% of whom both work and sleep in the streets.[5]

Poverty in the urban sector of the world will continue to grow. This fact alone should challenge the church to become creative, in new ways of reaching the urban poor. Case studies, such as the ones in this book, should trigger insights toward helping people overcome obstacles and progress beyond meeting basic needs, while attempting to make Christ known to them.

## Ethnic and cultural diversity

As a city grows, there will be an increased number of people of various ethnic and cultural backgrounds. The city will become a magnet for drawing people from surrounding rural neighborhoods as well as commercial and professional persons from other cities and immigrants from other countries. Within many of the world's cities there exist large ethnic and linguistic enclaves. People are naturally drawn to people of their own kind. People with high intensity ethnic consciousness are least likely to assimilate into a dominant cultural group and are likely to join their own ethnic churches.

In our urban strategy we must affirm the ideal of oneness in Christ, whereby people of various ethnic and cultural backgrounds can worship together by prioritizing their identity in Christ over their ethnic and cultural heritage. People with low intensity ethnic consciousness are likely to join multiethnic, assimilationist churches. Others on the opposite end of the scale of consciousness may prefer monoethnic churches or multiethnic mutually autonomous churches. The latter is the model of autonomous ethnic churches cohabiting a single church building, such as Immanuel Presbyterian Church in Linthicum's chapter. Or, people with a strong ethnic consciousness may choose to join one of Linthicum's "cluster churches," which are essentially monoethnic. The goal of urban ministries is to help people learn to identify themselves with the Christ who tears down the dividing wall of hostility among various ethnic groups. The gospel dictates that all believers, regardless of their backgrounds, reconcile themselves with others so that their unity becomes a testimony to those yet to come to faith and obedience in Christ.

**Guidelines for an urban strategy**

In developing an urban strategy, we must consider doing the following:
1. Identify the mosaic of people and their needs within the ministry area.
2. Focus on a ministry niche.
3. Embrace the holistic ministry approach, always demonstrating love of people and love of Christ.
4. Recruit staff with the conviction that salvation is possible only in Christ.
5. Develop a cadre of dynamic witnessing associates who would communicate a fervent faith in Christ.

6. Incorporate planting of a church as a part of the total urban strategy.
7. Place a high premium on prayer.

The chapters that follow will introduce you to the people of an urban world that is rich in diversity and full of God-given potential, one which is at the same time steeped in the realities of poverty, disease, crime, drugs and other social ills. More than any other place on earth, God's presence is desperately needed in the city. The irrevocable mandate given to the church today is to occupy the city by helping the urban poor help themselves, and thus reconciling them to Christ, the Healer.

In closing, and as we complete the current series of consultations and book publishing, I would like to recognize Howard and Roberta Ahmanson for their belief in the importance of holistic ministry, so much so that they personally invested their resources to enable the project. Because of their encouragement and support, we have been able to raise the interest of many around the world to the effective implementation of holistic ministry.

---

## NOTES

[1] Roger S. Greenway, "Introduction," in *Planning and Growing Urban Churches*, ed. Harvie M. Conn (Grand Rapids, Mich.: Baker Books, 1997), p. 17.

[2] Paul Hiebert, *Anthropological Insights for Missionaries* (Grand Rapids, Mich.: Baker Book House, 1985), p. 289.

[3] Harvie M. Conn, "Urban Mission," in *Toward the 21st Century in Christian Mission*, ed. James M. Phillips and Robert T. Coote (Grand Rapids, Mich.: Wm. B. Erdmans Publishing Co., 1993), p. 321.

[4] Alan Gilbert and Josef Gugler, *Cities, Poverty and Development: Urbanization in the Third World* (New York: Oxford University Press, 1992), p. v.

[5] Bryant Myers, *The Changing Shape of World Mission* (Monrovia, Calif.: MARC, 1993), p. 42.

# Part one

# Case Studies

# 1

# Take a walk

## Urban mission in the United Kingdom

*Colin Marchant*

Come to London. Join the tourists. Look at Big Ben and Tower Bridge, walk into Trafalgar Square and visit Buckingham Palace. Find your way to St. Paul's Cathedral and then walk into the City of London, the financial center crowded with banks and brokers.

Don't stop there. Walk on to another London—dense housing, industries, busy roads, changing conditions. This is East London, once the heartland of the English working class, now the swirling, cosmopolitan haven of waves of immigrants and settling ethnic groups.

Head a little north to Wesley's Chapel. It stands back from the road, silently marking the place where John Wesley was converted in 1738. Here Methodism began. Inside, a great central pulpit dominates the church. The Foundry Chapel is now a prayer room.

Across the road is Bunhill Fields with its rows of tombstones. This is the nonconformist cemetery, pitched outside the old city walls, and filled with the famous dissenting Protestants—John Bunyan and Isaac Watts, William Blake and Daniel Defoe. Now fenced in. A leafy retreat. A useful cut-through path. History interred.

Nearby is the London City YMCA. The first YMCA grew out of a prayer meeting and Bible study led by George Williams. Its primary objective was to win young men and boys for Jesus Christ through the agencies of care and provision. Now setting out "to be a caring Christian-based asset in the community," housing, community program, restaurant and chaplaincy cluster together. Other agencies including the Shaftesbury Society and Dr. Barnados, which also sprang up in London to meet the needs of the urban poor of the nineteenth century.

Walk on to Aldgate East. Stop off at Toynbee Hall. The very first settlement began here. Tucked away from the main road, a courtyard surrounded by halls and housing today continues as home to the work begun by an Anglican vicar in 1884. Here university students came to learn—and to serve. The names of Atlee and Beveridge remind you that the first Labour prime minister and the architect of the welfare state both served here.

Just around the corner, along the Commercial Road, stands a small statue of William Booth, founder of the Salvation Army. Here began, in 1865, an international Christian organization for evangelistic and social work. But no bands march this road now. Only a hostel for the homeless stands to remind. And opposite that is the largest mosque in East London, claiming 10,000 members.

You've walked through history. Mission history. The beginning of the urban mission story.

It's a stirring, salutary—and sometimes sad—walk. The city has moved on. Needs have changed. Other faiths compete. The secular process erodes faith and removes control from Christians.

But much began here and spread across the world. Early efforts in evangelism and struggles to "earth" the gospel; the call to whole mission and the emergence of political concern; recognition of cultural divides and the missionary failure. All are here.

So is the world. Now black churches and Asian fellowships witness alongside the projects and programs of traditional denominations. A reverse missionary flow has occurred.

## Urban Mission UK

### In the beginning

The Industrial Revolution began in the U.K. as industries developed, road and rail communications expanded and cities grew with the in-rush of workers from rural areas.

Traditional carriers of Christian faith since the Reformation were either left behind or proved too inflexible to carry the task of mission in a rapidly changing society.

In 1851, for the first and last time, questions about religious worship in the U.K. were asked alongside the national census. That census came to two significant and clearly linked conclusions:

> ❖ More than half the U.K. population was now urban—the first time ever in the history of any large nation.
>
> ❖ The working class did not attend church.

## The response

Churches' and Christians' two great waves of response to this situation make up the story(ies) of urban mission in the U.K.

The first wave began in the 1820s and peaked in the 1890s—as city missions, agencies, armies, settlements and central missions emerged as urban models of mission alongside the movements of Christian Socialism and the Catholic Orders. The second wave developed in our lifetime, in the aftermath of two world wars.

Models or movements of the first wave shared certain characteristics:

> ❖ Most spread across the world to become parts of urban mission strategy, often replicated in large cities.
>
> ❖ All struggled with the balance of holistic mission, moving between evangelism and social action, but rarely touching political justice.
>
> ❖ The Western cultural imprint is on them all. Produced in a specific context, first-wave missions were exported along the lines of commerce, language and power.
>
> ❖ Many are still in use, often adapted.

### CITY MISSIONS

City missions have a Scottish ancestry. Thomas Chalmers of Edinburgh engaged in city mission work, and David Nasmith began the city mission in Glasgow in 1826. He established city missions in Dublin and the U.S.A. before starting the London City Mission in 1835. Nasmith is credited with founding 36 missions in the U.S.A. and Canada and 50 or more in the U.K.

City missions recognized that millions of people were out of touch with the historic churches, and that the worship and evangelism of traditional churches were alien to the majority of urban people. Across the U.K. evangelicals formed a citywide voluntary society, raised money and employed agents to "visit the inhabitants of the district assigned, bring them to the knowledge of Salvation through faith in our Lord Jesus Christ and do them good by all means in your power."

Characteristics of mission-work were person to person, lay-centered, patch-working, people groups, hands on and practical. Individuals were targeted in their setting. Agents were drawn from the working classes, were not ordained. Intensive concentration on small "patches" (door to door visiting) replaced the overwhelmed parochial system. Specialized ministries to transport workers, prisoners, markets and prostitutes focused on people groups. And the combination of "living on the job," opening soup kitchens and day centers brought a down-to-earth practicality to the programs.

Motivations were mixed. Biblical mandates of reaching the unreached, compassion for the needy and affirming the worth and value of every individual were tangled with middle-class self-interest (keeping vice, crime and disease at bay and revolution underground) and anti-Catholic sentiments.

The significance of city missions included acknowledgment that large areas of the U.K. were now a mission field (statistically and morally); recognition that cooperation between different denominations was both essential and possible; and the realization that new models of mission were required to supplement (or supersede) traditional churches and chapels.

City missions have kept going. Twelve of the missions founded in the nineteenth century go on, together with four more started in the twentieth century. The largest is the London City Mission, which in 1870 had 500 agents or missionaries and in 1997 had 150 evangelists working with 21 people groups, and many mission halls.

The strengths of personal faith, scriptural basis, direct evangelism and focused targets are tempered by failure to move beyond "personal" or "ambulance" strategies to communal and justice concerns.

## AGENCIES

Voluntary societies have long been a feature of British life. Many drew together the well-to-do and responded to social need. During the eighteenth century they were concerned with education of the poor (through charity schools and Sunday schools) and with opening hospitals and dispensaries for care of the sick.

From 1800 to 1851 other Christian agencies emerged to respond to the developing urban situation. Some sprang directly from churches and worked closely with them. Others started with a cluster of concerned individuals and became autonomous, but often with specific Christian constitutions and charters. Some were transplanted from other nations. This incredibly diverse and dynamic flood of agencies acted on behalf of, represented or coordinated Christian mission in the towns and cities.

Many agencies were evangelical in basis, ethos and action. From 1851 to 1900 three-quarters of voluntary charitable organizations in the U.K. were evangelical in character and control. Many leaders and workers had been influenced by the Moody and Sankey Revival Meetings. (A similar pattern was to follow the Billy Graham Crusades in the mid-twentieth century.)

Growing awareness of urban social problems and a deepening sense of guilt at inequality and conditions of urban living grew alongside resources as national financial wealth increased and Christians recognized that traditional church programs were inadequate.

Two theological notes dominated—compassion and justice, buttressed by the often quoted parables of the Good Samaritan (Luke 10:25–37) and the Final Judgment (Matt. 25:31–46). Social justice lay behind the emergence of the cooperative movement and progressive social work and found political expression in the Christian Socialist Movement.

Many of the agencies have continued their work in the cities of the U.K., often changing their targets or merging with others but keeping to their constitutional roots and theological ethos. They are an integral part of urban mission, and agencies like the YMCA and YWCA have spread across the world.

They face the double challenge of being authentic and appropriate:
* Remaining true to the original, faith-rooted motivations and mandate; and
* Staying in touch with contemporary realities.

## THE SALVATION ARMY

The Salvation Army (1865), followed 17 years later by its Anglican echo, the Church Army, brought fresh, disciplined response to both evangelism and social care in the urban situation.

17

William Booth's conversion in 1844 and his belief in personal evangelism led him out of established Methodist congregations to become an undenominational preacher, increasingly aware that "we can't get at the masses in the chapels." He put up a tent in Whitechapel, East London, in 1865 and launched the "Christian Mission to the Heathen of Our Own Country," which became the Salvation Army.

Uniformed, with military-style discipline and brass bands in the streets, the Salvation Army became an evangelistic agency, a religious community and, later, a network of social ministry. For the first time, women and men enjoyed equal status as officers.

Lively hymns, vivid advertising, face-to-face evangelism, open-air meetings and the publication *War Cry* carried the gospel in direct and contemporary ways—"they were the only group of Christian evangelists of their time who approached working-class non-worshipers at their own cultural level," it was said.

Motivated by the doctrines of the evangelical revival and with a global mandate from General Booth, the Salvation Army was seen by many as a judgment on the churches for their failure to evangelize and their refusal to face the needs of urban dwellers.

By 1883 the Salvation Army had spread to Sweden, France, Switzerland and Germany in Europe; the U.S.A. and Canada; and South Africa, Australia and India.

A significant change of direction took place in 1890 through the publication of *In Darkest England and the Way Out*, described by Booth as a scheme of social salvation. It described England's dire social problems and outlined some remedies. This led to a range of social action initiatives (hostels for the homeless, agricultural colonies), which in turn polarized the Army's work between evangelism by local corps based in citadels and the developing social program centered in hostels.

This division has persisted, and contemporary Salvation Army work in the U.K. is characterized by a number of features:

- ❖ Decline in numbers, from 72,277 in 1980 to 57,124 in 1995.
- ❖ Continuation of evangelistic/social polarity.
- ❖ Disappearance or weakness in the inner cities, linked with suburbanization.
- ❖ Institutionalization of charisma.

## THE CHURCH ARMY

Wilson Carlile, a businessman changed by the Moody and Sankey missions, tried to take direct evangelism into the parish system of the Church of England, but moved instead into "slum mission" and launched the Church Army in 1882.

Parallels with the Salvation Army are clear—the initial vision and zeal of one man, use of uniforms and division of work under "spreading the gospel" and "social work." The difference is that the organization remained loyal in doctrine and discipline to the Church of England, working for conversion, consecration and churchmanship.

By 1900 the Church Army had 65 vans staffed by traveling evangelists, and more than 600 evangelists and nurses worked alongside parish clergy. Nearly 60 labor and lodging houses were erected in large towns.

Today 600 Church Army missionaries in the U.K. work at "evangelism through proclamation and social action."

Although respected (particularly for their social work), both Armies are in numerical decline and have a dated image.

## SETTLEMENTS

The Settlement Movement sprang from the public schools and universities of England. A group of university graduates "settled" in the inner cities to understand and to serve the surrounding community. The first was Toynbee Hall in Whitechapel, East London (very near the origins of the Salvation Army), with an Anglican clergyman, Samuel Barnett, as leader. The movement then spread from the U.K. into Europe, the U.S.A. and the then-British Empire.

By 1913, 45 settlements existed in the U.K.—27 in London. Of these, 18 were directly associated with a university, while others had university men and women working in them. Nonconformists and Roman Catholics added their own settlements in the predominantly Anglican network. But it was already noted that only 32 of the 45 settlements were religious (a trend becoming common to much urban mission work).

Centered in buildings, led by clergymen and staffed by university graduates, the settlements attracted financial resources and initiated an extensive program of social activities. Offering premises, funding and committed leadership, they drew in great crowds of people with a particular British ethos as members of educated classes came to work among the working classes.

A settlement was a bridge of goodwill between classes, built on religious foundations. But different theologies coexisted in the settlement movement: "A mission exists to proselytize. A settlement does not" (Toynbee Hall). "The outcome of the work should be the true acceptance of the fundamental doctrine of the incarnation, by which God and man are brought together. . . . A settlement should bear a Christian character and utter a Christian witness" (Oxford House).

The history of settlements in the U.K. has been that of a slow movement from religious foundation to secular social action. The British Association of Settlements and Social Action Centres is now a national association of multipurpose centers committed to helping local communities bring about social change. It is now an urban community network.

## CENTRAL MISSIONS

Congregations of Christians were to be found in every district in the U.K. before the Industrial Revolution. The Anglican or Church of Scotland parish system ensured that all areas were covered. The Nonconformist "gathered community" drew believers together from the wider community. Monastic orders and priests of the Roman Catholic Church served and centered Catholic congregations.

As the Industrial Revolution and increasing urbanization spread across the U.K., population shifts and growth followed. Great cities grew rapidly as huge working-class centers built up. All over the U.K., swathes of industrial-urban development followed the steel, coal and manufacturing industries. Established congregational systems broke down under the weight of population shifts and the inadequacy of buildings or ministry. A cultural divide began to emerge between middle-class church attenders and working-class absentees. Much of church life seemed distant or irrelevant to people struggling with new lifestyles often marked by poverty, unemployment and powerlessness. Churches responded by extending their schools (especially the Roman Catholics and Anglicans), using their premises for caring ministries, initiating agencies to meet social needs or backing evangelistic missions and crusades. All urban congregations and their ministers faced the pressures of change, and many struggled to "make the Word flesh" in new situations. The pastoral concept of church still persisted in the face of the demands of evangelism and community care. Maintenance often took precedence over mission. But some denominations and many churches began to engage realistically and creatively in urban mission.

Methodism contributed central missions. In 1885 the Wesleyan Conference broke free from some limiting and constraining consequences of the circuit and itinerary by allowing exemption for densely populated areas in London—and later in other large towns. The conference authorized central missions—described at the time as "probably the most significant and important event in the modern history of Methodism."

Central missions soon spread across the country. The London Mission was said to have recruited 7,000 new members by 1898, and was attended by 20,000 other people. By 1900 the Manchester Mission had more than 14,000 people in its 62 branches—mostly of the non-church-going class.

Central missions moved away from the traditional congregational styles of worship and evangelism to "Pleasant Evenings for the People," combining entertainment, education and evangelism. A program of social activities was intended to keep working-class people out of mischief, to civilize them and to coax them toward worship.

Methodism had moved a long way from the itinerant, open-air preaching of the Wesleys to a building-centered, program-based strategy. The institutional church in the cities replaced the circuit system and the class-meeting, which had been foundation stones of British Methodism.

Today the population shift from the inner cities of the U.K. has left Methodism with a massive problem with city-center churches. Many have been sold or adapted. Others are now community centers with a "rump" congregation.

## FIRST WAVE FEATURES

The initial urban mission models—city missions, agencies, armies, settlements and central missions—included a number of common features.

❖ The growth pattern from individual vision (Booth or Barnett) to localization (in place) and development (national and international).

❖ The process (especially in the Salvation Army) of moving from "charisma" to organization. This led to the banking and controlling of initial evangelical flow and vitality, to bureaucracy and suburbanization, and to loss of flexibility, initiative and spirituality.

❖ The struggle with holistic mission: holding tenaciously to "face-to-face evangelism" only (city mission), or moving rapidly to social concern and eliminating evangelism (settlements); polarizing evangelism and social action (Salvation Army), or failing to face political and justice realities behind much work among the poor (agencies).

❖ The cultural/class context, still unresolved in the U.K., exported from Western civilization (Europe and North America) to other parts of the world.

These features—and underlying theologies—were carried from the nineteenth century into the twentieth century through the models, through 50 oddly quiescent years, until two world wars brought upheaval and uncertainty and led to a second wave of U.K. urban mission.

## The Second Wave

In the early days of the Industrial Revolution, Christian organizations came into being to evangelize and look after the spiritual welfare of working people. The Navy Mission Society was set up in 1877 with working-class missionaries working in their own localities. This society amalgamated with the Christian Social Union to form the Industrial Christian Fellowship in 1919. City missions employed lay missioners to visit industrial sites, such as railways and gasworks.

During World War II, the Ministry of Munitions appointed "industrial chaplains" to their factories as a parallel to service chaplains. By the end of the war, industrial mission was an integral part of the church's work and witness in the world of mass production. A fresh wave of industrial mission emerged from earlier efforts, and for 30 years energy and commitment characterized the high-profile movement.

The William Temple College was an influential resource—breaking away from the traditional theological college pattern and encouraging a wide spectrum of individuals to understand and respond in mission to the industrial world. This influence recognized the modern separation of life from faith and the gulf between manual workers and the church. The Industrial Mission Association was set up in the late sixties and followed rapid growth in the work of industrial mission and the setting up of new teams in most Anglican dioceses. And although Anglicans led the way, much of industrial mission was ecumenical.

The style and action of modern industrial mission was initially pastoral and factory-based, adapting methods of its Victorian ancestors— regular factory visiting; talking with workers during work breaks, in groups; evolving projects growing from shop-floor contacts; and educating and training in courses. But recognition that the personal, moral and faith concerns of individuals were inextricably linked to the way that industry and society was organized, economically, socially and politically, led industrial mission into other fields. The move from the pastoral model (which other Christians saw as an extension of parish or congregational ministry) into that of industrial relations (requiring both professional expertise and different skills) led industrial mission away from the life of congregations and denominations.

Rising unemployment in the 1970s and 1980s gave industrial missioners the opportunity to share in the training and work experience of a new generation. As urban churches sponsored Manpower Service Commission schemes they built bridges with industrial chaplains. Increasing concern with local economies and the setting up of local economic forums brought together industrialists, church representatives, industrial mission and other groups to explore issues that affected the life and values of the area.

Current thinking about industrial mission strategy and technique concentrates on a lay-led movement (resourced by full-time industrial chaplains).

The story of industrial mission is threefold, passing through three generations.

I. 1940s–1960s: Sociological notion of the gap between church and world leads to factory-based chaplaincy.

II. 1960s–1970s: Theological stress leads to "doing theology," especially around the kingdom of God.

III. 1980s–1990s: Issue-centered concern leads to "prophetic ministry."

## Strengths of industrial mission

- ❖ Going where people were
- ❖ Being available
- ❖ Entering into stress-points at both personal and social levels
- ❖ Recognizing the gulf between industrial workers and the church—
  sociological notion of the gap
- ❖ Emphasizing the kingdom of God—the church as the instrument,
  with all of life to be under God's sovereignty
- ❖ Focusing concern on a new order of society rather than on a recall
  to churchgoing
- ❖ Reminding believers that God is at work everywhere
- ❖ Stressing "structural sin"
- ❖ Encouraging primary loyalty to the kingdom, not the church as an
  institution

## Weaknesses of industrial mission

- ❖ Failing to persuade local congregations, whose parishioners all too
  often did not really want to hear
- ❖ Allowing dependence on funding by Christian denominations with
  growing financial problems
- ❖ Becoming a separate, often judgmental, wing of Christian mission
- ❖ Allowing clericalism—takeover by the ordained, lack of lay in-
  volvement
- ❖ Accepting conformity to outdated patterns
- ❖ Not stressing personal sin
- ❖ Disappearing almost without trace

But industrial mission had picked up and emphasized key theologies that included creation, all "in the image of God," incarnation at all
levels and the kingdom of God (everywhere). Fundamental issues such
as the sacred/secular divide, and the wholeness of life and the individual were addressed.

The contraction and even disappearance of industrial mission in
the U.K. (matched across the Western world) has its own message—
both to the wider church and to urban mission practitioners. The

changes involve much more than that from "heavy" to "new-style technology."

## Networks

Since the 1960s, networks have been a central feature in urban mission. Drawing together individuals and groups, reflecting concerns and emphases, sharing information and insights while anchored firmly in urban centers, urban mission networks have become an enabling and encouraging component of mission. Networks link agencies and denominations, issues and theologies, areas and nations, individuals and ethnic groups. They match urban complexity and change at many levels—even in their emergence and disappearance. Key personalities appear as connecting nodules in many networks.

Training networks began developing in the Methodist-based Urban Theology Unit in Sheffield under the leadership of John Vincent in 1969. Concerned with new forms of urban mission and ministry, the Urban Theology Unit pioneered new styles of work, lay-training and radical theology. The "Seminary of the Street" and "Community of Study" moved forward alongside liberation theology and personal vocation and formation.

The Evangelical Urban Training Programme (1974) emerged as a counterpoint targeting working-class Christians and equipping them for mission in urban areas. International groups such as Youth With A Mission and Youth for Christ now share in training for urban mission.

Issue-centered networks range from Church Action on Poverty (1982) to the Churches National Housing Coalition (1994). They include the Frontier Youth Trust (1964), the Industrial Mission Association and the Churches Community Work Alliance (1990).

Two of the strongest and most widely known networks in the U.K. are denominational. The Methodist "Mission Alongside the Poor" and the Anglican "Faith in the City," which led to the Church Urban Foundation.

Denominational networks ran parallel to a group of national networks. The long-established Iona Community (1938) in Scotland sought new ways to live the gospel in today's urban world. The National Association of Christian Centres and Networks (1981) drew together a variety of intentional and dispersed communities in the U.K., while Corrymeela in Northern Ireland (1965) worked to break down barriers and build bridges between individuals and groups. The Evangelical Coalition for Urban Mission (1980) is a partnership of networks furthering the evangelical thrust in urban mission. The Ecumenical Urban Forum is a biannual meeting of denominations, agencies and groups concerned with urban mission in England and includes black-led churches, Roman Catholics and all the major networks.

A significant wave of black and Asian networks began developing in the 1970s. The African-Caribbean Evangelical Alliance (1984), Asian Christian Fellowship (1973), Afro-West Indian United Council of Churches (1976), South Asia Concern (1989), Centre for Black and White Christian Partnership (1978) and Evangelical Christians for Racial Justice (1972) were networks that reflected both the growing strength of ethnic minority urban churches and the realities of racism in the U.K.

In the 1990s political networks were represented by the renaissance of the Christian Socialist Movement (which grew rapidly in the years before the 1997 election and included Prime Minister Tony Blair) and by the Inner Cities Religious Council (a multi-faith body bringing government and faith communities together to look at inner-city issues).

In 1995 representatives from all these networks shared in the first U.K. Urban Congress, in Liverpool.


### Projects and community developments

The field of urban mission in the U.K. is now studded with projects. In church buildings, rented halls, community centers and shop fronts, there are hundreds of church-based or church-sponsored groups working away at an incredible variety of tasks. Within all the projects the underlying concern is that of the community and its development. Belief that communities are disintegrating, threadbare or failing has led to wider social concern expressed in community action, community care, community organizing and community work(ers).

Churches have been particularly concerned with the gap between themselves and their districts, the irrelevance of many church programs, usage of their premises and the unmet needs of individuals and groups around them. Beneath these pragmatic concerns pulse the theologies of service, incarnation, enabling and empowering—alongside uncertainty about "strings attached," loss of church control, the place of evangelism and the relationship between the "new community" of the church and the wider community.

26

The thrust of these projects is toward families and children; housing and homelessness; young adults; (un)employment; community care and self-help; new lives; community and race relations; and church growth and renewal.

"Control principles" for these projects include doing things with, rather than for; value and skills of every individual; partnership at all levels; "earthing" in specific community or issue; ownership by the "locals"; and redistribution and use of resources.

Although the Methodist and Anglican networks of projects are the most widely known, many others exist. Projects have continued to flow from the long-established agencies—the Shaftesbury Society, for example. And the armies have initiated new, responsive projects to run alongside or replace longstanding efforts. U.K. Action (Evangelical Alliance/Tear Fund) entered the field in 1995. Against the Stream funnels Baptist contributions to church-based projects.

Although many projects are church-initiated, a significant shift from "doing things for" to "doing things with" has earthed projects in urban realities and challenged previous paternalism or cultural imposition. But these projects also struggle with authentic Christian rooting, style and theology. Many projects move from their faith foundation to become autonomous and secular—as seen among hospitals, schools and social services, as well as in urban agencies like settlements.

## Urban faith communities

The waves of immigration have brought strength to the other faith communities in the U.K. Muslim mosques, Hindu temples and Sikh gurudwara now stand alongside Christian churches and chapels in the city streets.

The U.K. Christian Handbook (Religious Trends) estimates that by the year 2000, 675,000 Muslims, 165,000 Hindus, 52,400 Buddhists and 400,000 Sikhs will be alongside the 37.8 million recorded Christians. Almost all these other religions have their strength in the heart of the cities. There are 139 mosques in Birmingham and 89 Hindu and Sikh places of worship in Leicester.

In the U.K. only 13 percent of the population claims membership of a Christian church. In the inner cities and outlying housing estates of the U.K. church attendance is much lower (often as low as 3 percent) and urban mission is carried by a very small proportion of the population.

Yet some of these areas are now showing growth in the number of religious groups, in levels of attendance of worship and in the extent and intensity of religious belief. I have seen this happen in East London.

Some vivid strands within the urban church tapestry include:

❖ Independent and new churches. The evangelical resurgence, the charismatic movement and immigration are the forces behind the wave of community churches, black-led congregations and church plants.

❖ Other faiths. Judaism has been joined by Islam, Hinduism, Sikhism and other Eastern faiths to present alternative forms of faith community.

❖ Older denominations. Anglican, Baptist, Catholic, Methodist and URC congregations have all undergone great change. Patterns of worship, leadership, corporate life and programs, numbers, influence and age-profiles—all have been adapted, renewed or altered.

❖ Pentecostalism is on the march. The largest London congregation is the 12,000–strong Kensington Temple (Elim) with scores of ethnic and geographical groups. The fastest growing is the Calvary Charismatic Church (Baptist), which has grown from 30 to 1,000 in four years in East London.

Continuation, adaptation, new forms, death, renewal and planting all feature in the story of urban churches in the U.K. A characteristic of the best urban churches is their "togetherness," sense of identity and shared life. Ways and means include home groups, culture clusters, participating worship and intentional communities.

### Summary

The second wave of urban mission in the U.K. emerged with industrial mission, spread through the networks, was earthed in the projects and driven by the urban churches.

The first wave has continued beneath and within all this. Weakening or adapting, taken over or fading out, city missions, agencies and armies persist, while settlements and central missions change character or style.

Urban Mission in the U.K. as the century ends features:

❖ Local, national and global connections

❖ Concern with linking and earthing theologies and faith communities

❖ Flow of new life sown in church planting projects and mission ministries

❖ Centrality of holistic mission

❖ Concern with what is "authentic" and "appropriate"

### Phases and theologies

Those engaged in urban mission, whether in the inner city or housing estates, whether as pastors or community workers, whether in churches or agencies, have passed through changing priorities. In the last 40 years urban mission here has moved along a spectrum of five phases that overlap and interconnect. Each phase can be summed up in a key phrase and reflected in the experience and writing of urban-mission practitioners. The phases have each focused thought and action that led to new directions and patterns of response. Policies and programs that began to emerge in the 1960s in many denominations and church agencies fused together in urban mission in the U.K.

### Phases

*1. Inner city*

In the 1960s new initiatives in the inner city became preoccupied with place. Churches had witnessed the breakdown of parish and pastoral patterns, and had experienced the massive hemorrhage of membership from city churches to suburban congregations. So emphasis was placed on the indigenous laity. At the same time, immigrants and refugees moved into the inner cities in a stream that has made "inner city" in the U.K. synonymous with social problems characteristic of regions wedged between the commercial center and residential suburbs.

*2. Urban mission*

The progression to urban mission involved wrestling with appropriate programs for the inner city. Industrial mission had revealed that the gap between shop floor and management was matched by the gulf between the English working class and the churches. Emergence of new forms of ministry and recognition of ineffective styles of working led to experiments and projects that often centered in key personalities or cells which began to link together in supportive networks. In our programs debate about personal evangelism and social responsibility gave way to a more holistic gospel. Biblical emphases of the missionary mandate of Matthew 28:19–20 (go into all the world) and the Nazareth manifesto of Luke 4:18–19 (good news for the poor) came together. Under the umbrella of urban mission cluster the advocates of personal conversion, the practitioners of social responsibility, and the networkers of political involvement.

### 3. Urban poor

In the 1980s the focus moved to people categorized as the urban poor. In the U.K. they lived in the inner cities or outlying council estates, which ring British cities and attempt to rehouse, often in tower-blocks, families of the inner city. The 1980s began in the U.K. with urban riots and reaction. Social surveys told us that one in four lived in poverty. Disease and disturbance rippled through the city and stirred politicians and church leaders. Methodists launched Mission Alongside the Poor. The wider-based Church Action on Poverty drew together a consortium of individuals and churches, and the Evangelical Coalition for Urban Mission became a living network.

But the urban poor of the world were now with us in another way. Immigrants first, refugees later, began to pour into our inner cities from the Caribbean, Asia, Africa and Europe. They joined the left-behind white population struggling with economic and technological changes. They brought their own style of worship and faith, and soon hundreds of black and ethnic churches sprang up in homes, schools and community centers, sometimes alongside established congregations.

### 4. Urban priorities

By the mid-1980s, the fusion of concern for place and people exploded into the world of power and politics regarding urban priorities. The government now spoke of Urban Priority Areas, and a series of funded urban programs had spread across the U.K. In 1985 the Archbishop's Commission on Urban Priority Areas (Church of England) addressed both church and nation in the prophetic "Faith in the City" document, leading immediately to open conflict with the Thatcher government. The Anglicans were not alone. Networks including

COSPEC (Christians Organised for Socially Political and Economic Change) and Jubilee drew together radical, concerned Christians. Evangelicals began to talk about "principalities and powers." We were all in the deeper, murkier waters of social justice and political power, in which we are still struggling to swim!

*5. Urban regeneration*

As the 1990s opened the key phrase was urban regeneration at all levels. The holistic gospel covers all aspects of life. Regarding church planting and church growth, a wave of new churches, often springing from ethnic, cultural and charismatic roots, has enriched traditional mainline denominations on a massive scale. Urban mission in the U.K. is multi-everything: multiracial, and increasingly multi-faith, multipurpose buildings and multilevel programs. Networks like the Churches' Coalition on Housing draw together Christians committed to one of the many urban issues. Change and continuity, hurt and healing, pluralism and diversity—these are the realities that set the agenda.

## Trends and theological themes

Running through the phases are two central theologies and two widening themes. The central theologies are incarnation and holism.

*1. Urban mission is incarnational*

Urban mission in the U.K. is incarnational. It is local response to "making the Word flesh." Christian presence means being and belonging in the here and now. There is no room for the parachuting evangelist—continuity and credibility are the viable bridges for the gospel.

Evidence for the incarnational is everywhere. Roman Catholic Orders including the Little Sisters of Jesus in Liverpool or the Cappadocian Fathers in East London have left the great monasteries, becoming cells of witness and service, often dressed as all people are, echoing Philippians 2. Local people who become able to move out into more prosperous communities instead stay rooted as an act of missionary obedience—living, local signs. Professionals undergo "exposure" or "context training," with groups such as the Urban Training Foundation training hundreds of teachers nationally for inner-city schools using the "live in and learn with" process.

In biblical terms, "seed has fallen into the ground," and "the Word has become flesh." Demographically the Christian presence is now a blend of indigenous, incomer and immigrant. That is, a strong core of local Christians becomes committed to an area; a wave of incomers (often highly educated mobile professionals) moves in with mission motivations; and groups of immigrants (mainly from the former British Commonwealth or Empire) scatter and water seeds of their faith experience throughout the major urban areas. Taken together these groups provide an incarnational presence that is richer and stronger.

## 2. Urban mission is holistic (shalom)

Old, often bitter divisions between those engaged in personal evangelism and those concerned with social action have largely gone. Emphases remain, but renewed biblical understanding of the scale of the spiritual struggle has led to acceptance and collaboration. Whether talking about the need of a threefold conversion to Christ, church and world, or using the language of personal conversion, social action and political justice, we affirm the comprehensiveness of the gospel. That comprehensiveness is summarized in *shalom*. This "wholeness" is God's purpose for the individual (Rom. 5), the community (Ps. 122), the church (Eph. 2) and the universe (Col. 1:20).

## 3. Urban mission is cooperative

The gifted entrepreneurial individual has given way to the network. Coalitions, consortiums, alliances and associations buttress and support one another. "Joining hands together" is expressed in the informal, issue-centered groups that now mark the U.K. urban scene. The roll call of agencies and institutions backing the U.K. Urban Congress in November 1995 illustrates the current situation: evangelical groups (Evangelical Alliance, Evangelical Urban Training Project, Scripture Union, Alliance of Asian Christians, African-Caribbean Evangelical Alliance, London Urban Christians Together) came alongside the national mainline Methodist Church Urban Mission Committee, Baptist Union, Church Army, Assemblies of God and Church of Scotland National Mission.

## 4. Urban mission is global

U.K. urban mission is now also global—and this in a double sense. "God is stirring up the world," says Ray Bakke in *The Urban Christian*.

In East London half the population is now drawn from ethnic minorities, and the fastest-growing congregations are African, Asian and Caribbean (in that order). New styles of worship, evangelism and community life have swept into formerly white working-class areas like East London. The world is here. The reverse missionary flow has taken place. Once we sent missionaries to Africa; now we receive them. And other faiths, especially Islam, are here in great strength. In places like Bradford, Slough and East London, Muslims often outnumber Christian churchgoers. Nationally, the government has set up an Inner Cities Religious Council bringing together all the faiths. Locally, events such as multi-faith festivals or vigils develop.

### Contemporary agenda(s)

Urban Mission in the U.K. began and developed in the nineteenth century, especially in the 1880–90s. We know it has come alive again in the twentieth century, especially in the 1980s-90s—facing new issues and old enemies.

The sprawling cities of the U.K. have known a longstanding, deep-rooted evangelical failure among the urban white working class—even though much germinal Christian response began here in the missions, settlements, agencies, armies and orders. That failure persists. The urban church still struggles with two crucial questions:

1. The shift from maintenance to mission. How to become an outward-looking church; how to break from ministerial domination to "all in mission"; how to flow from tradition to vision, to prevent charisma from becoming locked into institution.
2. The holding together of holistic missions. Keeping personal evangelism, community concern and social justice in balance. Ministering to casualty and to cause, witnessing in pastoral care and prophetic signals, "doing the deed" and "naming the name."

# 2

# Ubunye Church
# and Community Ministries

## *Dan and Kathleen Sheffield*

Z anele (not her real name) came to The Haven following a phone call from Lifeline. Lifeline is a 24–hour crisis phone line in Pietermaritzburg, KwaZulu-Natal, South Africa. Zanele, a school teacher, had been beaten by her husband of two years and needed emergency accommodations for herself and her one-year-old son.

The Haven is a crisis shelter for victims of domestic violence, operated under the auspices of Ubunye Free Methodist Church (*Ubunye* is a Zulu word meaning "unity, together, harmony"). Zanele was welcomed into the shelter by Letty Mayephu, the house mother, a member and Sunday school teacher at Ubunye Church. Haven staff aided Zanele in obtaining counseling with a professional social worker through another non-government organization in the city; she received assistance in obtaining an interdict against her husband from the magistrate's court; a police escort was arranged to pick up belongings from her home; a phone call was made to a senior police superintendent to have the investigating officer on the assault case changed because the officer was a friend of the abusing husband.

During this period Zanele was invited to accompany the house mother and her family to worship services at Ubunye Church. Letty Mayephu and her husband, Joel, a ministerial student, are evangelists at heart, with a deep compassion for the people they work with. Zanele was from a Presbyterian background but felt comfortable worshiping at Ubunye Church, a multicultural congregation, because denominationalism was not overly emphasized at Ubunye.

After six weeks in the shelter Zanele came to a number of conclusions about her future. She had begun divorce proceedings against her husband and was looking for other accommodations. Through her connection with Ubunye Church she became aware of the low-income social housing complex that operated as Ubunye Cooperative Housing. She eventually applied for a room in this complex. Zanele perceived it as a safe place for a woman and child in the urban context, and it was affordable for her as a single parent. It also meant staying in fellowship with the people who had ministered to her through The Haven and Ubunye Church.

## MINISTRY DEVELOPMENT

The Free Methodist denomination started ministry in Pietermaritzburg in 1991. This city of over 400,000, located 45 minutes by car inland from Durban, was seen as a strategic starting point for a new development in the denomination's program in South Africa—urban, multicultural congregations. A small nucleus formed and began meeting in a particular section of the city center.

This geographical neighborhood continues to be the focus of attention, although people from all over the city now attend church services. Until 1992 this area was regarded as a white enclave in racially divided South Africa. However, with the discarding of the Group Areas Act, the neighborhood has almost completely become a multicultural community, with only four to five years' experience of relating together.

The neighborhood is a residential area with tree-lined streets and many single-story, turn-of-the-century homes. There are a few low-rise apartment buildings. The area is bounded by small retail stores on the south side, light industry and auto repair shops on the north, offices on the east, and park land on the west. Two traffic corridors cross the area; there are two taxi/microbus hubs within the area. Informal drinking establishments (*shebeens*) are dotted throughout. The neighborhood is less than four-tenths of a square mile in size, with over 6,000 residents.

The community is primarily made up of singles and single-parent families, with some whole family units as well. The average age is probably under 35. There is no primary school in the area, although there are several secondary-level tutoring schools and adult-education centers. Most households function at a subsistence level economically; most working adults are seeking employment in the formal sector and have a limited educational background. While ethnically diverse—40 percent Zulu-speaking blacks, 10 percent colored or mixed race people, 15 percent Indian, 5 percent Africans from other areas/countries, and 30 percent low-income whites—most share common aspirations of seeking employment and trying to better their circumstances. Almost all the blacks have come from rural areas into the city center, although some have just moved in from the peri-urban townships on the periphery of the city proper.

In 1994 Dan and Kathleen Sheffield joined Ubunye Church to develop the work further. At the time, ministry goals essentially involved growing a multicultural congregation to a size that could support a full-time pastor and provide for a worship center that could seat 150 to 200 people. As the Sheffields began walking the community's streets, however, they realized very quickly that other churches in the area were not ministering to new residents. Although there are between 10 and 15 churches within a 10–minute walk, they still serve congregations of whites who drive in from the suburbs. Thus there was a need for a congregation to be deeply rooted in the community's concerns.

The Sheffields and other congregation leaders, a group of individuals (three whites and four blacks—all community residents), began analyzing and discussing community issues that were of significant concern to the majority of residents. Issues were brought forward to the larger congregation for discussion and interaction. Four issues kept rising to the surface: housing, employment, women's safety and civil cooperation.

During this period of analysis and reflection the congregation grew through a consistent, multicultural worship service that appealed to a broad spectrum of the community. Most attenders were competent in English, although at least five languages are represented in the congregation.

In April 1995 church leadership initiated a pilot housing project. A house beside the building where the congregation meets had been a matter of prayer for several months. About 20 or 25 people lived in this three-bedroom house, renting individual rooms. An informal drinking establishment was located in the backyard. Electricity had been shut off for several months; water was restricted to a trickle. This is a fairly typical situation in the area. Finally city officials ordered the place to be shut down; all residents were evicted. Church leaders went to the building's owner, a Muslim investor, to inquire about managing the place for him. When an agreement was made with the owner, church members spent a month cleaning, painting and repairing the house and property. The first residents were a single mother with three boys who had been attending the church for some time. Other residents were admitted through referrals. Our goals were to keep rent affordable, maintain the property and tolerate no violence.

Another ministry stream being pursued was the issue of women's rights and safety, the new frontier for the humanizing of South African society. Rape and domestic violence are endemic in the country. Only now are adequate laws being put in place to protect women, but justice system personnel are inadequately trained to understand the issues at stake. One congregation member is a family and marriage counselor with a non-government organization that is reaching out to combat some of these basic issues. Kathleen Sheffield became involved with this organization in developing a support-group program for victims of domestic violence. Dan Sheffield is now a board member for this organization. Ubunye Church's work with this group made the congregation increasingly aware of the need for emergency accommodation for domestic violence victims and their children. In this city of 400,000, there was no women's shelter.

As the congregation grew, we needed a larger space for worship. We also sensed a need for further involvement in the provision of low-income housing. And the lack of a women's shelter was weighing on us. We began looking for a facility that would allow us to combine all of those concerns. In 1996, following the establishment of a trust that could function independent of the church structure, we purchased a building that had been a residential hotel, right in the heart of the community we were ministering in. We began renting out the sixty rooms in the complex, we renovated and opened the women's shelter in early 1997, and we are making plans for converting one section into a worship center/preschool facility.

## MINISTRY GOALS

The goals for this church and its ministry have been built primarily around the need to establish a credible witness for the gospel. The gospel has been disparaged because of the overwhelming "Christian" participation in maintaining the apartheid system. We want our growth to come from people in the community seeing a consistent witness to Christ, who is concerned about every aspect of their lives. This is a challenge in a city that is church-saturated, where evangelism is primarily slick advertising and flashy programs, and where faith and the rest of life are often disconnected.

The Ubunye Trust was established as a separate body from the church. Its purpose is to aid in responding to the needs of urban workers and their families who are functioning at the subsistence level. At this point those concerns primarily address housing and women's safety. Those needs will probably change. For instance, another concern we are becoming aware of is the need for affordable and safe childcare.

The themes found in Isaiah 58:6–12 serve as a guide. Identifying injustices and acts of oppression, and providing for basic human needs form a basis for actions that build a credible reputation in the community. Developing a sense of community and basic civil cooperation is done by establishing relationships in the area, networking with service providers and providing centers of stability, such as the housing complex and women's shelter.

Stated more succinctly, our goals are:

1. To develop a multicultural, worshiping congregation of earnest Christians and God-seekers.
2. To grow this congregation through Christian presence and ministry that is rooted in the community.
3. To develop and administer social ministries that correspond to the community's relevant needs.
4. To aid in developing a sense of neighborhood in our geographical home.

## MINISTRY DESCRIPTION

Attendance at Ubunye Free Methodist Church is between 50 and 60 persons for Sunday morning worship service. The converted carpenter's workshop that currently serves as our worship center only holds 70 people. It is located in the backyard of the pastor's home and not highly visible from the street. About one-third of the congregation are members of the Free Methodist church, but they hold membership in other local churches elsewhere in South Africa—or other parts of the world. The rest of the congregation consists of persons with some Christian background but who belong to other denominations. Many believe they should retain the membership they have in their home churches in the rural areas. However, in the urban context they have not found the "white" congregations of their denomination to be an accepting environment.

People in the congregation come from varied backgrounds: Bible college lecturers, nurses, teachers, social-service professionals in non-government organizations, tertiary-level students (university, technical college, Bible college), tradespeople, streethawkers and domestic workers. About one-third are children and teens, and at least 80 percent of the congregation is within walking distance of the worship center.

The primary church gathering is the Sunday morning worship service, led by a multicultural worship team. While most of the service is in English, the unifying language, Zulu is also used in singing and in presenting the message (when deemed necessary). Once a month communion is served, and the service is followed by a communal meal and congregational social interaction. An age-level children's program is offered in the second half of the service for children up to age 12.

In the Sunday worship service we attempt to engage with the realities of peoples' experience as they live in the city. Time is given for sharing comments about the joys, struggles and concerns of peoples' lives. Mutual prayer draws people into their priestly role in one another's lives. Multi-generational interaction and participation make this an experience in worship rather than just a service. Sermons are developed that address concrete issues while providing solid, biblical teaching. Tea is served after the service, facilitating social interaction.

Weekday evenings are generally considered unsafe for people to be on the streets; it is dark by 7 P.M. and street lighting is generally inadequate. Many people work long, exhausting hours before coming home to cook and spend a few moments with their children. Therefore any prayer/study groups are limited to a few close neighbors meeting informally. Thus the primary focus of church life is the Sunday worship service, along with individual and corporate participation in the community, upon which the church leadership place a high premium.

We have attempted to focus our people, time and finances on a limited number of church activities, so that we may do these well, rather than attempting to do many things poorly. Our corporate worship gathering is seen as a symbol of Christ's presence in the community, which has a redemptive function in and of itself. This Christian worship then becomes a spiritual protest against the forces of evil that overshadow the community.

*Ubunye Cooperative Housing* presently rents out over 65 rooms to low-income families, from two separate facilities in the community. The first project, begun in 1995, is still operational, with very little turnover in residents. The second project, of a much larger nature, is the primary focus of our Co-op Housing staff. Dan Sheffield continues to serve as volunteer managing director until financial and infrastructure stability is achieved. One full-time maintenance supervisor, a long-time participant in our church, lives in the complex and carries on most of the day-to-day operation of the complex. There is one half-time cleaning person under the supervisor's direction.

This complex presently houses more than 150 persons. A resident's association was elected and meets regularly with Co-op Housing staff. The primary purpose of these meetings is to disseminate information, raise issues of concern, and serve as a grievance structure. The bias in terms of criteria for allocating rooms is in favor of female-headed households. Women and children tend to be the most vulnerable group in the community. They often have the lowest-paying jobs, are exploited unfairly and are most susceptible to violence.

*The Haven,* our emergency shelter for women and children affected by domestic violence, has been operational for one year. We work with a broad network of social-service providers, including non-government organizations, government departments and the police. Kathleen Sheffield is the shelter's volunteer coordinator of services. The Haven is primarily an accommodation ministry. While we provide support and access to various resources for the women, the counseling and group-work process is delegated to existing groups in the community who have this as their primary function. A church member serves as the full-time house mother and lives in a self-contained flat adjoining the shelter. In the past year an average of eight women and children per month have occupied the shelter. This ministry is funded completely through grants and donations from various bodies. When the housing complex is financially secure, rental income from rooms will provide a subsistence budget for the women's shelter, promoting in-house sustainability for this program.

## RESULTS

After only three to four years of focused ministry it may be a little early to substantiate any significant results. We feel we are still in the foundation-laying stage. At the same time there are indicators that encourage us.

Ubunye Church is building a reputation in the local geographical area and in the wider context of the city. Within the section of the city we call home, the church and the housing project are becoming known for trying something tangible. People are inquisitive, wondering how genuine we are. They ask, "Why are you staying here, when everyone else is leaving?" There is almost a kind of begrudging respect. There is also high demand for a room in our complex because of affordability and safety; word has gotten around.

In the wider context local government, social service providers, police and development organizations keep aware of our activities. A local government official responsible for developing policy for the city's social housing visits our complex because "you are the only ones doing anything!" A development organization asks us to submit a case study of our project for inclusion in a national government policy paper on social housing.

Results can be seen in the congregation's steady growth, which has seen a growth rate of 20 percent in the last two years. Community contacts are the primary means of drawing new people into our fellowship. The connection with people living in the housing complex brought an almost automatic attendance boost as people came to investigate the building's owners. The women's shelter ministry has not had as significant an impact because many women go back to their own communities after a stay in the shelter.

We can also see results in the lives of people touched by the church and its ministries. One young man, surviving in the underclass and trying to improve his education, was introduced to Christ by a member of our congregation. At 26 he completed his high school education; two years later he was accepted into university bridging courses. He now has a job that provides a living wage with which he supports family members back in the rural areas. He has grown and matured in Christ, giving testimony to the changes in his life.

41

## Process of Coming to Christ

The process of coming to faith in Christ, in our understanding, can be related loosely to Engel's evangelism scale. First, there is the need for a credible "messenger" who is accepted by the target audience. We believe this messenger is composed of the individuals who make up our congregation, as well as the collective presence of our church's ministry in the community. Both our individual and corporate characters are relevant.

The next step is a kind of "flag-raising"; that is, identifying ourselves as Christians in appropriate contexts. Once again, this is true for both individual believers as well as our community ministries.

Following on credible presence and Christian identification is the need to communicate the gospel. We do this through personal conversation as well as through the church's public meetings. After conversion there is the ongoing process of Christian growth and transformation, aided by personal and group contexts for study and integration. We also identify those who are prepared for more focused discipling. Then we come full circle as we consciously draw these into the process of providing credible witness through their involvement with community ministries.

In our congregation we have persons at all stages of this continuum. Because we have a number of participants who are either students or lecturers at a local seminary, we have a high degree of Christian maturity often uncommon in young churches. Many of these, however, are weak in their integration of faith and deeds. Our church then becomes a kind of modeling studio as students do their required field education through our ministries. Many of these students will go on to minister in Free Methodist churches in other centers throughout the country.

We also have seekers who have many personal issues to deal with before they will ever come to conversion. One area resident, a middle-aged, single woman, brought her dog with her into the service on her first Sunday in attendance. Halfway through the service the dog began wandering around, frightening the children. When asked to remove the dog, the woman said her dog needed to worship God too! When the dog was removed, its owner stormed off. The next week, to our astonishment, she was back, without the dog, and has been with us for more than a year. She may or may not have crossed the threshold of conversion, but she has come a long way through loving acceptance, Bible studies and concerned prayer. There are other similar stories.

## EVALUATION

Why congregational development first?

One question raised regarding this case study is the model we adopted by starting with a worshiping community that moved toward community ministries, rather than starting with a community organizing model that moved toward conversions and congregational development. Two factors influenced our approach: one is theological, and the other is practical. We have to be honest in stating that perhaps the practical reason carried more weight.

As a denominationally initiated assignment, the task given to the original nucleus and then to the Sheffields was to plant a church in Pietermaritzburg. Inherent in that assignment was the commitment of resources and personnel for a limited time. If a viable congregation (that is, self-propagating and self-supporting) did not develop within a certain period (4 years), the denomination would withdraw personnel and resources. A congregation that could engage with community issues needed to be established.

Theologically, there is the egg and chicken debate. Which comes first, a worshiping community or community organizing? Our group felt the need to develop a worshiping congregation that would support our involvement with the community and its concerns.

## WHY MULTICULTURAL?

Ubunye Free Methodist Church chose to adopt a multicultural model, consciously rejecting a homogeneous approach, for several reasons. First, the South African context, in which legally sanctioned separation of peoples has profoundly affected the nature of the church in this country, needs to have some models of how to be church differently. A multicultural church is an anomaly in the evangelical community; it becomes a symbol, a kind of firstfruit, and a prod to the wider evangelical community.

Second, the multi-ethnic nature of the geographical area in which the congregation was started was a consciously chosen target for such a model. In essence, given the desire to plant a multicultural congregation, an appropriate community was chosen as the target. Most South African cities are still functionally operated under apartheid-era urban-planning models, with various suburbs dominated by one racial group. Only city centers have undergone massive social change, taking local council planners offguard. While high ethnic consciousness is usually antithetical to developing multicultural churches, the level of interrelatedness in this particular community suggested many people with a willingness to forgo such a perspective for the sake of economic improvement and social mobility. Many Africans in this community are actively engaged in educational upgrading or are working in English-language-based, intercultural workplaces. Almost all children and youth attend English-language, intercultural schools.

Finally, the church's original nucleus was multicultural in makeup. The church's present leadership represents two racial groups, four languages and five cultural groupings. Leadership decisions are made by consultation, identifying areas of commonality and cultural divergence. There is a conscious desire to bring various cultural distinctives into the church's public gatherings in an affirming manner. We believe this approach is drawing persons of like mind into our fellowship. A homogeneous approach would likely provide for explosive growth given the lack of such churches (other than white) in the community, but we have chosen the idealistic high ground.

## WHY THE STRONG CONCERN FOR WOMEN?

In reading the case study the reader will note that the church operates a women's shelter and has a bias toward women with children in our rental allocation policy. A black woman is a member of our six-person church board.

A first response is that women form a large visible presence in our community, but they do not command the level of public power and access to services that their numbers should dictate. Women in South Africa represent the new face of gender-apartheid.

Second, the Free Methodist Church, as an evangelical body, has ordained women for almost a century. This says several things: that our denomination has a long tradition of recognizing the role of women in the life of the church, that we have an undergirding theology regarding the equality of women, and that we have been willing to take a divergent position from most evangelical denominations. Our congregation has five ordained ministers, including one black woman, and seven ministerial candidates, including three women. This number of persons, at this level of denominational rootedness, keeps our view of women at a conscious level.

Third, we have women in leadership who continually bring us to the issues at stake.

### How Can a Small Congregation Have Such a Large Impact?

From the beginning Ubunye Church has not set itself to replicate the traditional gamut of church-based ministries that most churches view as necessary. The vision has always been to find ways to have the most impact on our community so we may create opportunities to lift up the name of Christ. We have focused our time, energy and resources on areas we identified would allow us to have maximum impact in the community. We do not have a traditional approach to children's ministries or to adult discipleship, so traditional levels of energies and resources are not expended in these areas.

Another factor has been our choice to network with the community's existing bodies so we do not replicate services and to seek advice so we can do our niche ministries better. One example is our relationships with an emergency hotline service and a family counseling agency regarding our work with the women's shelter. We don't have to market our services to the community at large, just to the social-service agencies who are on the front line with women. We only provide the accommodations these agencies want for their clients, and we send them back to the counseling agencies for personal and group contexts for dealing with domestic-violence issues. With the housing project we have interacted closely with a social housing-development organization. This organization has sponsored us to national conferences on housing management and aided us in securing government funding to pay off our loan and significantly develop the housing property.

One issue we must address is that the present pastor's salary is not paid for by the congregation but from outside sources. The congregation must develop to a size that can fund not only the ministries budget, as it does presently, but also a pastor's salary package.

## What Has Been the Role of the Pastor/Church Planter?

Dan and Kathleen Sheffield have sought to play a vision-casting and facilitation role in developing this congregation and its community ministries. Dan's ecclesiology and sense of the worshiping community as a Christian presence in the wider community, and Kathleen's studies in sociology and human geography, have played a key role in casting a vision of the possibilities to both the leadership and the congregation.

For the first six months of their ministry with Ubunye, the Sheffields pursued a listening, learning, consulting, information-gathering approach. They lived in the community and interacted with residents, struggled with access to education for their children, bought household goods in the community-based shops, and visited in the homes of church attenders. Information and ideas were exchanged in weekly meetings with the church leadership team. Ideas that gained acceptance with that group were brought to the larger fellowship about once a month. The first concern to be worked through this process was the basis for functioning multiculturally and the pragmatic issues of style, language, and common symbols and rituals. The church's name, *Ubunye*, came out of this process. The next major issue was the need for safe, affordable housing.

As ministry possibilities were identified, the next step was to discover those in the congregation with a burden and gifts for the different ministries. A process of spiritual gift identification was introduced; as individuals and groups of persons came to the forefront, skill-capacity was developed by networking with existing bodies in the city. Ministry plans and procedures were developed in a consultative manner among church leaders and ministry group leaders. Dan served as teacher/discipler where needed and also as facilitator for most of the discussions.

Dan Sheffield continues to function as pastor and vision-caster for the church and its ministries. He serves as the housing program's coordinator, working with a management team and staff. Kathleen Sheffield serves as coordinator of the women's shelter program. The listening, learning and consulting continues.

## Where Are We Going?

The next phase is clearly leadership development. As Canadians, the Sheffields do not intend to have a long-term involvement with the church. They would like to see leadership developed for the church, the housing program and the women's shelter in the next two to three years. That leadership may come from within the existing fellowship or through an internship process with people presently not involved in the church's ministry.

The church members believe we are engaged in a process, but we have not arrived. We are still establishing our base of ministry. While we have built many relationships, there is still a need to go deeper into the existing community, particularly in identifying more of the local social role players. While our ministry center, housing complex and the women's shelter now have a high profile in the community, we need our worship center and its educational opportunities to have higher profiles. This will only happen through a move to a more prominent position in the neighborhood.

Ultimately, we want to have more of a role in bringing stability to the community. We believe this will happen as we continue to extend our presence in the community.

# 3

# Clustering

## A new approach to urban ministry

*Robert C. Linthicum*

Immanuel Presbyterian Church was at one time one of the great churches in the United States. In the heart of what was once the most thriving business and residential community of Los Angeles, Immanuel Church reached its zenith in the years immediately following World War II. It was among the largest churches in the Presbyterian denomination and had an average Sunday attendance in excess of 4,000. It had built a magnificent Gothic cathedral for itself, with a sanctuary seating 2,000, a chapel of 500 and a second chapel of 150, two attached buildings with nearly 200 rooms, and a tower that climbed 20 stories into the southern California sky. Immanuel Church was surrounded by the mansions and luxury apartment buildings of the wealthy and upper-middle class of Los Angeles's movie and oil industries. Although you may never have visited Immanuel Church, you know it quite well because its rooms, chapels, sanctuary and exterior have been the sets for countless motion pictures, from *Sister Act II* and *Only in America* to *Mouse Hunt*!

Five years ago Immanuel Church was in real trouble. Sunday worship attendance had plummeted from 4,000 to under 100, still worshiping in that 2,000 seat sanctuary. The church had gone through a string of pastors, the most recent lasting only three weeks after his installation. Its rooms were empty during the week, and it was avoided by the community as too imposing. What had gone wrong?

What had gone wrong was that the community had changed. Stepping out the church's front door in 1993, one faced a canyon of high-rise office buildings with so many businesses within them that the corridor rated its own zip code. Interspersed between these high-rise office buildings are hotels, upscale shopping centers primarily catering to business community clientele; a string of cathedral-like churches and temples; and many expensive restaurants, boutiques and places of entertainment.

But to step out the church's *back* door means stepping into a different world. The community is no longer made up of wealthy and upper-middle-class Anglos. The community now boasts its all-time highest population of 421,000. But all the former mansions have been torn down, the luxury apartments divided and subdivided again, and cheap apartments have been built on empty lots. The community is now 53 percent Hispanic, 22 percent Asian, 9 percent Ethiopian Africans and African-American and only 16 percent Anglo. Nearly 43 percent of the adults are not married, nearly 60 percent are under 35 years old, and most are poor. More than 82 percent of the community's residents speak another language than English, work either in manual-labor jobs or are unemployed, and are refugees from another country. Concern about gangs and crime dominates the community.

Thus, by 1993, Immanuel Church was following the path of so many churches in the city—a rapidly declining and aging congregation in a community reaching its highest population, a church held together only by its remembrance of its former glory, irrelevant and unable to minister effectively to the people living around it.

Today, a visit to Immanuel Church reveals a congregation profoundly "born-again." Approximately 1,200 people gather on Sundays to attend a choice of five worship services conducted in English, Spanish, Korean and Ethiopian. Four congregations now make their home in Immanuel Church. From 600 to 800 youth gather five days a week for after-school athletic, art and academic pursuits. Hispanic ministry is an integral part of the life and work of the church, with many committee meetings conducted in English and in Spanish. A community organizer and a community worker spend all their time in the neighborhood, organizing the community around its issues. An economic development corporation supported by neighborhood banks is now coming into being, enabling poor residents to start vest-pocket businesses outside the church's front door. The building is filled with community activity seven days a week, from 8:00 in the morning until 10:00 at night. Immanuel Church is now the center of both the residential and business communities, and precious new life has flowed back into the congregation and ministry.

What has happened to bring Immanuel Church back from death to life? There have been several contributing factors. But one such ingredient in Immanuel's rebirth has been the Hollywood-Wilshire Cluster.

## THE CLUSTER: AN IDEA WHOSE TIME HAS COME

The clustering of congregations is an urban-ministry strategy that has developed in numerous ways over many generations. But it has only recently emerged into its own as a mature and sophisticated paradigm for ministry. The essential idea of clustering comes from the insight that churches working together can create a critical mass of power and motivation to accomplish far more than if they continued to work and exist independent of one another. It is the rediscovery of the whole church in an urban community as the body of Christ, perceiving each church's unique role and working together from that perception for the transformation of both the neighborhood and its churches.

Here are the essential principles of the cluster model of urban ministry.

### The magnet church

Most urban churches operate out of the self-perception that they are regional churches. That is, they perceive themselves as substantive congregations carrying out a wide spectrum of ministry, seeking to be all things to all people in order to attract some. This is the model of church as "department store"—and it is the primary model embraced by churches today.

The church as department store is one that tries to do all things equally well to reach the most people. A department store is a supermarket of wares, in which every conceivable item for sale is available in its specific department. One who enters that store shopping for a specific item simply goes to the appropriate department to find and purchase that item.

50

The department store has been the reigning model of retail marketing for over 50 years in the Western world, and throughout the Two-thirds World for at least the past generation. Churches have replicated themselves in the same way, modeling moderate-sized or even small congregations on the large regional churches sprinkled through our cities and suburbs. Thus, all churches function with the perspective that they must offer a wide spectrum of services—not only worship, but graded education, excellent music programs, a variety of fellowship and age-specific groups—everything any visitor might find inviting.

No model of ministry is more disastrous for the urban church than the department store approach. And the reason why is simple—resources. Every church has only so many members, so much building, so much money—and no more! And smaller, declining churches have extremely limited resources. When a church falls into the trap of seeking to be a super church, trying to do all things equally well, then it will squander the limited resources it has at its disposal. It uses up its people, buildings and money in a vain attempt to remain competitive with the church down the street. And in so doing, it becomes less and less able to maintain its viability as a congregation.

There has to be a better way. And there is—the *magnet* model of ministry.

A magnet by its very nature both attracts and repels. It attracts only metal that has sufficient iron particles in it. It repels all other material. The magnet is the boutique of the retail shopping world, not the department store. It does one thing supremely well—and doesn't try to do things it is not capable of doing! And it is the boutique that is overwhelmingly successful in today's retail marketing world, not the department store. Because of its enormous overhead, the department store has become the lumbering dinosaur of today, fast facing extinction. And boutiques—stores that seek to do one thing, and only one thing, extremely well—are rapidly becoming the only retail act in town.

The cluster model of ministry is built around the magnet understanding of urban church. First, it assumes that a given congregation—particularly a small, struggling, urban congregation— will be effective and successful only insofar as it embraces a clear, single focus of mission for itself and then mobilizes its people, buildings and money in an all-out effort to carry out that mission. Therefore, the cluster works to enable each of its member churches and agencies to discern and embrace that level of self-understanding (how that occurs is developed later in this chapter).

What would a focus of mission look like? Here are several samples from churches and mission agencies in the Hollywood-Wilshire Cluster:

❖ *a Korean congregation:*

> To reach second generation English-speaking Korean-American youth with the gospel of Jesus Christ and to build with them a strong Christian community, while continuing a vital full Korean-speaking ministry to the first generation Korean-Americans.

❖ *a neighborhood outreach built around resident interns:*

> To empower the South Hollywood neighborhood . . . to experience fullness of life in Christ by:
>
> 1. Providing a City Dweller internship program
> 2. Fostering a strong Christian community
> 3. Implementing a strategy that will:
>    - effectively share the gospel;
>    - enable the neighborhood to successfully address its own issues;
>    - identify and develop the leadership capabilities of the people; and
>    - work for the spiritual transformation of the neighborhood.

❖ *a neighborhood church:*

> To show Christ's love for all people (of the neighborhood) by being a beacon of acceptance, loving community and hope to the surrounding neighborhoods where these are often lacking.

❖ *an Hispanic congregation:*

> To reach with the gospel of Jesus Christ the Hispanic families that live around the church, sharing our faith, serving that Hispanic community, and building our life together as a church.

❖ *an economic development corporation:*

> To facilitate the economic growth of poor families in the Hollywood-Wilshire community through the development of locally owned businesses, in order to contribute to our mutual economic and social transformation.

❖ *an anchor congregation:*

> To embrace and join with the Wilshire Center for our mutual transformation, especially encouraging our youth and their families in a revival of faith.

### Anchor churches

A second ingredient in the cluster model of ministry is anchor churches. Just as a shopping mall and the boutiques of the mall are built around anchor stores, so must a cluster be built around anchor churches.

An anchor church is a congregation that is in a more secure position than many of the churches within the cluster. This security might be built upon the congregation's larger size, a solid financial base (such as large endowments) or a stature within the community or denomination that guarantees its continued existence (such as being a cathedral or a university chapel).

The role the anchor church might play in a cluster will differ according to the church's personality and the particularity of that cluster. But the importance of the anchor church is the sense of stability and permanence it brings to the partnership—an assurance that, just like the anchor church, the partnership of the cluster will be long-lived.

Besides providing stability, anchor churches can play a number of roles. Often they will be the logistical center of the cluster, or a primary education center, or a center for celebration and entertainment (often because an anchor church will have a sizeable and well-funded music program). If it is a moderately large to large congregation, the anchor church might act as a regional congregation, or as a regional church with a strong magnet focus—as opposed to being solely a magnet church. Its larger size and/or financial base might allow it to play that role. It can become a gathering place for the cluster and its churches, much as a medieval cathedral acted as the center of art, music, education and citywide worship and celebration for its community.

The anchor church may specialize in a particular area of ministry difficult for other cluster churches to undertake. Hollywood Presbyterian Church, one of the two anchor churches in our cluster, carries on a particularly effective and complex ministry to the entertainment industry; its location and its connections with people prominent in "the industry" make it a logical center for such a ministry. It is in the self-interest of each church in our cluster to encourage this ministry on behalf of all.

There may be several anchor churches in a cluster. There is no need for there to be only one. Several such churches will bring an even-greater stability to the cluster. In one cluster with which I am consulting, for example, there are two anchor churches and a large suburban church—one anchor church is an extremely well-endowed "tall steeple" church, the other a large church in a nearby wealthy enclave of the city.

The anchor church concept provides the opportunity for a large suburban church to participate in inner-city ministry. The suburban church mentioned in the example above is not at all in geographical proximity to that cluster; it is 24 miles distant. But it is a strategic player in that cluster through the services and volunteers it provides, for the sense of mission it receives and the significant relationships its volunteers have built with inner-city church members and community residents.

This is a clear example of the potential of partnership between the intentional suburban anchor church and the churches of an inner-city cluster. To that partnership the suburban church can bring both a high quantity and quality of skilled volunteers, leadership and funding. The suburban church's involvement need not be one-way, because the cluster's ministry can provide an avenue for that church for outreach, involving congregational members in strategic ministry, and strategic and personalized use of its mission money. Such involvement, then, can serve both the self-interest of the smaller cluster churches and that of the suburban congregation.

### The unique role of the cluster

The cluster assumes the role of integrating these individual mission foci into a single comprehensive mission thrust that seeks to reach all the people and to work for the transformation of the whole community. To continue the shopping motif, the cluster becomes the "mall" of "boutiques" and "anchor stores" (more about that later), providing the coordinated means to enable each store to be far more profitable by banding together than by remaining isolated and solitary.

The cluster approach, therefore, does not operate on the assumption that the church should not be concerned with all people or should not seek to minister at the point of each person's need. It assumes, instead, that only the largest and most resource-rich of churches can carry on such a comprehensive ministry. Instead, the cluster operates on the assumption that it must enable each of its member churches and mission agencies to discover and act out Christ's unique call and equip each of them for its individual focused and dedicated ministry.

By working together as a cluster, all these focused churches and mission agencies can *together* create that mission effort which reaches all types of people in that community and can *together* carry out the most comprehensive and effective of ministries.

Note this more comprehensive mission focus of the Hollywood-Wilshire Cluster as it pulls together and integrates the individual mission foci of its member congregations and mission agencies (some of which were sampled earlier):

> We, as an intentional Christian community of Presbyterian churches and mission organizations, are called by God to proclaim Christ's love through partnership with the neighborhoods of the Hollywood-Wilshire area in order to build bridges of mutual empowerment, reconciliation and transformation.

In a very profound way, it is the cluster model of ministry that enables previously insulated congregations to discover what it really means to be truly the body of Christ. It lives out Paul's admonition concretely:

> The body does not consist of one member but of many. If the foot would say, "Because I am not a hand, I do not belong to the body," that would not make it any less a part of the body. . . . The eye cannot say to the hand, "I have no need of you," nor again the head to the feet, "I have no need of you." On the contrary, the members of the body that seem to be weaker are indispensable, and those members of the body that we think less honorable we clothe with greater honor. . . . If one member suffers, all suffer together with it; if one member is honored, all rejoice together with it. Now you are the body of Christ and individually members of it. (1 Cor. 12:14–15, 21–23, 26–27)

### Building a community of trust: The role of the coach/mentor

We have described the cluster as a grouping of smaller congregations within a common geographical area that are claiming and acting out their self-understanding as magnet churches, each with a single mission focus. We have examined the role of anchor churches within the cluster, acting more as regional as well as focused congregations and providing stability to the cluster. Finally, we have examined the

55

cluster itself as the catalyst that enables all of the churches—each with its unique mission focus and gifts (both magnet and anchor)—to minister as one body of Christ, becoming in its actions and its theological rhetoric a dynamic manifestation of the church's unity amid unbelievable diversity, even in the heart of the city.

A critical question, however, is what moves the individual churches and mission agencies from the traditional understanding of congregations to the cluster concept? What enables a church to claim a single mission focus for its life and ministry? What motivates a regional congregation to assume the responsibility of becoming an anchor church toward churches around it or across 24 miles? What enables all these churches and mission agencies to bind themselves to one another in a cluster and work as one? The answer is vision, prayer—and strategic planning! First, let's look at vision and prayer.

A truly effective cluster cannot be built by the orders of a bishop or presbytery or by the planning of a denominational council or regional body. It cannot be built by fiat from the top-down. It can only come from the bottom-up. And it will come about only by building trust.

If a cluster is ever to succeed in an urban community, it will succeed only if significant investment has been made in its people. Hours and weeks and even years of time must be dedicated to fostering relationships of respect, trust and integrity. Those relationships must be built through pastors and laypeople sitting around with each other, sharing concerns and visions and fears, being supported by each other in both personal and church-centered crises and turmoils, and learning that they are there for one another.

The Hollywood-Wilshire Cluster came about, for example, because pastors from the seven Presbyterian churches in that community met together twice each month for four years. They shared hopes and aspirations, fears and congregational conflicts. They listened to each other's pains. So it was that they came to trust each other and even to depend upon each other in their respective struggles. Particularly important to this cluster's formation was one pastor's struggle, as all in the group became aware that his church would have to close and he would be without work. It was the other pastors' support of him and prayers for him that enabled him to move through one of the most difficult times of his ministry and that bound them together in love. The later work of the cluster came about because sufficient time had been given in its early years to listening, sharing, struggling, visioning and praying together.

Particularly strategic to this process is the role of the coach-mentor. Most successful clusters have had someone play that unique role within them. Sometimes the coach-mentor has been an informal role assumed by one of the pastors. In some denominations it is a designated role, involving selecting a person from outside the cluster who has considerable experience in urban ministry and a strong pastor's heart.

The coach-mentor is a strategic role. It is one of listening to people, encouraging them, coming alongside them and, out of this common sharing, building a relationship together that allows formation of the future. Most effective coach-mentoring relationships include time spent with pastors individually as well as time spent together in groups. One particularly effective cluster is built on the premise that each pastor will spend two hours each month in a single meeting, one-on-one, with the coach-mentor. For that meeting they work on issues dealing with the pastor's personal and professional development and spiritual formation—not on problems of the pastor's church.

The coach-mentor coaches. That is, he or she works with each pastor and with the gathered assembly of pastors and church leaders on problems of their churches, issues of the community, or common concerns they all face. The coach-mentor does not so much tell them what to do as work with them to figure out collectively and individually what needs to be done. This includes sharing from his or her own experience in doing urban ministry and from knowledge of what others have done. But the coaching role is always that of enabling people to do for themselves.

The coach-mentor also mentors. That is, he or she discerns the strong characteristics of each pastor and leader with whom the coach-mentor is in relationship and calls forth the exercise of those gifts. The coach-mentor comes alongside each pastor or church leader, teaches by example, encourages them to learn from one another, and seeks to develop the entire group as a learning laboratory.

It may seem wasteful to spend so much time in a cluster's early stages in building a life together through strengthening relationships and the "pastoral" work of the coach-mentor. But unless a foundation of trust, mutual respect and confidence has been laid, there is no way that pastors and churches will be willing to sacrifice their independence and self-determination for a mutual ministry that builds them into an active and shared body of Christ.

### Planning is next to Godliness

The coach-mentor works with the cluster to provide a safe environment for sharing problems and joys, to examine and evaluate their respective ministries, and out of such examination to move toward new ministry efforts in which they can jointly share. When the foundation is sufficiently set, the cluster must move beyond maintaining relationships into building a mission together. And that is done through shared strategic planning.

To be truly effective, planning must occur at three levels: regional, local and cluster. Regional body planning provides the larger context within which cluster planning can occur. Local planning should include each church and mission agency of the cluster, as they set mission directions for themselves and the development of their interior life and institutional development to support the carrying out of their mission. Cluster planning should be done in the light of priorities developed in regional planning and the mission directions of the local church and mission agency planning.

Mission study at the local congregational or mission agency level should have two primary characteristics. First, it should bring *clarity of mission*. There should be a clear discernment of God's call to that church or agency. Each church or agency should create through this process that body's primary mission focus—a statement in 25 words or less (if you can't say what you're about in 25 words or less, then you don't know what you're about!). From that mission statement the church or agency should develop mission objectives and clarity as to how that mission focus informs the strengthening of interior life and institutional development of that organization. Emerging from the mission objectives should be concrete, specific, measurable and achievable strategies, the use of that body's limited resources, and effective means for evaluation.

The second primary characteristic of such strategic mission planning is *ownership*. Most strategic planning processes do not bring about the people's ownership of the results. The reason is simple: people only own that in which they participate, and most mission planning is done by a small committee of people who seek to convince everyone else of the wisdom of their plans. Building the planning process around people's involvement is crucial for the success of that planning.

Thus, in the strategic planning done by the Hollywood-Wilshire Cluster and its six participating churches and mission agencies, each body held a congregation-/constituency-wide "Discernment Week-end," where between 35 percent and 85 percent of the people from each group gathered on retreat to study its respective neighborhoods, to engage in Bible study to discern the mind of Christ, to create a mission focus for each group and to work on implementing strategies. This resulted in high ownership by each congregation and mission agency of the directives for their communion. The effort reached its climax when 100 percent of the delegates to the cluster from each participating body met on a three-day retreat to set the directions for the cluster. The result? *Empowerment.* That is, strong acceptance by each church and mission agency, enthusiastic participation of its people, and empowerment of each church and agency and the cluster in their respective and shared work of ministry.

There are several planning vehicles that enable a regional body, churches and clusters of churches to gain clarity of mission and ownership. One is the three-phase "Vista" process developed by Percept (151 Kalmus Drive, Suite A104, Costa Mesa, CA 92626, USA). Another is "Church: Discover Your Calling" by Partners in Urban Transformation (3300 Wilshire Blvd., Los Angeles, CA 90010, USA). Percept is particularly effective in bringing about mission clarity, Partners in Urban Transformation in enabling congregational ownership to occur. Intriguingly, Percept and Partners, aware of each other's strengths and their own weaknesses, have recently begun working together to enable clusters to undertake a coordinated approach to mission planning, using the best of both systems.

## A Case Study: The Hollywood-Wilshire Cluster

An example of effective clustering is the Hollywood-Wilshire Cluster of Presbyterian Churches in Los Angeles. Immanuel Presbyterian Church, with which we began this paper, is an active member of this cluster, and much of its transformation has been due to its cluster participation.

The Hollywood-Wilshire Cluster was formed in 1992, made up of the pastors of the seven Presbyterian churches in that four-mile-by-four-mile area. Their first several years were spent sharing with each other their problems and frustrations and building relationships of trust and support. In this task, they were guided by an extremely skilled coach-mentor, Rev. Michael Mata, director of the urban studies program of the School of Theology at Claremont and a Nazarene pastor.

In 1995, however, an event occurred which was to profoundly shape the cluster's future. One of the seven churches made the decision to close! That shock caused the cluster churches to undertake a strategic study together and make studies of each congregation. I was asked by the churches and the presbytery to direct that study when Rev. Mata resigned his coach-mentor responsibility to complete work on his doctorate. The cost for these studies would be covered by the sale of the dissolved congregation.

On October 1, 1995, the study began. Five of the six churches and two of the three Presbyterian mission agencies in the area decided to conduct self-studies as part of the larger strategic study. Each study of each church and agency was built around the concept of magnet churches.

Through this strategic-planning process, each church and mission agency was able to determine a single "magnetic" focus of mission, and each involved its entire congregation or constituency in determining that focus. Each church and agency created objectives and devised a strategy and plan of action to implement that focus. The leadership of all six churches and the mission agencies then gathered together to study all the individual strategic plans; they discovered there was no overlap or competition in the respective foci chosen. What all did need, however, was support for each church and common areas of ministry that needed to be undertaken as a cluster of the whole.

The result was the formal creation of a cluster strategy, in which the six churches and the three mission agencies determined three primary foci of cooperative ministry: community organizing; youth outreach to Hispanic, Korean, Taiwanese, Filipino and Anglo neighborhood youth; and the strengthening of a "hands on" incarnational ministry program. In the past year all three foci have been greatly developed, organizing around neighborhood and church issues in three neighborhoods, developing four distinct community outreach efforts to neighborhood youth and joint activities of all the youth groups, and providing experiences to 15 college graduates in urban ministry.

Courses and learning opportunities for church officers, church school teachers, evangelism and community workers have also been developed, as well as joint worship opportunities and retreats for spiritual formation. Nine staff were employed (two full-time, seven part-time) for deployment to the churches and mission agencies to carry out the commonly agreed upon strategy. Staff salaries were paid by the presbytery from the invested monies from the sale of the seventh church building. I agreed to be director of the cluster on a half-time basis.

The success of the Hollywood-Wilshire Cluster was built around turning a *ministry liability* (the seventh church that was no longer viable) into a *funding asset* (using invested monies from the sale of its building) to enable a significant *mission advance* to occur. And all this happened because six churches, three mission agencies and a denomination's regional judicatory were willing to "color outside the lines" of how ministry ought to be done! This is the cluster approach to ministry in urban communities.

# 4

# Dawn of new life

## Value change through community organizing

*Franklin Joseph*

India covers an area of 1.27 million square miles or 2.4 percent of the world's area. India contains 16 percent of the world's population, making it the second most populous country in the world. The UN estimated India's population in 1996 at 953 million.

India's urban population has seen enormous growth since 1950. In 1950 there were only five million-plus cities in India. By 1991 there were 24 cities with a population of more than a million people. According to the 1991 census India's urban population was 217.2 million.

India has four metropolitan cities: Bombay, Calcutta, Delhi and Madras. According to the 1991 census Bombay has a population of 12,569,978; Calcutta 10,860,399; Delhi 9,370,475; and Madras 5,361,468. Approximately 27.7 percent of the urban population lives below the poverty line. A total of 9 million in these four cities live in slums. National trends indicate that, while rural poverty is declining, urban poverty is increasing. Despite the various programs the Indian government has initiated to alleviate poverty, only 18 percent of the resources allotted for the poor actually reach them.

## URBAN INITIATIVES

In 1980 a number of staff in a Christian non-government organization engaged in urban ministry in India's cities. In the early stages the primary focus was on providing health and education services for the urban poor and loans for income-generation projects. Community organizing was not yet part of the approach to development.

It was only in the late eighties that the concept of community organizing was introduced as a strategy for working with the urban poor. The Christian non-government organization began its urban community organizing initiative in 1989. Madras was selected as the first city in which to begin this effort.

## THE CITY OF MADRAS

Madras is one of the fastest growing cities in India. Its current population is over five million, with expected growth of up to seven million by 2000. Estimates are that one-third of the population live in slums and squatter settlements. Houses are usually one room, with mud walls and thatched roofs made out of coconut branches, scrap metal, cardboard and other available materials. Most of these dwellings are found along the roads, railway tracks and canals, dangerous areas that are also subject to flooding.

Most of the people are rural migrants and come from the lowest caste in Indian society. Hinduism is the predominant religion, though mostly in a form of folk Hinduism with strong elements of animism, distinct from the philosophical Hinduism of the higher castes. Each person can have his or her own individual god from the pantheon of gods. Folk mysticism in the form of witchcraft and fear of evil spirits pervades the people's religious practice. They are landless, illiterate and extremely poor, living constantly under threat of eviction and fire. Most of the men are unskilled and cannot find employment within the economy's formal sector. These men turn to drugs and alcohol as a way out of their frustration. This, in turn, leads to tensions within the home and causes family breakdown. Women are forced to take on the role of the family's primary caregiver and provider.

In spite of these difficulties there exists a strong sense of community. People have an expectation that life will get better. They often help one another by working together in times of need and crisis. They are courageous, strong and resilient, and they work hard to make the community a better place for the sake of their children. Even in the midst of the most adverse conditions they seldom lose their sense of humor.

## COMMUNITY ORGANIZING

For our group's first effort in community organizing we wanted a community that was central, fairly small, not too diverse, open to change, and manageable, given our limited resources. After an initial survey of impoverished neighborhoods in Madras, we selected an area with approximately 600 families. Work in this community began in July 1989.

We followed five basic principles in our community organizing:
* ❖ Networking
* ❖ Coalition building
* ❖ Action and reflection
* ❖ Leadership empowerment
* ❖ (resulting in) Rebirth of the community

## NETWORKING

We began by calling on the community's leadership. Initially, these leaders questioned us about our motives for getting involved. Our explanation that we wanted to work for the community's welfare did not satisfy them. The leaders were concerned that we were coming to convert their community to Christianity. They had good reason to be suspicious, as others had come supposedly to help but had their own interests at heart. It took several months to impress upon the community that we were there to work *with* them and to be a part of their struggle.

We did not rush in to address the problems we saw. Rather, we wanted the people to set their own agenda. They had a long list of issues they wished to address, from educating their children to improving their health. We suggested that they confront the most urgent and important issue. The first thing they wanted to do was rid their slum of the rubbish that had accumulated over the years. But who would do it? They came to realize that they themselves were the best people to address this issue, since they were the ones most affected by it!

## Coalition building

We brought together a coalition composed primarily of women and discussed with them the issue of the rubbish in their community. They decided to meet with the local government official to present their grievances and demand action. The coalition members visited the government office and presented their demand to clean up their slum. The official responded favorably and sent a team of sanitary workers to clean up the whole area. It took almost a week to complete the work. At the end of the week the community arranged for a celebration and extended an invitation to the official, which the official accepted. At the celebration the community thanked the official and presented other community needs. The official agreed to look into the community's list of demands.

Throughout this process the community organizer from the non-government organization stayed with the community as one of its members. He encouraged them to take leadership of the process. He acknowledged that the rubbish issue was successfully addressed by the community's collective bargaining. The community organizer gave credit for this first success to the coalition members. This enabled coalition members to develop trust in the community organizer. They could see this community organizer's different approach. They asked the organizer to help them start an organization that would represent community needs to the government and work for the people's welfare. Thus the Women's Association was born.

Women's Association members come from all walks of life. The primary reason for starting with the Women's Association was because it was easier to bring the women together due to their availability. During the day the men went out to work, but most of the women stayed at home to look after the children and do household chores.

The organizer enabled the community women to come together, select their leaders and draw up rules and regulations for the association. The association was formally registered with the government in November 1990. The registration legitimized the association as the community's representative body to the government and non-government organizations.

A Youth Association composed of youth and men was formed soon after. Together the youth and women's associations work to address the community's major issues. These associations have successfully addressed issues such as drinking water, roads, electricity, health, education, government loans for small-enterprise development and getting access to resources from non-government organizations.

## Action and reflection

The action-reflection process is an important part of community organizing. The coalition's first action was a success. Community reflection on this first success led to the formation of the Women's Association. The association began to address issues such as water, electricity and roads; they did not always meet with success.

Further community reflection led to planning for agitation within the democratic framework. For example, the community did not get enough drinking water. The leaders presented this need several times to the local government but did not get any response. Finally they decided to block the main road to get the government's attention. On the appointed day men, women and children blocked the main road. Traffic came to a standstill. Police and officials rushed to the area and pacified the crowd by restoring the water supply. On another occasion the community organized a day-long hunger strike to get the government to construct public toilets in the community. The government relented, and new toilets were constructed. Through their constant struggle and advocacy the association enabled 78 widows and aged destitute to receive government welfare. When the community was affected by a flood, the association persuaded the government to extend assistance by giving RS 300 (US$10) to each affected family. With the experience gained in this community the non-government organization began community organizing projects in three more slums.

Throughout the organizing process the community organizer from the non-government organization assisted the people in the community in understanding their own power. The non-government organization did not provide any money for this program but arranged for leadership training of the coalition members. This training provided the opportunity for coalition members to reflect on their successes and failures. Through the action-reflection process they could evaluate their actions and plan their next steps. Work and words, action and reflection became an integral part of training and community organizing. Through the action-reflection process the community came to understand the role of local government. They realized that government's primary duty is to provide basic amenities for the community. Moreover, government implements various programs for the community's welfare. So the association began to focus on securing government welfare schemes for the community. The Women's Association successfully obtained loans for small businesses from government banks. Community-organizing efforts also secured vocational training for the community's young people. Altogether, 62 youth underwent training through this program.

A matching grant was provided to the association to start a credit union with 26 women. The members manage the credit union and use funds for small-business projects. These kinds of experiences are repeated in all the slums the non-government organization works in. In another slum 74 widows receive government welfare, and 65 women received assistance to start small businesses. Tree planting is another important activity; over 500 tree saplings have been planted in these slums.

## Leadership empowerment

During the first two years of its work in the slums of Madras the non-government organization conducted 10 training events on leadership and community organizing. These training events provided an opportunity for association members to acquire leadership skills and clarify their value system. For example, city tours for the members of the Women's Association were arranged. These tours were not for sightseeing but for gathering information from various government departments. The women went on these tours in pairs. They visited various offices and gathered information on government programs. This information was shared with association members and plans were made to gain community access to these programs.

During leadership training much importance was given to values clarification and good leadership qualities. Often stories from the Bible were shared as examples of good leadership. As a result the community began to challenge corrupt local leadership. For example, distribution of drinking water was controlled by one person, who collected money for this service. The Women's Association challenged this individual and wrested away control of water distribution from him, distributing water freely to all. Within two years the corrupt leaders became powerless, and the community ignored them. Association members began to meet to discuss social and moral issues. The association center became the focal point for values clarification and values change. Community transformation began to take root in the hearts of the association's members.

## Rebirth of the community

In the six years of the non-government organization's involvement in the first slum, staff members led a few individuals to Christ. Staff enabled community children to cultivate good behavior and values through moral-education classes. The children often challenged the wrong values of the adults. One such example was when children made a procession through the area, denouncing those who were addicted to alcohol. This brought an awareness regarding the need to address the issue of alcoholism. Because of this action some alcoholics gave up drinking and others were referred by the Women's Association to the addiction center for treatment.

Another example of a community's rebirth was our work in a resettlement colony of 15,000 people. These people were brought together with the promise that they would be provided with good housing, a promise the government did not keep. Only a few houses were built in the first year. During the monsoon season in 1990 the area was flooded and the community approached us for assistance. We provided some emergency food supplies and worked with the community in organizing them. The first issue this community wanted to address was housing. The community decided to present the government with its housing concerns but was unsure how to go about doing so. The community organizer said he would lead a team from the community to meet with a government official but would not present the problem—the community members should do so themselves. On the appointed day the community organizer led the community representatives to the official. The people did the talking and the official, faced with a large group of determined people, promised to meet the community's demands. This experience gave the community boldness to approach the government on other issues. Since then, community associations have successfully addressed various issues, such as health education and economic development.

Currently the non-government organization is involved in more than 12 slums in the city of Madras alone, not counting its involvement in eight other cities in India. There is a movement of people coming to Christ. The people who played key roles in the successes recounted in this chapter are the community organizers and the association leaders.

Our involvement in these communities as the staff from the non-government organization has been in organizing the community and providing training. Funds were provided for income generation and a vocational-training program based on the idea of partnership. We asked association members what some results of their initiatives were. They observed these seven important changes in the community:

❖ The educational status had improved through adult non-formal education and formal education for children.

❖ The people, especially children, were in better health because of health programs implemented by the government and non-government organizations. The association played a major role in gaining access to these programs.

❖ The government provided basic amenities such as roads, water, electricity, housing, a park and day-care centers for children.

❖ Household belongings had increased because of the additional income generated through association programs.

❖ A clean environment has been created because of awareness of health and sanitation issues.

❖ There was peace in the community because of the love and concern shown to one another because of new life in Christ.

❖ The land value has increased because of the improvement of the neighborhood.

Overall, there is a greater sense of responsibility and civic conscience in the community, so much so that people pay their taxes and housing loans to the government regularly.

When we, the staff from the Christian non-government organization, first entered the resettlement colony in 1990, there were only two Christians among a population of 15,000. Today more than one-third of the community are followers of Christ. Four new churches have been established. Worshiping groups have formed in other slums. When the members of the Women's Association were asked about this change, this is what they said:

❖ The love and concern shown by the Christians are primary reasons. All improvements that the community can point to are due

69

to the Christians. No one cared for us in time of need except for the Christians. The community center, the public park, the houses, roads, water, electricity, the trees, healthy children, and income-generation programs are signs that someone cares for us.

❖ The Christian community organizers developed our leadership abilities so our association could address issues of importance to the community. We are empowered. We write letters to the government and other non-government organizations to gain access to resources and to initiate programs.

❖ Community organizers began every program with prayer. People in the community have seen that God answers prayer. Whenever we prayed to Jesus, he guided us and gave us success. For example, the community had sent repeated requests to a government official to construct public toilet facilities. Association members made several visits to government offices without success. The community organizer encouraged them to try again, which they did. On the appointed day association members gathered to go to the government office. The community organizer suggested praying to God that their mission might be successful. The members in turn requested the organizer to pray. God answered the prayer. When the members met with the official, to their surprise he granted their request. Construction began within a week. Association members and the community believed in the power of Jesus after this event, and there was an openness to learning more about Jesus. Further, association members had a number of personal problems. We shared these problems with the organizer. She encouraged us to pray and also prayed with us. God answered these prayers. This strengthened our faith in Jesus. Soon we began to witness to others.

❖ God's power is another important reason. We arranged for a special film show about Jesus. When the film was running, a community member objected to screening a Christian film and cut the power supply. A few days later police arrested this community member for a crime he had committed. The community attributed this punishment as God's punishment. There was a sense of fear and respect in the community about Jesus.

❖ The association's ongoing success further confirms that God is blessing us. The association's credibility in the community and government is very high.

## PROGRAM EVALUATION

Evaluating the entire process helps us uncover the following reasons for this program's success.

First, the community organizer integrated Christian witness in all program activities. This assisted the community in understanding that Jesus is concerned about the community's economic and social life.

Second, nearby churches and missions stood with us from the beginning and helped new believers grow in their faith. They did not pursue an independent course of action. They always identified with our organizing effort. They complemented our work with prayer and Christian nurture. We have been bringing pastors of various churches in the slum areas for monthly gatherings where communities and churches share mutual concerns. We explore ways and means of working together and fostering fellowship among various churches. Eventually we hope to move these various faith groups toward a coalition that will work together for the welfare of the poor.

Third, the community organizers' personal witness and counseling of association members in their time of need enabled many to understand Jesus' relevance in their individual lives.

Fourth, weekly review meetings among the organizers helped them to plan and to pray for the community. Monthly prayer and fasting enabled staff to receive needed strength and guidance.

Above all, it is the Lord who draws people to himself. All praise and honor to God, and God alone.

# 5

# Working with the street people in Zimbabwe

*Toniel Marimba*

Zimbabwe's rate of urbanization has more than doubled its population growth since 1984. The number of people living in towns and cities increased drastically between 1970 and 1990. Now, more than 40 percent of the country's population lives in urban areas.

This rural to urban movement was the result of many factors, including the liberation war, which reached its height in rural areas in 1970–79. This war ended when the country gained independence from British rule at the end of 1979. Persistent harsh droughts and food shortages between 1982 and 1992 added to the problem by pushing large parts of the population from rural communities to urban streets. Landlessness and population congestion after the liberation war were other contributing factors.

Harare and Buluwayo are two of Zimbabwe's major cities, and these cities experienced the highest influx of people migrating from rural to urban communities. Most of these people became homeless and squatters. This unplanned urbanization uprooted and dislocated communities and created new inequalities between rich and poor. The result has been a threat to traditional values and structures that once served to restrict criminal behavior and recover social values as families have become isolated, alienated, less constrained by social norms and exposed to poverty.

Adding to the problem is that Zimbabwe's cities were developed as colonial administrative and trading centers rather than industrial and commercial centers equipped to support large populations. As a result, urban authorities providing administration and services have been unable to keep up with the explosive growth of squatter communities and shanty towns. Local authorities in Harare and Buluwayo, hit by their own cash-flow crisis and competing priorities, have found it increasingly difficult to deal with the influx of people seeking a better life in the cities. In Harare, for example, overcrowded living conditions, poverty and soaring unemployment contribute to ill-health and the outbreak of disease. Poverty is a serious issue in Zimbabwe's cities. In rural communities people could share a small piece of land, water, food and other services communally, but when they arrived in the city they found a situation of "every man for himself and God for us all." Basic human services were lacking; only the necessities of air and sunshine were shared by rich and poor at no cost.

Because of vulnerability to attacks, people would gather in groups at night, sleeping in rows on the pavement and waking early to search for food. These groups continued to grow in certain areas of Harare: the main railway station, Mbare high density suburbs, Mukuvisi effluent stream at the city's eastern periphery, and the Government Vehicle Inspection Department, also near Mukuvisi stream. More groups gathered in other areas of the city, becoming an eyesore to city administrators.

Numbers of street children and street beggars continued to grow daily. As their numbers grew, so did social ills and the crime rate, causing concern among law-enforcement agencies and authorities. The public also became concerned, and many forums were held to no avail, seeking to solve the problem of homelessness and the street people's plight.

The unemployment crisis was getting worse by the day. Statistics indicated that more than 20,000 workers had been laid off since January 1991. To cope with the unemployment problem, the formal economy had to grow at a rate of over 10 percent a year. According to *The Zimbabwe Herald* (April 1996), the country's economic growth rate from 1991 to 1994 stood at 3 percent annually. Only an average of 10,000 jobs were being created yearly for over 300,000 school leavers who entered the labor market annually to compete for between 20,000 and 30,000 formal sector opportunities in the job market and tertiary-training institutions.

## THE URBAN ADVANCE PROJECT

For many years World Vision Zimbabwe's focus was on community development with people living in the country's rural communities. In 1989 the organization began a new initiative to respond to the needs of the urban poor through a project named Urban Advance. The purpose of the project was to listen to the cry of the poor, walk side by side with them, help them to have a voice, and give them the capacity to change their situation. The Urban Advance project employed one person, a coordinator whose role was to identify the urban poor, create and build relationships with them and find out who else was involved in alleviating their plight. The coordinator was also responsible for building relations with local churches in the city. After a year on the job the coordinator found the street people's problem undefined, work with them was unfocused and their plight was subject to many interpretations from various quarters.

There was an obvious need for a professional study of the problem to assist in coming up with recommendations for a strategy for effective work among the street people. World Vision Zimbabwe commissioned such a study through Urban Advance to determine the magnitude of the problem, identify causal factors, establish various means of livelihood for the street people and survival or coping mechanisms to determine a plan of action.

## PROBLEMS IDENTIFIED BY THE STUDY

The study identified the following problems: homelessness, street begging, child abuse, massive unemployment, drug trafficking, substance abuse, economic decline, high divorce rates and regional conflicts.

Twenty-one squatter camps of varying sizes scattered within greater Harare were identified. The biggest of these was at Mbare Musika. Mbare Musika is a congregating place for people on the move, where all the routes for passenger transport in the nation begin and end. Passenger transport from cities and towns in the country and from all rural areas in the nation end at Mbare Musika. Road transport and passengers traveling to and from neighboring countries also pass through Mbare Musika. Many people have settled at Mbare Musika because they have lost belongings as a result of criminal activities in this area. Large numbers of the street children that flock the streets of Harare come from Mbare.

Mbare Musika is also a beehive of activities of various kinds throughout the whole week, day and night. In this respect it outdoes the city center, which is usually quiet during weekends. The street beggars who frequent the city center during weekdays are at Mbare Musika during weekends.

There are three categories of destitute at Mbare Musika. The first one is the stranded traveler who becomes homeless. The second is the person who is in the process of becoming destitute but pretends to be a traveler. The third is the settled destitute who does not live in proper living quarters; some of them have family-like units built of plastic or cardboard materials.

### WORKING AMONG THE SQUATTER CAMP PEOPLE

The Urban Advance project encouraged coalition-building and triggered the process of community organizing through creation of forums, enabling people to deal corporately and collectively with issues that kept them in a squatter situation. Coalition-building was done by forming committees or associations that looked into various issues that affected camp inmates and took action to address the problems. Associations also organized themselves to deal corporately with the forces that were exploiting their community and causing their powerlessness. Though project staff worked alongside three squatter camps in Harare—Porta Farm, Glenview and the Vehicle Inspection Department along Mukuvisi effluent stream—they concentrated community-organizing facilitation in Porta Farm Squatter Camp.

In 1991 the government rounded up street people from all the squatter camps in and around Harare. Zimbabwe was hosting a Commonwealth meeting, which the Queen of England would be attending. During this round-up many people lost what little they possessed, and police incarcerated 300 of them in Chikurubi, a maximum security prison. Of the more than 2,200 individuals who were rounded up, most were put into a camp 20 miles away from Harare's city center.

This camp, called Porta Farm, was not a concentration camp but a city government established holding camp. There was no forced labor; there was no war going on. Nevertheless, there were rifle-toting watchmen, high fences and guarded gates. Today the guards and fences are gone, but many of the forces that drove the urban poor there in the first place remain. Authorities originally designated the camp a transit place for three months, after which inmates were going to be settled elsewhere permanently. The city government never honored this promise, though half the community has now moved to other areas.

At Porta Farm Camp the people found themselves in a community with no traditional authority structures or natural cohesion; confusion and chaos reigned. In the first two weeks Urban Advance project staff provided food aid and organized meetings to help provide leadership for this community. A skeleton leadership was created to at least get the community going. Project staff invited churches to assist with the work at Porta Farm. The Salvation Army, the Anglican Church, Martin Luther Church and Hear the Word Church responded with food and counseling services.

Project staff assisted the community to form committees, associations and clubs, where the people could corporately and collectively work together to solve important issues. The people created leadership structures that looked into the community's social, political and spiritual life. One leader now oversees the whole community's affairs, assisted by four community branch leaders. These branch leaders are responsible for the four sectors that make up the community. Sector leaders dealing with education, health and security issues are responsible to the branch leaders.

Besides these structures the community has associations or committees that oversee the community's socioeconomic matters. These groups create savings plans to help prepare for building homes when they are finally resettled. Groups and clubs that do income-generating activities— such as basket-making, tin smithing, knitting clothing, creating wall hangings and fish selling—were also created. Sports clubs also prosper.

### Education sector

Under the education sector, the community—with the assistance of Urban Advance and Martin Luther Church—established a primary school with classes for grades 1 to 7 in 1993 and was granted an informal education status by the government. The government now pays the teachers, while the community provides books and the school's infrastructure. Thus far, 2,600 children have passed through this school and some have moved on to secondary education.

## Health sector

The health sector has a housing committee, which is responsible for negotiating with the government on the resettlement issue. The committee of three men and three women resisted eviction orders by city government if no alternative housing was made available for people by contesting eviction orders three times in the courts; the case is now under consideration by the high court of Zimbabwe. Urban Advance, through its advocacy role, helped the housing committee to work with human-rights organizations in the country to get legal advice and representation in the courts of law.

This committee also leads savings clubs for housing projects. Besides looking into housing problems, this committee also looks into the community's health affairs. This includes water and sanitation, temporary infrastructures built by the community, repairs to broken water pipes, latrine maintenance, and ensuring that roads and the environment are clean. They see to the health of the people by ensuring that the sick are sent to hospitals, the dead are given a decent burial and the bereaved are comforted.

## Security sector

This sector is responsible for maintaining public order. It controls the spread of information, community influx and ensures the safety of camp inmates and their property.

## Spiritual life

When it comes to worship and the spread of the gospel, most of the community leadership had become Christians before their eviction from squatter camps and placement at Porta Farm. Preaching and studying of the Word and the practice of church ritual continue at Porta Farm.

In their interaction with the people Urban Advance project staff facilitated every activity in such a manner that it pointed to Jesus Christ as the solution to all human problems. The lifestyle of the staff became a living witness to the gospel of Jesus Christ.

Martin Luther Church, a partner with Urban Advance in Porta Farm, also integrated its development work with the gospel of Jesus Christ. The result was that 75 percent of Porta Farm's residents became Christian by July 1996. The percentage has since risen, with two pastors and fourteen lay leaders residing in the community. An indigenous church called Apostolic Faith Johane Marange, which believes and practices the preaching of the Word and self-reliance, has spread like wildfire in this community. Through this church's work many residents are now involved in income-generating projects. Muslims tried to introduce Islam in 1995–96 by providing material aid and staying in the community for nine months. But three months after the Muslim leadership left, their followers converted to Christianity. The small building they used as their mosque has now disappeared.

Urban Advance project staff and members of Martin Luther Church and other churches are always invited to celebrate with the community whenever there is a ceremony or important ritual taking place in the community. The people believe God has enabled them to continue despite the difficulties they have faced while living in Porta Farm Camp.

## Epworth Community

While work at Porta Farm Squatter Camp was initiated, families from Epworth Community sought assistance from project staff to locate their children, who had been placed in Porta Farm when the street people were rounded up. Epworth Community is a peri-urban community, a zone between modern urban life and traditional life. Chaos rules in this community as the urban people exploit the unsuspecting from rural areas. The community has a high crime rate, a high unemployment rate and serves as a drug-trafficking center for Harare.

Urban Advance staff managed to locate these children, but though they returned to their families, the children could not remain unless food, clothing and opportunities for education were somehow made available. More than 50 percent of the children ran away from home within the first week of reunion with their families. They walked the streets again and did not trust project staff, who wanted to instill in them social values through counseling. The aim of the counseling was to ensure that the children became useful members of society who would not disrupt established principles and values.

Contrary to society's basic values, street children have values of their own. Theirs are the values of survival. For them, "good" is what enables them to satisfy their stomachs. Stealing is no shame, it's a job. The children organize themselves in different types of gangs, because organization is necessary for survival. Street children—boys and girls—

take drugs to overcome fear or to accomplish acts that basically go against their nature. They have to act in order to survive.

Project staff faced the challenge of enabling these families to become self-reliant and care for their children. Staff felt it was wrong for children not to have loving families, to be out of school and alone on the streets as gang members. They stressed the following values regarding the children:

- ❖ Children should lead healthy lives in which their basic needs are met so they won't steal or take drugs.
- ❖ Children should live in a protected environment, whether a family or an institution, where they are subject to discipline and authority and taught society's basic values.
- ❖ Children should be in school, where their daily activities are organized and directed.

Urban Advance formed networks with seven churches in the city, including the Anglican Church, Trinity Methodist, the Dutch Reformed Church, the Roman Catholic Church, Central Baptist Church, the Presbyterian Church and the Salvation Army Church, to respond to the needs around them by forming the Harare Shelter for the Destitute.

The Anglican Church opened the doors of St. Mary's Cathedral to Harare Shelter for the Destitute, providing a place for the shelter's rehabilitation activities. All seven churches supplied food for the soup kitchen, which provided the poor with one hot meal per day, cooking utensils and spiritual counseling. Classes teaching children to count, read, write and do craft work were introduced.

From the start of the vocational training and education program street children stole teaching materials and teaching aids, training tools and articles ready for sale. Those who revealed the culprits would be harassed and beaten at night. Sending the wrongdoers to government reform centers didn't do any good, because the children returned to the streets even worse than before. Controlling street children in a cathedral environment became a nightmare, and the children's lack of discipline slowed the pace of activities. Despite these initial problems, of the 2,100 children who went through the program 280 were admitted to formal schools and some have attained a secondary education.

As the rehabilitation of street children progressed, project staff continued relationship-building with the mothers of Epworth Community. Two women's groups were formed within two years. The first group, Kubatana Co-operative, chose to engage in market gardening.

They grow vegetables throughout the year to feed their families and sell some of the produce to earn income, which they use to send their children to school and to buy clothes. They also engage in home craft activities. Kumboedza Food Catering Club is the second group, composed of former commercial sex workers. These women exchanged prostitution activities for food preparation, processing and selling.

The groups and project staff faced many hurdles in getting land for gardening purposes, getting the local administering board to allow them to establish selling stalls for their products, and delays by authorities in processing official documents. Some of the community residents became jealous and blocked the speedy sale of products by these women. But the former sex workers had changed their lifestyle and earned respect from their community, which now supports the women's efforts. Most of these women are now Christians, and they pray daily for their food project to succeed. They even pray for the clients who buy their food. Both groups meet twice a week to pray for their project activities and their community.

Besides the gardening and food catering, these two groups have subsidiary projects that increase their earnings. For example, some women perform bicycle repairs, usually a man's job in Zimbabwe. After training for six months at bicycle manufacturing companies, three women can now assemble new bicycles and repair broken-down ones. The Urban Advance project helped by sending them to receive their training. Some of the women also sell crocheted and knitted materials.

Now the local administrative board has warned the gardening group that their land may be taken away through upgrading activities by the Ministry of Local Government Urban and Rural Development. The whole area is to be upgraded, including roads, water sources and human settlements. This upgrading will require good housing that meets Zimbabwe's housing policy standards. It is definite that these women, with no garden as their major source of income, cannot provide shelter and food for their families. Urban Advance is in the process of negotiating with local authorities and community leaders to enable these women to find alternative land with adequate water for gardening purposes.

The impact of Urban Advance's facilitation in the development process in Epworth Community is seen and recognized by the people of the area, where more than 200 households have benefited from community mobilization and training in various development methods and approaches. The children of those families directly involved in the project are no longer roaming the streets but attend school activities; those who are grown assist their parents by selling the garden produce and foodstuffs processed by the food-catering club.

## YOUTH OF POOR COMMUNITIES

The third category of people the Urban Advance project works with are the young people of poor communities. These are the street children who have grown up, and the unemployed school leavers of Harare and the poor communities of Dzivaresekwa and Epworth. The project trained these youths in the area of employment creation so the youths would do microenterprise projects that keep them occupied and that generate income. This involved developing the youths' minds and skills.

Youths who had moved from Porta Farm Camp to Dzivaresekwa walked the streets in search of jobs. The project mobilized these youths and merged them with those already in the vocational training at St. Mary's Cathedral.

Besides these two groups of youths, another category emerged: youths from poor communities surrounding the city. Most of these are young people who completed their secondary education but could not pursue tertiary education or find employment. They learned of the project's training program from either the press, through other trained youth, or by seeing items made by the trained youths being sold at marketplaces. Combining the training of these three categories of youths was an enormous job, difficult but rewarding. These youth were trained in communication methods, leadership techniques, project planning and management, financial controls and how to start small businesses.

From 1992 to 1996, 325 youth were equipped with knowledge, skills and ideas of starting and implementing their own projects as individuals or as groups. By 1993 a number of these youths started small projects including trading, sewing, metal fabrication, photography, leather crafts, carpentry, wood and stone carvings and hairdressing. There were 12 of these groups at the end of 1994. Seven of the groups were a combination of girls and boys working together. All groups began managing their activities with help from Urban Advance staff, who offered ideas and provided information on where to go and whom to see for assistance. Some of the groups disbanded by 1995 due to lack of capital, and some continued to struggle on until 1996. Of the 12 groups formed in 1993, 5 continue to this day, and 4 more groups began in 1995–96.

The groups that braved and overcame the effects of the government's economic structural adjustment are the Right Choice Leather Co-op, now manufacturing all sorts of leather products, and Chitungwiza Integrated Youth Survival Alternative Project, which has three groups engaged in auto mechanics, training other youths and trading. Quality Wood Cooperative manufactures household furniture, and Shoe Doctor Company specializes in shoe manufacturing. The groups that began in 1995–96 are the Fountain Blue Soap Cooperative, specializing in manufacturing laundry bar soap; Dzivaresekwa Youth Project, which manufactures candles; and Young Stars, a Girls' Sewing Group that manufactures school uniforms. Besides individuals who went through the training program and now run their own successful small businesses, these nine groups are doing very well.

The Shoe Doctor Company and the Fountain Blue Soap Cooperative begin their work every morning with a time set aside for devotions and prayer. Four executive members of Quality Wood Cooperative Society are members of churches and leaders in their denominations. Three members of the Shoe Doctor Company are leaders of a youth movement church ministry. This ministry embraces young people from many different church denominations and encourages teaching the Bible, praying and offering praise and worship to God.

This project activity has enabled many youth to become self-employed and earn money to buy food, clothes, pay for their living quarters, support church work and even support their parents. Work among these youth has also fostered a sense of unity and love among them and their families.

## PARTICIPATION, EMPOWERMENT AND LEADERSHIP

Among the people who responded to the gospel through the work of the Urban Advance project were Kenneth Musanje, who in 1990 became a community mobilizer for Urban Advance. Christopher Phiri, Aaron Tembo and Teddy Dende are some of the leaders who became friends and continued to work with Urban Advance. After his conversion Aaron Tembo went to study at Rhema Bible College and is now a pastor working with Hear the Word Ministries. Christopher Phiri volunteers constantly to help Urban Advance with its community mobilization efforts in Epworth Community. Teddy Dende cares for orphans in Glen View Squatter Camp.

Some of the street children who came to know Christ also made great contributions to other people's lives. One of these was Mike Chimhondo. Mike became a leader for an Urban Advance street children's rehabilitation project in Epworth community. He cared for 18 children and trained them in leather craft, soap making and carpentry. Mike Chimhondo died of the effects of diseases he contracted while he lived on the streets.

After his conversion, Kenneth Musanje, Urban Advance's senior community mobilizer, became the project's main link with the street people's organization. He worked with the project coordinator to organize prayer and counseling meetings with the street people. He also assisted in cementing relationships with street people who had become thugs and interacted with various gangs. George Madziva, one of the converts from these gangs, is now a supervisor for an electricity construction company.

Urban Advance's work among the street people of Zimbabwe nurtured the creation of associations and committees, thereby establishing community leadership in the squatter camps, especially in Porta Farm Camp. Squatter-camp residents are aware of their problems and have the ability to take necessary action collectively and cooperatively against the forces that seek to disempower them. They now have the skills to take the initiative in mobilizing their labor and their hard-earned resources to manage their community environment.

The youths doing micro- and small-enterprise development activities are able to work and share their resources with each other. They manage and control their businesses on their own. The former street children are now gainfully employed and are also assisting those caught in the situations they once experienced.

**6**

# The Alliance of Basic Christian Communities

## People empowerment in a garbage dump

*Benigno Beltran*

I n the year 2000, 52 percent of the world's population will be living in cities. The world is in the midst of a massive urban transition unlike that of any other period in history. In the coming decades population growth will be virtually synonymous with urban growth. People from rural areas will continue to flock to cities because they offer jobs, entertainment and advantages in the delivery of education, health and other social services, apart from access to information (newspapers, television and radio are all headquartered in cities), creativity, diversity and innovation. In the year 2025, 75 percent of the world's people will be living in cities. The focus for evangelization and ministry efforts will have to be in the urban areas.

If present trends continue, tomorrow's mega-cities loom as urban nightmares. More than a quarter of the world's population in the year 2000 will live in slums and squatter settlements in the urban centers. Rapid population growth brings with it a host of social and ecological problems, some of staggering proportions: poverty, crime, environmental degradation, substandard housing in slum areas and poor sanitation. Hundreds of millions live in squatter colonies in the world's cities and 220 million lack access to clean drinking water, while more than

420 million do not have access to latrines. Water-borne diseases kill more than 4 million infants and children every year. Conditions devoid of human aspirations breed crime, disease, addiction and alienation: "The people of the land have practiced extortion and committed robbery; they have oppressed the poor and needy, and have extorted from the alien without redress" (Ezek. 22:29).

The Philippines had a population of 68,614,200 in the census of 1995. It is 48.5 percent urbanized. Metro Manila alone had 9,454,000 in 1995, and growth is increasing at a geometric rate. Home to the country's principal ports, government centers, financial institutions and markets for industries providing employment opportunities, Manila has grown crowded by manufacturing concerns over the years. And people from the provinces, pushed out by war, rural disasters or crop failure, lured by the promise of jobs, enticed by glittering mega-malls and glamorous movie stars, stream into the city and end up living in slum areas or, worse still, scavenging in garbage dumps.

Smokey Mountain is the popular name given to the huge garbage dump in the heart of the city of Manila. The site was once a peaceful village of fisherfolk before World War II. In 1954 the area was turned into a dumping place for Manila's garbage by the Refuse and Environment Sanitation Bureau. The fishermen and their families continued to live on the site, while many more families congregated around the dump to survive by scavenging in the trash heaps.

Eventually more than 25,000 scavengers lived in makeshift huts constructed from old wood, iron sheets, cardboard and plastic. They piled used tires and stones on top of roofs in efforts to prevent the huts from being blown away during typhoons. Some enterprising individuals tapped illegally into the lines of the Manila Electric Company and collected fees from households connected to the power lines. Community faucets existed, but there were not enough to serve most families' water needs. Many fetched water from outside sources and sold their haul to other residents. Every day was a struggle simply to live. Often riots erupted between groups of scavengers fighting over the right to pick up garbage in a particular area. Police seldom ventured inside the dump site, except in large groups with high-powered weapons, and the place became a haven for criminal elements, petty thieves, kidnappers, carnappers and drug dealers.

The mud and flies, the rats and cockroaches, the stink of burning and decomposing garbage exacerbated already deteriorating health conditions. During the rainy season the dump became a stinking morass of decaying garbage. In summer, smoke reduced visibility to a few feet. Deaths occurred regularly, mainly among infants and children, due to pneumonia, diarrhea and typhoid fever. Tuberculosis and childbirth mortality also claimed many victims.

In 1983 people living in the vicinity of the dump site were forcibly evicted and resettled in Bulihan, Silang, Cavite. Imelda Marcos wanted to turn the dump site into an orchidiarium and a golf course. Because no provisions or amenities, such as jobs, water or electricity, were provided in the resettlement area, the scavengers trickled back to the dump site and started to scavenge once again in order to survive.

The scavengers preferred to stay in the dump site despite the flies and the smell and the smoke. Reasons they cited included the sense of belonging to a community; sentimental attachment to the land where many of their children had died either from disease or by being run over by bulldozers; and the relative ease of finding odd jobs in the vicinity, such as stevedore work at the nearby docks. Before the dump was closed, more than 70 percent of its residents were dependent on the garbage.

In January 1988, when rumors of demolition and forcible relocation were rife, the scavengers prepared to march to Malacañang Palace to talk to President Corazon Aquino. People close to President Aquino got wind of the planned mass mobilization. When she heard that the residents wanted on-site development, President Aquino directed the National Housing Authority to conduct feasibility studies for a low-cost housing project in the dump site. The residents asked to be consulted in the making of the plans.

In 1992 political advocacy reached fever pitch because of fears that Aquino's successor would demolish the scavengers' shanties and forcibly resettle them again. Residents sought appointments to talk to government officials. They wrote to the archbishop of Manila, Jaime Cardinal Sin, who personally talked to government officials in Malacañang. On January 17, 1992, President Aquino ordered the National Housing Authority to implement the Smokey Mountain Development Plan and convert the garbage dump into a habitable site for a housing project. A private-sector joint-venture scheme would finance this, at the least cost to government. The plan proposed to close the dump site, temporarily relocate the scavengers, level the mountain of garbage and treat the soil's toxic content. Houses would be built for qualified residents in the rehabilitated area.

Community leaders met several times before the 1992 elections and decided to support Fidel V. Ramos as the candidate most likely to advance their cause. Soon after being elected, President Ramos issued a proclamation ceding the area to the National Housing Authority. On October 8, 1992, on his one-hundredth day in office, President Ramos inaugurated the housing project for the scavengers in Smokey Mountain by unveiling a scale model of the planned medium-rise buildings. On May 1, 1993, President Ramos formally closed Smokey Mountain as a dump site.

Community leaders of Smokey Mountain met with the heads of government institutions directly involved with the housing project. As soon as the plans for the Smokey Mountain Development and Reclamation Project were finished, the community leaders contacted students and professors of the School for Urban and Regional Planning of the University of the Philippines to evaluate the plans for them, especially the environmental implications of building on top of a dump site. After a few weeks the findings were explained to the people, who decided to support the government plans but asked that the area of each housing unit be increased from 195 square feet to 345. They also asked that the monthly amortization be affordable to the scavenger families. These requests were granted by the government, as well as demands for skills training and livelihood programs for the resettled families. Before the demolition of their shacks the residents asked for a document from the National Housing Authority to bind the government in assuring that each family would be given a unit in the permanent housing. This request was also granted. While the temporary site was being built, a 200–acre reclamation project was undertaken to pay for the project costs. Thirty five-story buildings are being constructed in the former dump site, and the former residents are slated to go back to Smokey Mountain in late 1998.

In 1995 scavenger families were transferred to the temporary relocation site. Thirty-two two-story buildings were constructed, with bathrooms, water and electricity. Eighty-eight families reside in each building. Some 200 families belonging to another organization refused to transfer to the resettlement site, because they wanted a piece of land where they could build their own homes. Others wanted to be left alone, even after it was explained that the mountain might explode because of the methane underneath. These people were forcibly relocated after several consultations.

## Basic Christian Communities: A New Way of Being Church

In the midst of the scandalous gap between rich and poor in the Philippines, which prides itself as the only Christian nation in Asia, much discernment has been attempted by the church in the hope of establishing a society filled with love, justice and harmony—values that characterize the kingdom of God. Inspired by the God of history, whose bias has always been for the poor of Yahweh, church people together with the struggling and disenfranchised in parishes all over the country started coming together to reflect and act as a community of faith. This ecclesial and sociological phenomenon became known as Basic Christian Communities, a community-building pastoral strategy.

During the past two decades Basic Christian Communities became the overall objective of pastoral efforts in the parish, providing an avenue for people's participation in the decision-making process in church and society. In building a church truly servant, prophet and people of God, community participation offers a framework for social action. The holistic model of Basic Christian Communities was enunciated by the Second Plenary Council, speaking for the Catholic church in the Philippines, which gathered in 1996 to propose a vision for the church in the third millennium as

> a community of disciples in mission called to become a Church of the Poor, a Church that lives in evangelical poverty which combines detachment from material possessions with a profound trust in the Lord as the only source of salvation; a Church that defends and vindicates the rights of the poor even when doing so spells for herself alienation or persecution by the rich and powerful; a Church where the poor, equal to all others in Christian dignity, are not only evangelized but become evangelizers themselves; a Church where no one is so poor as to have nothing to give and no one so rich as to have nothing to receive.

The mission is integral salvation: "Evangelization does not stop at the building of the church. It seeks to transform the whole fabric of society according to the values of the kingdom and of Christ."

Community participation is the life-blood of Basic Christian Communities, and participatory development increases people's capacity for self-help to decentralize planning and implementation. It is the reversal of centralized agencies' tendency to think that they have something to offer to improve people's lives without even asking what they really want or need. In participatory development, constituents and beneficiaries are involved in all levels of decision-making and implementation. It is the complete reversal of the so-called top-to-bottom approach, where people are passive recipients of development projects and interventions, which often characterized pastoral ministries in the past.

In Basic Christian Communities the people are the principal actors, playing the lead role in designing programs, planning budgets for personnel, equipment and support, and proposing job descriptions for each person in management. Participatory development is Christian community-building based on the early Christian communities described in Acts 2 and 4. This process values collectivity, communal consensus and a democratic style of work. People's participation initiates fundamental changes in the very structure of society.

## THE ALLIANCE OF BASIC CHRISTIAN COMMUNITIES

The Basic Christian Communities in Smokey Mountain were established in 1978 by the Divine Word missionaries, a religious congregation of 6,000 priests and brothers working in the more difficult places of the world to spread the Good News. In their Constitutions, paragraph 112, the missionaries have written:

> The poor have a privileged place in the gospel. In a world deeply scarred by injustice and inhuman living conditions, our faith calls us to recognize the presence of Christ in the poor and the oppressed. We thus commit ourselves to fostering unity and justice and to overcoming egoism and the abuse of power. We consider it our duty to promote justice according to the gospel in solidarity with the poor and the oppressed.

The idea of establishing Basic Christian Communities as ecclesial communities grew out of the African experience, with its dilemma of cultural disintegration and human underdevelopment, and out of the Latin American experience, rooted in desires to help the poor and oppressed know their own problems and assume responsibility for the solutions to these problems. Although first steps were initiated by priests and seminarians, the formation of the Basic Christian Communities in Smokey Mountain was motivated mainly by the scavengers' efforts to fight for their rights and free themselves from ignorance, injustice and poverty. This desire intensified after the demolition and relocation in 1983. This traumatic experience made the scavengers more determined in their struggle to be recognized as human beings with dignity and inner worth.

On March 27, 1989, the archbishop of Manila, Jaime Cardinal Sin, formally established the Parish of the Risen Christ in Smokey Mountain. The parish includes the dump and several other slum areas in the vicinity. The total parish population is more than 40,000 people, 95 percent of whom are Catholics, many of them nominal ones. The missionaries asked themselves, What can be done to mobilize the scavengers to take up the task of helping themselves? The question also challenged the dole-out mentality of many other organizations doing ministry in the dump site. Their good will and ministries often only served to prolong the dependency of many who are beneficiaries of the handouts, with no thought given to the sustainability of the assistance or to the liberation of the poor from the poverty of their imagination.

The Basic Christian Communities strategy was to root the church once again in the very heart of the Christian community. The form, ministries and evangelical thrust of pastoral action would be derived from the cultural, social, economic and political context of the garbage dump. The church would be brought down from the chapel into the hovels of the scavengers. The objectives of the parish responded to the need for a new sense of belonging and intimacy in the increasingly impersonal nature of relating to one another in the city, far from the personalized relationships and extended family structure in the rural areas where many of the scavengers came from.

Strategies experimented with included increasing lay participation and setting up lay ministries; focusing on Scriptures through Bible-sharing in small clusters of neighboring families; strengthening the integration of faith and life; deepening commitment to work for social change through the transformative power of the Resurrection; and providing a new vision, new hope and new meaning by rooting the community's need for unity in the mystery of the Blessed Trinity, the eternal self-giving at the core of the divinity of the three Persons in one God.

The Alliance of Basic Christian Communities in Smokey Mountain visualizes a self-sustaining organization corresponding to the morals, principles and values that guide its members to live as Christians. The Alliance believes its members should unlock human potential by making people realize and appreciate their worth as individuals. However, the organization also stresses mutual help, social involvement and fellowship, along with prayer and sacramental worship. Armed with a strong social commitment, these communities believe that the empowering of the poor is possible. They believe the scavengers' families can fully participate in this development and eventually in the transformation of Philippine society, which is structured in a way that favors the elite, resulting in the poverty of many.

With the start of the Basic Christian Communities in Smokey Mountain, the Divine Word missionaries celebrated the Eucharist regularly and conducted feeding programs for undernourished children. Seminarians were officially assigned to the dump during weekends for apostolate work as part of their formation and training. They lived with the people, sharing their joys and hopes, their griefs and anxieties. Summer camps allowed seminarians to do catechetical work and community organizing for six weeks during their summer vacation. Activities also included social investigation, enhancement of awareness about social issues and the structuring of collective experience for increased involvement in the community. The people of Smokey Mountain became an integral part of the spiritual and theological formation of future missionaries of the Society of the Divine Word.

In organizing the people the raising of awareness followed the traditional "See, Judge, Act" process initiated in Latin America but enculturated into the Filipino situation. There is an assessment of needs and wants, discussion of problems facing individuals and the community, formulation of a mission and a vision, establishment of goals and objectives, and discussion of obstacles hindering the community from attaining its vision and its goals.

In 1984–85, when the organizational work had just started, members of the Basic Christian Communities joined mass mobilizations for Benigno Aquino, carrying the name of the Alliance. They were not strong then, with few and untrained leaders and members. But they pressed on. Although members' vigilance still had no significant effect, more media focus was given to Smokey Mountain during President Corazon Aquino's time in 1986.

In 1988 the Alliance prepared for another mobilization to demand the development of Smokey Mountain. While the Basic Christian Communities struggled for on-site development against a government whose foreign consultants always advocated relocation as the only solution to congestion in the cities, leaders of the Basic Christian Communities also experienced oppression from local warlords. These were often officials of the local government in cahoots with criminal syndicates. Because Basic Christian Communities leaders fought against drug dealers, they were often threatened with death and bodily harm. In 1990 a fragmentation grenade thrown on top of the roof of the parish house could have killed scores of children playing nearby while their parents engaged in Bible-sharing in the chapel. The people attributed to divine intervention the fact that a part of the firing pin broke off and so the grenade failed to explode.

The parish eventually divided into 18 zones, and each zone comprised a cluster of Basic Christian Communities. Each zone is registered with the Securities and Exchange Commission. The Basic Christian Communities were federated into an Alliance of Basic Christian Communities in Smokey Mountain, also registered with the Security and Exchange Commission, thus attaining a legal personality. The *sambahayan* is a communion of families, the zone a communion of *sambahayans*, and the parish a communion of communities federated under the *Alyansa ng mga Sambayanang Kristiyano sa Smokey Mountain*. All of these are based on a democratic structure, where people have ultimate authority over their leaders in a mutual-benefit organization. The organization thus becomes increasingly self-reliant. Its continued existence no longer depends on outside initiative or funding.

The president of each zone or area automatically becomes a member of the Parish Pastoral Council. There are 24 members of the parish along with the six clusters of the *Kabataang Sambayanang Kristiyano*, the youth arm of the *Alyansa ng Sambayanang Kristiyano (ALSAKRIS)*, who help in administering the parish. Vice-presidents of each zone supervise the youth and the children's Basic Christian Communities.

Other community-based organizations are the Basic Christian Communities for children 7–12 years old. They have their own activities, centered mostly on catechetical instruction and Bible-sharing. They have their own set of elected officers. The youth arm of the Alliance is the Youth Basic Christian Communities, young people aged 13–24, who also have their own set of elected officers and committees. Their programs stress Bible-study every Saturday and solidarity with other youth groups. They conduct outreach programs for prisoners, drug addicts and unwed mothers. They also actively participate in discussions and mass actions regarding the government housing project.

The Alliance divides its tasks through committees. The Spirituality Committee supervises formation programs and liturgical activities in the parish, especially prayer breakfasts and the assignment of sponsors for the daily Eucharist from the different zones. The Health Committee manages the parish's small clinic, oversees the training and activities of health volunteers from each area, helps out during medical missions, and plans to establish a health cooperative and its own drugstore. The Livelihood Committee consults with the Board of Directors of the parish cooperative to assure more participation.

The Education Committee supervises the scholarship programs of the parish, which has close to 400 children ages 4–6 years old in its day-care centers, more than 200 students in its Alternative Learning System for adults and out-of-school youth, and more than 100 students in its vocational training program studying automotive mechanics, computer secretarial preparation and computer technology. The Legal Committee links with volunteer lawyers for seminars on legal procedures and human rights and also helps in looking for pro bono advocates for members who have a case in court.

The Sports Committee organizes tournaments in basketball, volleyball and indoor games for intramural competitions within the area. The Committee for Women's Concerns seeks to raise the consciousness of women regarding their rights at home and in the working place; it is currently setting up a counseling center for battered women and abused children. The Cultural Committee organizes concerts and programs to increase members' love for their own songs and dances. It also supervises the Children of Mother Earth, an environmental group of young people from Smokey Mountain who have already gone on concert tours to Europe and Australia. The Disaster and Relief Committee distributes relief goods during typhoons, fires or other calamities. The Research and Documentation Committee is responsible for official papers and minutes of meetings.

Since 1991 the *Alyansa* has embarked on various activities and livelihood projects through the *Sambahayan ng Muling Pagkabuhay* Multi-Purpose Cooperative, Inc., which is registered with the Cooperative Development Authority. Its various divisions include the Garments Cooperative, the Merchandising Cooperative and the Transport Cooperative, among others. Funding for these projects came from local and international sources. Economically, the people are independent from the parish. However, they still rely on the parish for their spiritual needs. Right now, periodic retreats and recollections are conducted. Groups are invited to give Marriage Encounter seminars and Bible seminars. Seminars on health and livelihood are also given. Celebrations of the Eucharist have increased, especially area-based masses. The youth groups are involved with the Archdiocesan Youth Council in Manila and often join with youth from other parishes in religious and cultural activities. In all, one can easily see the significance of the spiritual aspect and the theological nature of the Basic Christian Communities in Smokey Mountain.

## MISSION-VISION-GOAL

In December 1996 the Executive Committee of the Alliance met for three days to reformulate its mission, vision and goals in the light of the changed situation.

*Vision:*
> We, the members of the Alliance of Basic Christian Communities strive for a peaceful life, unity and human dignity as we work with Jesus the Christ in propagating the Kingdom of God, the Father, Son and Holy Spirit.

*Mission:*
1. To help in proclaiming the Word of God and to live it in the community in order to have a personal relationship with Jesus through the reign of God, the Father, Son and Holy Spirit.
2. To improve the social and economic conditions of the urban poor through self-help for the triumph of everyone.
3. To learn how to actively participate and how to value Filipino culture, customs and history to improve social interaction.

*Goals:*
1. To educate the community in active participation in and submission to Christian living.
2. To assist members in skills-training and finding livelihood opportunities.
3. To actively participate and improve skills and capabilities to raise social conditions, especially regarding the Smokey Mountain Development and Reclamation Project.
4. To engage in activities that will raise the consciousness and motivate members to actively participate in issues concerning the housing project, construction of the incinerator near the housing project, and issues concerning women.

## PARTICIPATORY RESEARCH

This case study is based on participatory research conducted by professors and students of the University of the Philippines in 1994. Participants took part in conceptualizing, data-gathering and analysis. The concept of holistic ministry exemplified by the mission, vision and goals of the Alliance of Basic Christian Communities in Smokey Mountain assumes that the people themselves should shape their own destiny and create their own history. Perceptions, opinions and ideas expressed about the organization being examined came from the people themselves.

The research was conducted a year before on-site development of the garbage dump, a project the Philippine government started after years of lobbying and advocacy by the Alliance of Basic Communities in Smokey Mountain. Additional data from the socio-demographic study conducted by the National Housing Authority in 1995, as well as data from annual strategic planning seminars of Alliance leaders, are incorporated in the case study.

In participatory research community members are not just asked to be involved for effective gathering of information. Rather, they participate actively, from formulation of the statement of the problem to design for evaluation and research, up to validation and planning. This makes it easier to become active participants not only in identifying but also in resolving problems that affect them. Action for developmental change can then be elicited and evoked from their ranks. Eventually participants are educated and mobilized for action as they engage in ministries to fill the needs of the whole person, foster the values of the kingdom of God (Mark 1:14) and anticipate the *shalom* of the new heavens and the new earth (Rev. 21).

The vision of the Basic Christian Communities in Smokey Mountain is based on the belief that human beings should become the best they can be. Human potential should be developed to the utmost through the transformative dimension of Christian faith. A holistic ministry must serve the needs of the whole person in all dimensions of human life. Communities of faith in Jesus as Lord and Savior seek at the same time to engage in communitarian reflection, to become communities of mutual help and assistance with strong commitment for economic and political transformation.

Paolo Freire claims that the first step to liberation is when people articulate their own problems and then start owning and identifying with these problems. In effect, participatory research is in itself an agent for change. It is much more than research. It is research leading to community reflection and group action that transform participants from oppressed and miseducated individuals into a self-empowered group of human beings who feel a sense of responsibility for and control of their lives.

In the Philippines *empowerment* became a byword after the nonviolent revolution in 1986 where "people power" prevailed against the armored personnel carriers and battle-hardened storm troopers of the Marcos dictatorship. The poor's involvement in dismantling oppressive systems in the Marcos regime resulted in a heightened sense of self-confidence and ability to collectively change their situation. The model for holistic ministry assumed in this case study is based on people empowerment as the most appropriate concept for teaching people, especially the poorest of the poor. We teach how to fish; thus people no longer need to be given fish all their lives.

The participatory evaluation included the following objectives:
1. To determine and assess the status and levels of performance of the Alliance of Basic Christian Communities (ABCC) in terms of its holistic ministry in the following dimensions:
   a. the spiritual dimension
   b. the economic dimension
   c. the historical dimension
2. To determine and assess processes and methodologies adopted in undertaking activities under these three basic concerns of the ABCC.

3. To determine perceived and objective impact of the ABCC programs on the lives of people in Smokey Mountain.
4. To identify recommendations for strategic planning and development of the Parish of the Risen Christ in Smokey Mountain.

METHODOLOGY

## Preliminary workshops

*1. First workshop: Orientation and identifying research problems*

The first formal workshop was attended by about 80 *Punong Alagad* (servant-leaders) and presidents of the Alliance. In this meeting the rationale, objectives and methodology of the study were explained. Participants discussed their situations and aspirations.

A workshop was conducted to identify problems the people would like to answer in the research. Participants were divided into three groups to discuss the spiritual, economic and historical dimensions. A volunteer classified problems participants listed by clustering together related questions.

*2. Second workshop: Validating variables and identifying indicators*

The second workshop focused on validating variables the evaluation team had identified from questions the leaders raised in the first workshop. But before the validation, the evaluation team explained the concepts, relevance and uses of variables, measurements and indicators used in the evaluation process.

Three committees (spiritual, economic, historical) formulated guide questions to be used in the data-gathering.

*3. Third workshop: Sampling and preparing for data-gathering*

In the third workshop the three committees learned different methods to use in data-gathering. They also offered input on the concepts and methods of sampling.

## Data-gathering, analysis and feedback

*1. Focused group discussion*

Eighteen separate focused group discussions were conducted for different cell groups targeted by the research team. Each discussion was attended by an average of 10 *sambahayan* members and facilitated by the evaluation team. A *sambahayan* is the smallest unit of the Alliance, a cell of 10 families each. The discussions applied the guidelines formulated by the committees in the preparatory workshop.

## 2. Officers and staff of the cooperative

To get a better picture of the economic aspect of the Alliance, a separate workshop involved the cooperative officials and staff. In this focused group discussion several problems, issues and conflicts surfaced. Thus the discussion became a venue for setting and ventilating conflicts not verbalized before. Solutions to problems and issues were also identified.

## 3. Workshop with youth members and focused group discussion with youth leaders

Two separate meetings explored the status, problems, activities and suggestions of youth members and leaders.

## 4. In-depth interview with parish priest and parish staff

The evaluation team conducted an in-depth interview with the parish priest. Members of the parish staff and leaders of the Alliance also attended.

## 5. Focused group discussion with servant-leaders

After the 18 discussions with the *sambahayan*, three separate focused group discussions were conducted for the servant-leaders. This constituted the second level of data-gathering and analysis.

## 6. Workshop with Alliance presidents

In the third level of data-gathering and analysis—presidents of the Alliance who serve as the Executive Committee and as members of the Parish Pastoral Council—participants identified problems and weaknesses as well as strengths of the Basic Christian Communities. After the workshop the evaluation team presented initial findings for validation and feedback. Dialogue with the leaders later sorted out some problems that cropped up in the discussions.

## 7. Other data-gathering techniques

The evaluation team also collected in-depth interviews with non-members of the Alliance and leaders of other organizations, participant observation, on-the-spot interviews and relevant documents.

### MEMBERS' PERCEPTION OF ALLIANCE OBJECTIVES

The research showed that the general membership of the Alliance and each Basic Christian Community had a clear understanding of the organization's goals and objectives. The following are their perceived objectives:

*Spiritual:*
1. To provide venues for spiritual worship.
2. To enhance value formation and development of a Christian character.
3. To work for peace and order in the community.
4. To enable members to share their problems with others.
5. To reconcile strained relationships among the people.

*Economic:*
1. To work toward realization of the housing project.
2. To work for improvement of housing and community facilities such as school, health clinic, pathways, and so on.
3. To increase employment opportunities and raise income levels.
4. To provide educational support for the children.
7. To provide capital for livelihood.
8. To provide material assistance in times of need.

*Historical:*
1. To enhance unity and cooperation among residents.
2. To develop leadership potential of members.
3. To ensure a good future for the children.

The general membership are able to discuss the objectives pertaining to socioeconomic and spiritual dimensions. In the historical dimension, enhancement of unity and cooperation was mentioned in all the *Sambahayan* workshops; development of leadership potential was mentioned by a few. It seems, therefore, that members have a better appreciation of what the Alliance and their organization can do in terms of the socioeconomic and spiritual dimensions.

The head servants were able to articulate the way objectives of the historical dimension are rooted in the spiritual dimension. The servant-leaders and presidents of the zones have a greater understanding of Alliance objectives in terms of the historical dimension. Thus, they cited the following as additional objectives:

1. Develop the people's capability, to enable them to respond to their problems.
2. Develop the people's awareness of their rights and how to exercise these rights.
3. Establish links with other organizations and agencies in Smokey Mountain and in the surrounding areas.

The Alliance claims membership of about 2,000 households living in the Temporary Housing Site. This does not include adjacent areas covered by the parish, about 75 percent of 2,879 families now living in the area. Thus, a significant number of adult residents are members of the Alliance.

Reasons cited among members for joining the *sambahayan* and the Basic Christian Communities included:

1. The socioeconomic benefits of the organization—many believed that membership in the Basic Christian Communities is a requirement for them to avail of the scholarship, relief, job placements, loans and other services facilitated by the Alliance.
2. Spiritual development—based on the desire to worship and serve God, and to bring oneself and the family closer to God.
3. Identification with and strengthening of the organization—the desire to be a part of the Basic Christian Communities and people's perception that the organization has good intentions for the people and the community. Some joined because they heard the Basic Christian Communities are "good" organizations.
4. Getting to know more people, fostering unity and cooperative undertaking—people joined the Basic Christian Communities to improve their personal and working relationships with other people.

These are the same reasons they continue their membership in the Basic Christian Communities. Gains and achievements of the Alliance serve as further reinforcement to continuous identification with and involvement with the *sambahayan*. It is also significant that more than 70 percent of Basic Christian Community members are women. Due to time constraints and the perceived religious nature of the organization, membership is usually delegated to women of the household.

An ordinary member in a *sambahayan* is normally involved in Bible-study and sharing once a week. Occasionally a member is tapped by the servant-leader to help in activities such as preparation for religious activities, fund-raising, benefit dances and food preparation during seminars. Members also attend meetings convened by the *sambahayan* or the president. Others attend only the Bible-sharing and the Holy Mass.

Most members of the *sambahayan* acknowledge that good relationships exist among them. This is manifested in the following:

1. They help each other in times of emergency, for example, by lending money to those in need.
2. Conflicts do arise among members but can be settled easily, especially with the mediation of the servant-leaders.
3. Members identify and appreciate being part of the *sambahayan*.
4. Members enjoy participating in the religious activities, especially the Bible-sharing where they can express their problems to others.

## LEADERSHIP PRINCIPLES

Leaders of the Basic Christian Communities are the servant-leaders of each *sambahayan* and the presidents of each area. Members are generally aware of the leadership structures and know the leaders personally, as shown by the research. Members have a high regard for their leaders, describing them as having good personal attributes. They expect their leaders to be responsible in following up with members.

According to the research, members' nonparticipation should serve as a cue to leaders that something has gone wrong. The servant-leaders are more aware of their terms of office and of their duties and responsibilities. While good qualities mentioned by the members are generally true, validated through observation by the research staff and actual interaction with the leaders themselves, these leaders are aware of their own weaknesses, which, they said, have to be changed.

Leaders, particularly presidents and some servant-leaders, generally think critically and possess analytical skills in perceiving things. They are able to comment on issues and to draw out insights and analysis. They can raise pertinent questions and can respond to queries posed to them. Leaders' commitment to the organization is very strong.

In leadership seminars for newly elected servant-leaders the model proposed is leadership that can motivate active participation of all members. Consensus-seeking in decision-making is also stressed as the best means to increase members' commitment and cooperation.

101

The leadership process and communication patterns are group-centered, focusing on constant feedback, evaluation and dialogue. "Bring it down to the people" is the constant refrain. Clarity of expectations and responsibilities is the greatest factor in group cohesiveness. The ideal set for the Alliance is to become increasingly goal oriented, with a leadership trained in interpersonal competence and capable of creative and independent thinking.

Both members and servant-leaders claimed that objectives of the Alliance and of the Basic Christian Communities are usually set by the leaders, although consultation takes place. In most cases members become recipients of plans, intentions, requests, instructions and even commands from the higher echelon. Consultation with members takes place regarding issues, such as the type of housing scheme to be proposed.

## SPIRITUAL DIMENSION

Members of the spiritual committee articulated that their objectives are focused on "person/other orientation" and humility. Inclusive in these are unity, understanding one another and giving time for the Lord, that is, learning the Word of God and living God's Word in one's life. Members found Alliance objectives in the spiritual dimension attainable. One activity started in line with these objectives is Bible-sharing, initiated by seminarians. This activity bore fruit in deeper understanding of the Bible. It also made giving advice to children and youth easier, because the Bible-sharing has made them familiar with Jesus' teachings. Members also cited Bible-sharing together as making life's hardships easier to bear.

In strengthening spirituality, principal activities include celebration of the Eucharist and Bible-sharing. Members also participate in some devotions to the Virgin Mary and attend prayer meetings and seminars on the charismatic movement.

They have great faith in prayers; that is, that prayers answer problems and God does respond to human pleas. It is further observed that prayers provide strength, endurance and clarity of mind in confronting any problem that comes. Prayers assist members in their daily activities. In terms of problem-solving, members of the Spirituality Committee readily assist each other. People have more opportunities to relate with each other. During free time they tell each other stories and express problems or concerns in life; thus, interpersonal conflicts are no longer as glaring as before.

Concretely, the riots that previously pervaded the community have stopped. Criminal activities have decreased. Members attributed the elimination of riots to prayer and to the presence of soldiers in the area. People take more initiative in doing and finishing whatever spiritual task is at hand. They facilitate Bible-sharing among themselves.

Other programs that make concrete spiritual objectives include livelihood programs, building a cooperative, setting up of spiritual training and advocacy for their envisioned housing project. Members do not find difficulty in reconciling objectives of spiritual activities with livelihood projects and joining mass actions and mobilization. This shows that holistic ministry has resulted in an integrated spirituality that confronts sinfulness—committed by persons or embedded in social structures—as the root cause of social problems that beset their cities and the whole nation today.

The research showed that members are aware of the strengths and, at the same time, areas for improvement in members' ability to do liturgical services. The present status of the Alliance's spiritual activities remain limited. Liturgical and biblical activities can serve as avenues for conscientization but, if not regular, these might not take root in the general population. Most of those attending are women, and no specific program exists for the men; therefore their horizon for developmental change may remain narrow.

## ECONOMIC DIMENSION

According to members' perception, the parish cooperative is the main component of economic development. Although not every member belongs to the cooperative, almost everyone sees the cooperative as a lending, helping and financial refuge center. For some, the cooperative can be a source for alternative livelihood and a recourse in times of emergency.

Leaders, rather than the general membership, have a clearer knowledge of the cooperative's objectives. They know that apart from the livelihood programs of the cooperative, education is also an integral part of the economic dimension.

The cooperative is generally perceived as an authentic organization that endeavors to provide alternative livelihood and to alleviate community economic problems. Some members' responses to the question of what economic needs the Basic Christian Communities respond to included:

1. It helps provide alternative employment for the unemployed.
2. It helps alleviate economic difficulties.
3. It provides opportunity to access aid from other institutions.
4. It provides credit and financial loans.
5. It facilitates capital benefits for economic enterprise.

A general observation among members is that the cooperative has actually facilitated several services, including:

1. Providing capital for microenterprises such as stores, soap manufacturing, candle making, and other means of alternative livelihood.
2. Providing savings investment for the cooperative's members.
3. Grants of credit loans for emergencies (hospital bills, burial expenses or school fees).
4. Providing alternative employment.
5. Providing assistance during crises (food and clothing during fires and typhoons, nails and lumber for house repairs).
6. Making help available for basic needs (rice, water, electricity).

The cooperative is generally perceived as an organization with collective decision-making, hoping to unify members through its organizational policies. Leaders, officers and a board of directors are assigned respective tasks to perform in order for the cooperative to function. As perceived by both leaders and members, benefits, policies, and communications are favorably delivered to the people. Leaders' inefficiency can be corrected by regular elections of officers. Benefits are delivered to the people. Members have positive regard for the leaders, parish and staff of the cooperative. In spite of some deficiencies, benefits are administered concretely and tangibly, and even nonmembers of the co-op avail of its services.

Alliance members offered the following recommendations for improving the cooperative:

❖ clear guidelines and orientation for all members
❖ participation by all, with the general membership to be consulted on decisions regarding more important issues
❖ improved and continued credit access
❖ benefits for nonmembers of the co-op

- ❖ a clear recruitment program, so everybody in the community becomes a member
- ❖ two-way communication between leaders and members, especially for orientation and policy consultation
- ❖ concrete resource-generation program and planning
- ❖ credit monitoring and collection system
- ❖ a clear package of benefits, especially regarding rebates for capital shares and interests on savings
- ❖ alternatives for the unemployed, especially the men and their participation in planning this
- ❖ technical and vocational training in preparation for the transfer to permanent housing.
- ❖ regular general assembly, for economic discussion, planning and management
- ❖ involvement of the broader number of members in all cooperative endeavors

Cooperative principles rely on communal capital, participatory management and collective benefits. These remain ideals to be sought after by the parish cooperative, even if several steps have been taken in this direction. Present endeavors of the cooperative function around capital, consumer goods and marketing. For capital to flow, cooperative members need to invest their savings. It appears that such an approach may not be the most feasible economic resource to mobilize in Smokey Mountain. The capitalist and consumerist state of the global economy may not allow small-scale production to flourish, such as production and marketing of soap and other products.

## HISTORICAL DIMENSION

The Alliance has established links with a number of both local and foreign-based non-governmental and government organizations. This is facilitated through the parish, which initially identifies and establishes contacts either with individuals or organizations that can assist Smokey Mountain. The parish priest introduces these organizations to the Alliance for whatever undertaking and resources might be required by the Smokey Mountain community. Thus, most resources tapped by the parish for Smokey Mountain are channeled through the Alliance. In some cases resources or projects are first managed by the parish until such time when the Alliance is ready to take over.

In areas near Smokey Mountain, Basic Christian Communities have also been organized, often with the help of servant-leaders from Smokey Mountain. These have the same organizational structure and also work on the spiritual, economic and historical levels of holistic ministry. Nearly 5,000 families belong to the Divine Word Basic Christian Communities in the slum areas nearby. They have engaged in concerted action together, especially in combatting illegal drugs and in activities of the cooperative. The Alliance, like the Divine Word Basic Christian Communities, is accredited with the local government and belongs to the Urban Poor Coordinating Council of the Presidential Commission for the Urban Poor. The cooperatives also belong to the National Capital Region Cooperatives Union.

With regard to organization-building, members consider the unity and cooperation of the people as the most significant impact. For the leaders, the most significant impact is recognition of the Alliance and the Basic Christian Communities by the government and non-government organizations. Thus, the Alliance and the people in general now assume that they must be consulted by the planners in drawing out alternative programs for Smokey Mountain, as a God-given right.

Members focus on the need to be united so that their voices can continue to be heard, especially on specific issues of reblocking and housing problems the community is confronting now. One observation expressed was that development is slow in terms of spiritual and community life.

### IMPACT OF THE ALLIANCE OF BASIC CHRISTIAN COMMUNITIES

The Alliance was established as an integrated approach to community building and mobilization of the poorest of the poor in the garbage dump. It has employed different strategies to call people to action, strategies that carry with them certain incentives and community benefits. This is very encouraging because in an organization sustainability is always fostered by clarifying benefits. People join an organization also because of its services.

Most of the impact of the Basic Christian Communities as perceived by members is related to psycho-spiritual and socioeconomic welfare, including nurturing of members' spiritual life, improvement of public facilities (pathways, electrical and water supply), education and better

106

health conditions for the children, improved peace and order in Smokey Mountain, and less drug addiction among the youth.

The support staff of the parish ensures that the whole parish community life moves as a team and a network. Seminarians render support services when they come for the weekend apostolate. Liturgical venues include prayer reflection with *agape*, seminars on skills-training and critical reflection and liturgico-biblical celebrations to gather the people for consolidating their solidarity. Cultural remolding and formation are initiated by the youth through their dramatic guild or *sandulaan*. Environmental issues are brought to the fore by the performing artists, *Mga Anak ni Inang Daigdig* (Children of Mother Earth).

Comprehensive training and education would unify the development perspective of members and even nonmembers of the Alliance. Currently only top leadership receives this training and education. The scope and parameters of development are also limited by spiritual formation, especially for those who are not too religiously oriented or belong to other religions. Finally, the extreme poverty and long years of historical passivity and silence still influence lack of critical consciousness and creativity. Thus, in the absence of an ongoing regular conscientization program and alternative source of income, community building will be very difficult. Many will still depend on handouts and will not act to liberate themselves from their misery.

The participatory research summarized the impact of the Alliance as perceived by the members thus:

*1. Improved relationship and community building*

There is consensus among members, community leaders and parish workers that the Alliance has been instrumental in creating closer interpersonal relationships throughout the community. This is manifested in verbalized identification with the organization, recognition of Alliance leaders, expressed sentiment to support the organization's activities for the general welfare of the residents, and participation in the organization's mutual support systems, for example, "helping each other and listening to one another's problems" in times of emergency and family problems.

Awareness of belonging to an organization has brought about social security and better support systems. In the Basic Christian Communities, people from different areas are brought together for common concerns. In the *sambahayan*, in which neighborliness seems to be the governing value, social relationships are enhanced by spiritual activities. This closeness has increased in the buildings at the temporary relocation site, where people live even closer to one another.

*2. Value formation and attitude changes*

Testimonies show the Alliance has helped members transform their values, attitudes and character as human beings. This transformation is exemplified in the following:

   a. Increased desire for and frequency of worship, prayer and study of the Bible;
   b. Greater self-control;
   c. Improved self-esteem and confidence;
   d. Willingness to serve and do volunteer work for the parish and the Alliance;
   e. A sense of justice, and desire for human rights, especially among Basic Christian Communities leaders; and
   f. Increased happiness among the people.

It is surprising to discover that people living in the dump site, despite their socioeconomic and physical conditions, say they are happy. As members said, they have hope and faith, and these make them see the day, and the days to come, with greater enthusiasm. These positive attitudes toward life were also very evident in their visions of what Smokey Mountain would be. The Alliance is looked upon as one of the mechanisms by which these dreams have been attained. It therefore implies that the success of the Basic Christian Communities can bring further positive attitudinal change.

*3. Improved people's welfare and access to alternative services*

The Alliance is considered very effective in providing access to external resources, both local and foreign. Alternative services for health, education, employment, housing, enterprise and trading, cultural and recreational amenities and other facilities are made possible through active intervention of the Alliance. Through activities in the historical dimension—resource-sharing and networking—a solidarity network with civic and religious organizations in the Philippines and abroad has slowly been built.

*4. Developed leadership*

The research showed that presidents of the Basic Christian Communities and the servant-leaders manifest leadership characterized by the following:

a. A high level of commitment to the Alliance and to the general welfare of the people of Smokey Mountain.
b. Critical awareness about issues pertaining to rehabilitation of the dump site, particularly the issue of land and housing.
c. Ability to express feelings and ideas well.
d. Satisfaction and fulfillment in volunteerism.

*5. Improved mechanism for people's participation*

The Alliance has provided people with mechanisms to participate actively in the various undertakings in the area, from relief operations to developmental planning. They consider it a personal triumph that the government acceded to their demands for on-site development and point with pride to their new housing units as the fruit of years of struggle as a community.

Leaders of the Alliance realize that they have become more influential now, vis-à-vis developing alternative plans for Smokey Mountain. Now government agencies, such as the National Housing Authority, have learned to consult the Alliance in developing the community in Smokey Mountain. The organization through its Executive Committee attained official recognition as spokesperson for the community. Members, too, perceive the Basic Christian Communities as their instrument to block government plans that would be detrimental to them. Ordinary members expressed that they would be willing to join mass mobilizations again if their rights are not respected.

*6. Meeting members' emergency needs*

The Alliance can respond to some of the emergency needs of the people, particularly during fires, typhoons and other calamities. Assistance is also given for hospitalization and burial expenses upon recommendation of the servant-leaders. Legal assistance is provided to those unjustly accused and imprisoned without cause.

More sustainable assistance is provided through the livelihood programs and placement services of the parish cooperative, the livelihood arm of the Alliance, and through education programs for children, adults and out-of-school youth. Close to 100 young women have found employment in a semi-conductor factory through the placement services of the cooperative. Most were graduates of the Alliance's vocational program.

*7. Greater public awareness and sympathy for Smokey Mountain*

The popularization of Smokey Mountain here and abroad was due primarily to attention that media focused on the dump site. The

Alliance also contributed to this through linkages the parish and Alliance established with both church and secular groups, government and non-government organizations. The Cultural Committee, through youth performances, has been very effective in depicting the conditions and aspirations of the people in Smokey Mountain and advocating for on-site development during the long years of the Alliance's struggle.

Public awareness and sympathy generated for Smokey Mountain have brought in more resources. However, there were also sentiments expressed that the people and situation in Smokey Mountain are being used by other entities who would like access to resources for their own benefit.

*8. Organizational and personal rifts*

An unfavorable impact attributed to the formation of the Alliance is the emergence of organizational rivalry and personal jealousy between members and nonmembers. It is true that members take pride in acknowledging and identifying with the Alliance. However, members perceive that other organizations do not have a smooth relationship with the Alliance. Others are jealous of the Alliance and leaders because of the perception of mishandling of resources coming in for the people of Smokey Mountain. The bigger cause of the rift is differing ideas about how the rehabilitation and development of the dump site should proceed. While the Alliance, after consultations with experts, supported the government plan, other groups opposed it. Wounds caused by this division have not completely healed, although many members of other organizations joined the Alliance soon after the resettlement.

## RECOMMENDATIONS

It can be said that the future of the Alliance of the Basic Christian Communities in Smokey Mountain depends on the success of planned development for the area. As experienced by many urban poor organizations, many were promised units in government housing projects only to see these units go to other people. While this is a major consideration in the formulation of the recommendations, it is assumed, unless otherwise stated, that the Alliance of the Basic Christian Communities will remain as the majority organization in the area.

*1. Streamlining program direction and planning processes*

The Alliance of Basic Christian Communities needs to spell out clearly what it wants to achieve given a specific period of time before the transfer to permanent housing. Although the general goals and objectives of the Alliance are clear, specific operational objectives are not laid down. Thus, the Alliance tends to react to changes brought about by events. More systematic planning and more strategic planning workshops can help to respond to needs identified.

*2. Revitalizing and strengthening the economic component of the program*

The economic impact of the Alliance on the lives of people in Smokey Mountain has been felt only by a small number of beneficiaries. Even among those who benefit, the sustainability of efforts and benefits poses a big challenge. The Alliance must strengthen and diversify schemes for capital provisions and entrepreneurship.

More capital and loans should be made available to members willing to undertake family-based economic ventures such as production and processing, trading and vending. The Grameen Bank system is slowly being set up among women micro-entrepreneurs to address this need. A revolving fund exists from capital shares of the members and grants from funding institutions abroad. More capital is being requested from the Cooperative Development Authority and the Technology and Livelihood Resource Center. More people can then benefit from the relending program and set up their own small businesses. Lately, the board of directors established guilds as a strategy for increasing the beneficiaries.

*3. Membership expansion program for men*

As observed, Alliance membership is composed mostly of women. Thus, basic concerns being addressed are planned and implemented by women, while the men remain inactive, if not unconcerned. Involving more men would not only help in resolving some of the problems and issues, but it would also make them partners of the women even in family formation, especially in the upbringing of children.

*4. Sustaining the development of current leadership*

While recognizing that the Alliance has strong leadership, some areas require intervention:

a. More values formation, monitoring, accountability and constructive criticism are needed.

b. Consistency is required in ensuring that leaders come from Smokey Mountain.

111

c. Further deepening of leaders' socioeconomic and political consciousness is needed.

A greater number of presidents of the Alliance and relatively fewer
leaders at the servant-leader level have analytical and critical consciousness (are able to analyze critically situations in their area and relate
these to outside conditions; are able to analyze programs and be vocal
about their feelings and ideas). However, it would be much better if
more leaders had these analytical skills and consciousness. Leader training should therefore consider the kind of consciousness being propa-
gated. Identifying and developing leaders can be facilitated if specific
training programs are conducted to suit leaders' specific needs.

*5. Providing more educational opportunities for members*

Very few members have undergone or participated in the training
and seminars conducted by the parish or the Alliance. In most cases
participants are presidents or servant-leaders. Of course, training
should start with potential leaders first. However, ordinary members
also need training in other fields such as development perspective,
community organizing and leadership, in addition to Bible-sharing and
other values formation activities. To do this, it would help if local train-
ers could be developed, who later would train other members. A monitoring system must be designed to determine and track progress of
members' development.

*6. Enhancing more dynamic communication between upper and lower con-
stituencies*

Communication between upper leadership and the membership has
to be more democratic and dynamic. From the top, more information
in terms of updates, policies and developments regarding issues have
to reach ordinary members at the *sambahayan* levels. Organizational
mechanisms instituted for this purpose do not seem to work as envisioned. A lot of things happening at the top do not filter down to members. Similarly, information coming from below should contain more
of the needs, aspirations and suggestions of ordinary members. This
information should go to the Executive Committee, so that felt needs
determine decisions arrived at. This means more dialogue and consultation with members.

*7. Improving relationships with other sectors and organizations in Smokey
Mountain*

The people of Smokey Mountain have to work collectively regardless of their religion, ideological perspectives and status in life. The

Alliance should work with other organizations and strive to heal the wounds of divisions. Leaders should lead in remaining humble and should respond to accusations from nonmembers that they favor Alliance members, especially in times of relief distribution intended for everyone.

*8. Further enhancing the spiritual dimension*

While it is true that the greatest impact of the Basic Christian Communities is on the spiritual dimension, the research indicates suggestions to improve overall values formation and spirituality of the people:

    a. More dynamic liturgical expression by contextualizing the gospel and the Christian faith to the indigenous understanding of a developing nation and within the life-situation of former scavengers.

    b. More pastoral visits by pastors, in addition to visits and Bible-sharing done by seminarians.

    c. More Bible distribution and seminars on how to study the Bible. As of now, only leaders have participated in Bible-study seminars.

    d. Developing leaders' capabilities in handling liturgical activities.

*9. Consolidating and streamlining activities pertaining to permanent housing in Smokey Mountain*

Since the rehabilitation plan and relocation to a temporary site occurred, recommendations of the participatory research regarding the plan have been overtaken by events. Dialogue with the National Housing Authority continues, along with the seeking of technical assistance from other organizations. The main problem facing people now is paying monthly amortizations for their housing units. For this, the parish cooperative is doubling its efforts in job creation and placement. This will not be enough, however, and the Executive Committee estimates that up to 30 percent of the people might lose their rights to the units after a few years.

Another problem regards the environmental safety of living in a former dump site. People fear that the toxic gases trapped in the mountain will pose a hazard. The Executive Committee has decided that unless environmental engineers will certify the safety of the area, no one will transfer to the permanent housing.

A housing cooperative is being planned to take over administration and maintenance of the buildings in the permanent site. Efforts have also been made to coordinate with the organization that opposed the government's plan, so that a tactical coalition with a common objective can ensure the majority's participation.

CONCLUSION

The prophet Isaiah proclaimed long ago that ambitious people would "cover the face of the world with cities" (Isa. 14:21). This prophecy is being fulfilled in our generation. Whether we are terrorized or compassionate, cities should command our attention. What is God saying to us through the millions of people in the cities who are trapped by the tyranny of poverty, filth, illiteracy, hunger, unemployment, overcrowding, mass violence, helplessness and degradation? How can we proclaim the lordship of Jesus to the countless people in the cities? And of what value for them is the salvation we proclaim?

The city has always had a primary significance in the Bible. The phenomenon of urbanization and globalization presents a dilemma to the church: to work out a strategy for holistic ministry in the cities, return to her biblical roots and make an impact in the city as the early church did. Toward this end the documents of the Society of the Divine Word enjoin its members engaged in holistic evangelization to experience the "passing over" to the poor. This "passing over" presupposes a profound experience of God as the source of all compassion, the realization of one's own inner poverty and powerlessness, the need for continual conversion of heart and the belief that the poor possess the power to shape their own destiny.

The setting up of Basic Christian Communities especially in urban centers is a strategy for holistic ministry, a new way of being church, a church of the poor as ministering and being ministered to. Founded on the Trinity, energized by the Divine Word, born and guided by the Spirit, the Alliance of Basic Christian Communities in Smokey Mountain journeys together to the Father (the God-before-us) in the company of the Son, the risen One (the God-with-us, Emmanuel), under the guidance of the life-giving Spirit (the God-within-us). It joins hands in building up and serving the kingdom of truth, peace and justice according to the gospel in solidarity with the poorest of the poor by actualizing salvation in the here and now in the spiritual, economic and historical dimensions of human existence.

The saga of the scavengers of Smokey Mountain has shown that faith in the risen Jesus can break the cycle of deprivation, conflict, devastation and failure in a garbage dump, although the fullness of the kingdom will come only with the advent of the new heavens and the new earth:

> "They will be his peoples,
> and God himself will be with them;
> he will wipe every tear from their eyes.
> Death will be no more;
> mourning and crying and pain will be no more,
> for the first things have passed away." (Rev. 21:3–4)

# Part two

# Reflections

# 7

# The church in the city

## A mediating and catalytic agent
## for social change

*Donald E. Miller*

I n the new millennium responsible Christians must face the challenges presented by the fact that the world's poor will increasingly live in cities, not in rural locations. This point was amply illustrated in the case studies from the Philippines, Zimbabwe and India. Examining global trends, 16 percent of the developing world's population resided in urban areas in 1950; by 1990 there had been a fivefold increase to 37 percent; by the year 2025, 61 percent of people in developing countries will be urban dwellers. During the decade of the 1990s, cities in the developing world are growing by an aggregate of over 160,000 persons per day.

Globally the world's urban population more than trebled between 1950 and 1990 (from 730 million to 2.3 billion). Between 1990 and 2020 the urban population will double again, to 4.6 billion, with 93 percent of this increase occurring in the developing world. Cities such as São Paulo, which had 2.8 million residents in 1950, are projected to grow to 22 million by the year 2000; similarly, Mexico City will increase from the 3.1 million residents it had in 1950 to 25 million by the beginning of the new millennium. In 1950 there were only two mega-cities of over 8 million people: New York and London. By 1990 there were 21 mega-cities, with

16 of these in the developing world. But there is also an explosion of cities with populations in excess of one million. For example, in 1950 there were 31 cities with one million or more. By 1990 there were 180 such cities. And by 2000 it is predicted that there will be more than 300 cities with a population exceeding one million.

In the developed world much of its urbanization occurred a century or more ago. Currently about three-quarters of all residents in the developed world live in urban areas. Consequently, urban population growth in the developed world is only growing at about 1 percent a year, compared to a 3.5 percent annual urban growth rate in the developing world. When viewed as an aggregate, only one-third of the world's population lived in urban areas in 1975. By the year 2025 two-thirds of the world's population will be urbanites.

With such massive trends occurring, the question surely arises as to why the world's demographic characteristics are shifting so dramatically. The answer to this question is multifaceted but largely reflects rational decisions made by people moving from rural to urban areas. The lure of cities is the possibility of better employment. In addition, health care is typically more available, reflected in the fact that life expectancy of city dwellers, on average, is higher, and infant mortality rates are lower, although these generalizations do not necessarily apply to the poorest groups living in the city. Also, education is more available, and the perception exists that upward mobility is more likely if one's family lives in a city. On the negative side, people are "pushed" out of rural areas due to war, famine, declining levels of agricultural work, lack of land to farm and poverty.

While city dwellers live more affluent lives in general, the case studies make the point that migrants to cities often arrive with few marketable skills and virtually no financial resources. They live in shanty towns or create squatter villages on the fringe of urban areas. Many of them end up working in the "informal" economy associated with garbage collection, domestic help, piecework in the clothing manufacturing industry—or they support themselves through criminal activity. For some people this is a transitional existence, but for others there is no easy escape. By the year 2000 it is estimated that half of the developing world's absolute poor will be living in urban areas. And children are too often the victims. Up to 100 million children currently struggle for daily survival on the streets of large cities in developing countries.

120

With urbanization comes high rates of unemployment, under-employment (urban markets cannot absorb the number of new job seekers), inadequate public transportation systems, congestion of streets, air pollution, inadequate sanitation and contaminated water supplies. Growth in the urban infrastructure simply cannot keep pace with the explosion in demand. In the developing world 40 percent of the population do not have access to proper sanitation, and in many cities in the developing world, 40–50 percent of the people live in slums and informal settlements. While cities are potentially very efficient centers of economic activity—especially related to manufacturing, trade and finance—there are also huge disparities in income in these cities. Consequently, people of wealth and power seek to isolate the poor, a point well illustrated in the Zimbabwe case study when the police rounded up Harare's poorest residents and put them in Porta Farm camp.

## URBANIZATION, MODERNIZATION AND ULTIMATE VALUES

The shift from rural to urban living exposes migrants to a new worldview. In rural life, associations are often intimate, bound together by years of interlacing family and village traditions. Cities, however, tend to foster impersonal relationships that are based on commodity exchange. One is valued for the labor one has to offer or one's role as a consumer, not for intrinsic values associated with one's personhood, reputation or family lineage. Stated more theoretically, urbanization is associated with modernization, a condition in which community values decline and individualism increases, with an enhanced emphasis on personal choice. In extreme cases individuals become completely dissociated from any communal attachments, making them vulnerable to self-destructive behavior, including, in extreme cases, suicide. Life's ultimate purpose becomes problematic as individuals imagine that personal meaning is strictly a matter of their own construction, unbounded by tradition, community or anything transcendent. Secularization and modernization often progress hand in hand. The idea of a world infused with gods and divine intervention gives way to a notion of the world being organized according to rational processes that reflect human initiative and nothing more.

The case studies clearly show that this is the context that Christians confront when they seek to serve the urban poor. Human community is in disarray. People may be living together, but very often they are

121

not bound together by common purpose. Family life typically takes a severe beating in this transition from rural to urban living. Men who were once proud of their ability to support their families are now humiliated by their failure to find regular and meaningful employment. Consequently, they turn to drugs or alcohol to anesthetize their pain. Children are not tended with the same care that village life or extended family living encouraged, producing a generation of poorly socialized youth. And tremendous burdens fall on women to perform roles to which they were not accustomed in more traditional societies.

The most extreme form of urban pathology is that people live relatively autonomous lives. Self-interest becomes the overriding value. Capitalist values result in people being treated as means to financial ends, rather than being valuable because they have intrinsic worth (for example, made in the image of God). The pluralism of different peoples and different ideologies presents the challenge of whether any single claim to truth is absolute. All of these various aspects of modernity and urban life call into question the status of ultimate values, as well as the common bonds that constitute the social contract that undergirds a civil society.

## WHAT IS THE RELEVANCE OF CHRISTIANITY?

The case studies in this book make clear the role of Christianity in confronting the problems of the urban poor. First, Christianity insists on the dignity of every individual, including women, children, the elderly and the infirm. All people have equal value in God's sight. Whether one references the story of the Good Samaritan or the parable of the sheep and the goats in Matthew 25, or simply observes Jesus' relationship with prostitutes and tax collectors, it is apparent that everyone has value. Jesus did not elevate the rich over the poor. Indeed, one might argue that his ministry was to the outcast. Hence, Christianity is an important counterpoint to politicians who might prefer to practice social triage—discarding the weak to promote the strong.

Second, Christianity strongly counters the ethic of individualism that characterizes urban life. The most fundamental aspect of Jesus' ethic is that one should love one's neighbor as oneself. Far from being an individualistic ethic, this summary of the Law and the Prophets suggests that one has an obligation to care for others, which is the basis for all expressions of community (for example, the Basic Christian Community at

Smokey Mountain). Christians have no right to live only for themselves. They exist to worship God, but also to be God's instrument for love and reconciliation in the world.

Third, Christianity is rooted in the vision of the Old Testament prophets, for whom justice was the axiomatic moral principle. The Hebrew Scriptures are filled with warnings to those who oppress widows, orphans or exploit the powerless. God is consistently on the side of the poor in the great narrative stories of the Bible, which is the point made in this book's case studies of Christian political action. For example, blocking roads in Madras to get the attention of government officials is a holy act, as are the many other collective acts of Christians described in the case studies (that is, when faith-based groups of people confront self-interested persons in order to demand that justice be done in policies related to the poor).

Fourth, modern urban society is in desperate need of mediating institutions, such as the church, which can be a point of connection between individuals and the larger body politic. As individuals within urban society it is very easy to feel powerless. The church, however, is a community of people with common purpose; it not only worships together but also exists in order to create a more just society. The Ubunye Church in South Africa is a superb example of a multicultural congregation that is committed to serving the residents of its neighborhood. Likewise we see an interesting example of how churches can band together and thereby multiply their effectiveness in the Hollywood-Wilshire Cluster described by Robert Linthicum.

Religion in these case studies is far from being an opiate of the people, as Karl Marx argued, drugging the masses by providing them with visions of the life beyond so that they will not confront the evils of their own society. Rather, these case studies illustrate Christianity's capacity to be a catalyst for change, enabling people to translate their vision of a just society into specific expressions of political power. Furthermore, these case studies challenge the Freudian image of religion, which assumes that Christianity is merely a crutch that supports weak-kneed individuals who want to escape reality. A religion that insists on the dignity of persons, that stands for justice and equality, that creates leaders who transform their society is scarcely the "illusion" that Sigmund Freud imagined it to be.

Indeed, the programs and activities described in these case studies challenge the processes of secularization described by many sociologists.

Religion is not disappearing, nor is it highly privatized—at least in the examples the case studies offer. Instead, religion is active in the public square, asserting values that counter some of the most viral pathologies present in modern urban life. Holistic ministry—the term coined by Tetsunao Yamamori to describe Christianity's active engagement in meeting the physical, mental and social needs of people—represents a reversal of the processes associated with secularization.

### Relief, Community Development and Community Organizing

Present in these chapters are different models of how to serve the urban poor. A rather traditional model is that Christians have an obligation to provide emergency relief—for example, in response to famines, earthquakes or other natural disasters. While this model is still practiced by some Christian groups and agencies, there is an emerging recognition that it is a highly unsatisfactory long-term strategy. Given the magnitude of the urban transformation that is occurring, it is impossible for Christians to deal with the immense human suffering in this world by taking such an individualistic approach to being Christ's instrument of love in the world.

An alternative approach is community development, which typically involves projects related to economic development, literacy training or housing. The activities of the Ubunye Church in South Africa is an excellent example—especially its involvement with low-income housing. Likewise, the shoe and soap cooperatives in Zimbabwe illustrate Christian community development at its best, because people are not only earning a living but are becoming self-sufficient.

A third approach is community organizing, in which people who lack political power form an organization that allows them to pursue their collective interests. This approach undoubtedly works best in democratic societies where people have access to decision-makers. Franklin Joseph's case study provides a clear outline of the steps involved in community organizing. First, one must listen to the needs of people, establishing friendships and letting them know that this is not one more scheme to exploit them. The residents of a community must establish their own agenda, it cannot be imposed by outside organizers. Second, a broad-based coalition needs to be developed, which results in intimate groupings of people who know each other and are committed to common purposes. These "people's organizations" in

Madras were made up principally of women, because of the lack of interest or availability of men. Third, a specific issue is identified (for example, drinking water, roads, electricity, health, education), and demands are made to public officials for these services. Inevitably these requests are ignored by officials in the first, second or third round of presentations. However, the Madras case study illustrates that even very poor people have power when they act as a collective group and are strategic in making their claims. The community-organizing model does not require ongoing aid from some outside organization; rather, it teaches people to demand their rights; to work cohesively as a community; and to decline any form of aid that engenders dependency.

LEADERSHIP

Each of the projects described in the case studies was initiated by someone with a vision. Sometimes this is a pastor, such as Dan Sheffield or Fr. Ben Beltran. Other times it is a nonclerical community organizer, who serves as a catalyst in developing leadership among disenfranchised people. What is unique in Christian community development and organizing is that this vision emerges out of the faith of people in a God who offers hope for the future. Christianity is a very non-fatalistic religion. The central symbol is that of the Resurrection, not an endless cycle of rebirths that, at its best, promises incremental progress.

The inspiration for social and political change emerges out of worship and, more particularly, the study of Scripture. Hence, each of these case studies is also a study in Christian community—crossing the spectrum from Catholic to Protestant. The power of community development and community organizing is when ordinary people—laypeople—seize hold of their responsibility and right to be agents of change. Leadership is not innate. It is something that is developed, and the good community organizer or pastor is one who is continually calling on people to accept the challenge to be God's instruments in his or her neighborhood. In turn, participation in regular worship is the experience that gives power, strength and longevity to pursue the task of social transformation.

In these case studies one is continually aware of the important role that women are playing in leadership. They appear to be less involved in drugs or alcohol, are more committed to the welfare of their community, and also more responsive to the importance of religion in their lives. While the role of women is to be applauded—and, indeed, many of them are heroic in the work that they are doing—it is also a commentary on the need to involve men at the grassroots level of community organizing and development.

CONCLUSION

In conclusion, it is important to note that Christianity does not always have a positive, transformative effect on its culture. There are times in Christian culture when it has been repressive, exploitative and even demonic. Hence, it is important for us to applaud the expressions of Christian witness that are present in these case studies. It is precisely the witness to life-affirming values that seems to be the reason why churches associated with these community-development and organizing projects are growing. In this regard holistic ministry can be viewed as a church-grown strategy, even though, biblically, it is also the heart of the Christian gospel.

And, finally, a personal reflection. The role of leadership and the power of Christ's love to transform were nowhere more evident to me than in visiting Smokey Mountain and then touring with Fr. Ben Beltran the new high-rise apartment buildings that were being constructed in response to the dump's residents' insistence that they be treated as people worthy of respect. In this context I was able to see the work of a skilled community organizer, as well as meet some of the women who were instrumental in achieving this victory. For these women religion and politics were completely interwoven, as was their worship and devotional life. During our group's conversation with these women, I noticed that Fr. Beltran stayed in the background. His achievement was not only in transforming a smoking dump into sanitary housing, but in developing leaders who could carry out the work of ministry by themselves.

---

**SOURCES**

Nick Devas and Carole Rakodi, eds. *Managing Fast Growing Cities: New Approaches to Urban Planning and Management in the Developing World*. John Wiley & Sons, 1993.

John D. Kasarda and Allan M. Parnell, eds. *Third World Cities: Problems, Policies, and Prospects*. Sage Publications, 1993.

Saskia Sassen. *The Global City: New York, London, Tokyo.* Princeton University Press, 1991.

*The State of the World's Children: 1995.* Oxford University Press, 1995.

*World Resources, 1996–97: A Guide to the Global Environment.* Internet: www.wri.org/wri/wr–96–97/

# 8

# Coping strategies
# of urban poor women

*Grace Roberts Dyrness*

T he unfolding story that is told through these cases studies is one
of God at work as the Spirit is allowed to move. These are stories of the human spirit, invincible, rising out of circumstances
that would otherwise bind and dampen that spirit. We see courageous
people who are living out the evidence that God is not pleased with
the way things are in our cities and thus has placed special instruments of grace and transforming power in the midst of some of our
most neglected and oppressed neighborhoods.

As I read these stories, I see also the story of women who have turned
difficult circumstances into situations of hope for the communities that
they live in. These women have reminded me of the many others that
I have encountered in fieldwork in Manila, Nairobi, and the inner cities of Oakland and Los Angeles. The urban environments in which
they live are very similar; yet the stories we read here are significant
because of the role that the power of God has played in leading them
into new and, in their own way, risky paths. Here I reflect on the lives
of these women from an anthropological perspective.

These stories are all rooted in a historical movement of people. The
rapid urbanization of developing countries is well documented. There
is a general acceptance that third-world cities have grown faster than
expected or anticipated. The growth patterns show that in effect the
greatest growth is in the largest cities. In 1950 only 31 cities in the entire

Third World had a population of one million or more. By 1970 that number had doubled, and by 1990 the 1970 figure had nearly tripled, to 171 cities. The growth rate for these large cities was 5.1 percent a year, faster than the average annual rate for the urban population of the rest of the Third World.[1] In Asia, for example, the Asian Development Bank says that the region is projected to be 51 percent urbanized by 2020, and 17 of the world's 27 mega-cities will be in Asia.[2] While much of the growth is due to rural-urban migration, much of it is also natural growth.

What makes people leave their homes and roots and move to an unknown, urban destination? Some are refugees. Having fled their countries of origin for economic reasons or for reasons of war, they find themselves in a city that is alien to their way of life. Others are internally displaced, having left their rural settlements as a result of drought, famine, ethnic conflict, natural disasters such as earthquakes and erupting volcanoes, and sometimes even for reasons of family tension. Toniel Marimba tells us that Harare, Zimbabwe, has grown dramatically after the liberation war in 1979. Persistent drought and food shortages in the rural areas between 1982 and 1992 have played a significant role in Harare's growth.

This movement of people reflects the massive urbanization that characterizes this period in history. Growing at an unprecedented rate, with the flow of migrants adding to their natural growth, "cities offer advantageous conditions for capital, and so encourage concentration of financial, commercial and industrial power, as well as the expansion of markets through the dissemination of tastes and consumer habits."[3] These conditions produce a more attractive environment for people than the agricultural-based area, which is perceived as poor and without possibility for improvement. In the developing world much of that growth is in slum and squatter settlements. Each of the cases that we have seen unfold here in this book has clearly delineated the urban-growth patterns of the country it is in. And we are made aware of the effect this has had on people's living conditions. Patterns have emerged that demonstrate the universality of many of the problems: massive unemployment, poor sanitation, unclean environment, landlessness, inadequate housing, general and pervasive poverty, resulting stresses and tensions often leading to drugs and alcoholism.

How, then, do poor households cope when incomes decline, jobs are scarce and securing the basic basket of goods becomes more expensive?

In a study conducted for the World Bank by Caroline Moser in 1996,[4] Moser compares four poor urban communities according to the strategies that individual households or whole communities use to mobilize their assets as a buffer against the declining situation they find themselves in. A major source of instability has been the labor market. The decline in formal-sector employment and the instability of the informal sector of the economy has forced them to mobilize the labor of additional members of the household. Moser underlined the importance of land and housing as productive assets that give stability and provide a secure base from which to launch entrepreneurial activity. She also found that investments in infrastructure can ensure that productive enterprises have a chance to flourish. By contrast, poor access to social infrastructure adversely affects the stability of the household. The stresses and strains of a declining economy can have a serious effect on members of the household. The social fabric of the community, the unequal distribution of labor, and the stock of social capital all influence the community's capacity to work on its problems. Moser's findings all resonate with the cases we have here, and thus I find it useful to reflect on them in this same way.

## LABOR AS AN ASSET

Since labor is one of the poor's greatest assets, one of the ways that households cope with declining income and increased poverty is to harness all of the household's labor forces. In the case studies presented here, we have found that most of the men are unskilled workers, and with the loss of employment in the formal sector many find themselves in marginal, temporary occupations or simply unable to find work. In the case of Madras, at least, the increased frustration at being unable to provide adequately for their families has led many of the men to turn to alcohol and drugs.

This has forced the women to find ways to contribute to the household income, not necessarily because fewer men are working but also because households must depend on multiple earners. Themselves unskilled, they turn to the informal sector of the economy to augment their income. In the Kubatana Co-operative in Zimbabwe some of the women have chosen to engage in food production through market gardening—growing vegetables throughout the year to feed their families and then sell some of the surplus produce to earn enough income to clothe their children and send them to school. Others have become involved in food catering—processing and preparing food for sale. The women have even ventured into a male domain: bicycle repair! They can assemble new bicycles and repair broken ones. In Manila the women have also opened up small businesses selling food and other commodities to one another, scavenging on the nearby dump site, and finding jobs in factories nearby, selling their labor as domestic servants and laundry women. In the Ubunye case, many of the women have been selling their labor as domestic servants.

Perhaps the most dramatic and sad coping strategy has been to harness the labor of the children to supplement the household income. In Harare, Manila and Madras children are put out onto the street as prostitutes and other child labor, often ending up on the streets completely and leaving the homes they came from. As Fr. Beltran points out, many are runaways from intolerable situations at home, but many are also pushed into prostitution and work by their own parents in an effort to survive.

## SOCIAL AND ECONOMIC INFRASTRUCTURE AS AN ASSET

Social and economic infrastructure is of vital importance to the ability of the poor to support a sustainable lifestyle. While social services such as education give people the skills and knowledge they need to improve their life, economic infrastructure such as water, transport and electricity—together with health care—ensure that the poor can use these skills productively. Service deficiencies and cuts in public spending can reduce income-earning capacity, and the poor find themselves unable to substitute private for public services. The urban poor have always had to pay for the services they need, often at a larger share of their income than higher-income households. Thus, where access to these services deteriorates, the poor find themselves spending much more time and money just trying to meet their daily needs. It is the women who are most severely affected by this: if fetching water, for example, consumes more time, they have less time to spend in income-generating activities. This can have important implications for household welfare.

It is not surprising, therefore, that in all of the cases the people desired a change in the social and economic infrastructure of the community. In Madras the first thing the women wanted to work on was the

131

removal of the garbage and waste in the community. They knew that this was vital to the health of the community, but especially to the health of their children. Another issue that was pressing for them was that of safe drinking water, and we read how they were able actively to engage the government in providing enough water for them. The Women's Association in another of the Madras slums successfully wrested control of water distribution from the hands of a corrupt individual. For the community in Manila the most important item to be addressed was also the health of the children. Located on the site where all the garbage from Manila was dumped, the community demanded changes in the environment and succeeded in gaining the attention of the authorities to address these issues. In Harare the focus of the efforts of the Urban Advance project was to provide education for the street children and for other destitutes because the city could no longer provide such services at an affordable level. This focus on education was based on evidence that as the educational level of the household increases, so does the income level. All the cases show the important role of educational services.

### HOUSING AS AN ASSET

Housing is an important asset that can cushion people from the harshness of severe poverty. Insecurity of housing, as when households do not hold formal legal title to their property, increases the vulnerability of the poor. When the poor own their homes, they can use them as leverage for additional income by renting out rooms, using them for micro-economic enterprises, selling part of the plot for additional income, or selling them altogether as a last resort. Furthermore, owning their own homes means saving on rent they would otherwise have to pay.

The people of Smokey Mountain in Manila have focused their efforts on gaining title to property and building houses that are permanent, safe from the onslaught of the typhoons that storm through the region each season. They succeeded in gaining title and building temporary structures that they live in now while the permanent ones are under construction. Those who live in squatter settlements, in makeshift homes that are vulnerable to natural disasters and fires, also live in fear of eviction, which can come at any time and can produce severe household trauma. Thus the people in Smokey Mountain can now harness their resources to increase the income and health of their families without these constant threats to their stability.

The Ubunye Church in South Africa has also focused much of its effort on securing housing for community members. With a primarily single and single-parent family membership, the intention of the housing program has been twofold: (1) to provide emergency shelter for women who are abused and thus very vulnerable, and (2) to provide a housing community for the families where children and their parents can have the help of additional adults in a safe environment, without the threat of a slum lord cutting off electricity or water.

The Epworth Community of Harare has succeeded in obtaining basic infrastructure, such as water and electricity, and is negotiating with the government for housing that meets Zimbabwe's housing standards but that also meets the needs of the women, needs such as garden plots on which to grow vegetables.

In Madras one of the projects is in a resettlement colony with 15,000 people who were relocated with the promise of housing. But we read that this promise was not kept, and the area was flooded during the monsoon season. The project staff members have assisted the people in getting the government to keep its promise and to begin construction.

Home-based enterprises have more of a chance of succeeding if the people own the home and can either increase the family's ability to move out of poverty, or at the very least from slipping so far into it that they are completely unable to seize new opportunities. All of the cases are examples of ways in which communities can leverage themselves to secure the land and the housing that they need to survive.

## INEQUALITIES IN HOUSEHOLD RESPONSES

Often strategies that a household uses to reduce its vulnerability can impose unequal burdens on different members of that household. Women, because of the multiple responsibilities they have, often shoulder a disproportionate share of the burden of adjusting to increased poverty and thus can be limited in their ability to take advantage of new opportunities. Because of the invisibility of domestic labor, women who begin income-generating activities spend more hours working than men, because the men often do not pick up domestic tasks when their wives are engaged in work for cash or kind. When the woman's paid labor is over, she still has the responsibility of managing the home. Child-rearing responsibilities and domestic tasks are carried out mainly by women; they are the nurturers, the caregivers, the preparers of food, the ones most concerned about the health of family members. In addition to these responsibilities women are often the ones who work for change at the community level, balancing all these responsibilities.

In Moser's findings, women often feel the social costs of all these responsibilities. Some women become despondent about their situation—worrying about their children; feeling deficient in their ability to provide adequately; afraid for their young daughters, who leave home as domestic servants or as sellers of their bodies. Many end up "burned out" after years of struggling to make ends meet. And men often respond to the decline in income and growing households demands through increased alcohol and substance abuse. This, in turn, often increases domestic violence and tension, as much needed cash is spent on these drugs.

Substance abuse had become such a problem in Madras that even the children took to the streets to denounce their elders' alcoholism. In South Africa the opening of the women's shelter is a direct response to the problem of substance abuse and the resultant increase in domestic violence. When earnings drop and hopelessness sets in, the level of frustration in the home can lead to an increase in violence, and it is the women and the children who bear the brunt of that violence. Zanele, we are told in chapter 2, had been beaten so badly by her husband that she was driven to leave in desperation and seek emergency shelter for herself and her one-year-old child. The pain and grief suffered by the women in all our cases cannot be glossed over. We do not know the stories of all the women, but we must bear their burden with them and share their pain. And what we have seen here is something beyond the pain. The cases here actually reflect a hope that change can occur through the power of the redemptive love of God.

## SOCIAL CAPITAL AS AN ASSET

The vulnerability of poor households in an economic crisis causes them to cope by turning to other members of the community in reciprocal arrangements. Short-term reciprocity is centered mainly on money and responding to crises such as death or illness, and longer-term reciprocity in food, water, space, childcare. The extent to which these arrangements in the community can be considered an asset depends on the stock of social capital, which is generally identified as the networks, norms and trust that facilitate such cooperation. These structures often have their roots in the rural-urban family links and networks based on kinship and place of origin. Indeed, many studies show that people tend to migrate in kin and ethnic clusters; they often form voluntary associations in the city that help them adjust and accommodate to the pressures of urban life. Moser's findings in her comparative study suggest that economic crises have pushed many households beyond the point where they can sustain any level of reciprocity. Poor women no longer borrow because they can no longer pay back. The struggle to survive becomes so intense that a household can only focus on itself and cannot help out a neighbor. Thus the stock of social capital is eroded. Furthermore, as women spend more time working, they have less time for the volunteer activities that build the community.

The cases presented in this book actually demonstrate that considerable social capital is put to use in these communities. In spite of the fact that the women are working, they still find the time to work in the women's associations for the sake of the community, and ultimately for the sake of their children. They have learned how to deal with government bureaucracy. They have learned what their rights are and what is expected of their government and other authorities. Thus they have organized to force the government to provide water, or to build houses, or to clean up the garbage. Story after story has unfolded of the power that has come from women understanding that together they can work for change.

The people in these cases have encountered the power of God at work. It is this power that has transformed them. They have seen it transform their neighborhoods and they have seen it transform their families and themselves as individuals. And it is this power that, far from eroding the social capital, has built it up and unleashed new energy, creativity and opportunities.

## CONCLUSION

It is no wonder, then, that the women respond so readily when they begin to see a way out of their situation, when they begin to understand that there is another way of life, that if they work together they can improve the lot of the family. Their families will have better food, their children will have a chance to get proper health care, they can be educated, and maybe there is even hope that their husbands will also understand that drugs and alcohol cannot ultimately bring a solution to the frustrations of being poor.

The stories included in this book have told us that while the women may have initially worked together for the sake of their children and families, in the process of doing so they have discovered something deeper. They have come to understand that they themselves have been created in the image of God and that therefore they themselves are of intrinsic value. There is something internal that is unleashed in each of these cases, something that is unleashed when given the opportunity. Each case has sprung out of and capitalized on what is actually there.

❖ *A collaborative spirit.* Before they ever moved to the city, women have worked together. In Zimbabwe, India, South Africa and the Philippines women have worked together to till the soil and produce the food that their family needs; they have joined cooperatives so that they can buy the clothing they need; they have watched each other's children so that work can get done. And now, in the city, this collaboration is harnessed in a variety of different ways.

❖ *A learning spirit.* The desire to earn and to provide for their families has led to the willingness to learn, to be educated, to be trained in order to get better jobs or to increase their income.

❖ *An entrepreneurial spirit.* These are incredible stories of women willing to take risks, to try things they have never tried before, to begin something new.

❖ *A sacrificial spirit.* All the efforts these women go through for the good of the community are at the sacrifice of their own private time. Already burdened with the task of being a homemaker and of also earning additional income for the family, a woman still gives of her time to work for transformation.

❖ *A hopeful spirit.* Given the circumstances in which these people live, there is no way they would be able to move forward, to work for change, if they did not have a great faith, a faith and trust in one another that working together will make things better, but most of all a faith in the transforming love of a God who has proven to them that God is on their side. Not that their faith does not falter, but when it does there are others around them to sustain and to help encourage them along the way.

136

Finally, I think there are lessons and insights in these cases that will help us all as we partner with the poor to change our cities. First, it is important to recognize that spiritual transformation has to be at the core of community transformation. Acknowledging the power of God leads us to ponder whether community organizing can ultimately be as effective as these cases have demonstrated without that personal spiritual transformation. Second, we need to validate the role of women in our communities. We need to validate the domestic work that they do and recognize the toll that increased work outside the home will take on their health, both physically and emotionally. We need to challenge men to take up their share of the domestic work and shoulder responsibility for home life as well. And third, we need to ask why these cases about women are told by men. Why are the women's voices not heard? Why are their stories interpreted by others? We must look at our own organizations and seriously evaluate the way power is brokered in them. This issue of gender equality is expounded on in more depth by Althea Spencer-Miller, and we need to take seriously what she says.

Nevertheless, we can celebrate the transformation that we have read about in these cases. Women who have traditionally born the brunt of changes beyond their control, who have been the victims of oppression from many different sources, have now become the leaders in their communities, a political force to contend with and a sign of hope to the rest of the world. They have succeeded in showing men that change is possible, and men, too, have joined in the community efforts. We are indebted to these courageous people.

## NOTES

[1] John D. Kaarda and Allan M. Parnel, eds., *Third World Cities: Problems, Policies, and Prospects* (Newbury Park: Sage, 1993).

[2] Johanna Son, *Asia-Habitat: Squatters Left by the Wayside of City "Development,"* Inter Press Service, Manila, January 23, 1997.

[3] Nick Devas and Carole Rakodi, *Managing Fast Growing Cities* (London: Longman Group, 1993).

[4] Caroline O. N. Moser, *Confronting Crisis: A Comparative Study of Household Responses to Poverty and Vulnerability in Four Poor Urban Communities* (Washington, D.C.: The World Bank, 1996).

# 9

# Face-to-face reflection

*Jayne Scott*

There's nothing quite like taking a good, hard look at yourself in a mirror—especially when someone else is looking over your shoulder. You not only see what you've seen so many times before, but you also see some things about yourself as if you were the onlooker.

Effectively, this is what this reflection is about. As a consultation group, engaged for five days in the task of meeting together each day, hearing case studies about working with the urban poor, sharing ideas, resources, and offering reflections on one another's contributions, we were in a situation where we were looking at one another and ourselves in new ways. We were peering over one another's shoulders, so to speak, as if accompanying our colleagues in their urban work and looking at what they do and how they do it. Simultaneously, we found that we began to see ourselves too—our strengths, inadequacies and potential.

We had set ourselves an imposing task, not least because we scrutinized what we do in our respective work with the urban poor, but also because we committed ourselves to being reflected on for the duration of the consultation.

To what extent were we able to use the principles that undergird holistic ministry with the urban poor of whom we speak? Would we adopt a process that demonstrated empowerment, integration, holism and faith? It could be that our credibility and integrity as practitioners, fund-holders and reflectors would depend on it—particularly if a book were to emerge claiming to speak with any meaning to those endeavoring to bring about holistic approaches to ministry with the urban poor. The stakes were high.

So it was that we were committed to consider how holistic learning and holistic-ministry principles can be applied to a consultation process such as ours, which aimed to have a clearly identified "product" (a book) as the end result.

The aims of this particular reflection are mainly twofold:

1. To consider to what extent the principles of holistic ministry were incorporated into our process for the week.
2. To explore (and perhaps identify) how holistic learning can be developed when different life experiences clash (that is, reflecting on the dialectic tensions between power and powerlessness, wealth and poverty, East and West, male and female).

The main themes of reflection were power, expectations and motivation. The choice of these three themes was deliberate, because for all those engaged in ministry with the urban poor, these themes confront them every day. Transformation can be made possible or completely confounded according to the levels, nature and direction of all three within the life of the community.

For us, as a short-term group with a specific goal in mind, these themes took on a shape particular to our task. But we wanted to ascertain whether there were some insights here for us to retain and develop in our shared endeavor to nurture holistic ministry. The particularity we experienced is purposely presented in a way that shows our approach is but one experience in the context of many. As a springboard, trigger, inspiration, "nudge," we encountered something of our own formation in considering integrated holistic processes in relation to community development and organizing.

## How Did We Do It?

In the course of the week each participant received and returned a reflection sheet on which there were three questions, each related to one of the three themes: power, expectations and motivation. As the week progressed there were several observations that emerged from the group members themselves concerning their own learning and awareness of how these dynamics changed. By the end of the week, when the time for evaluation arrived, the feedback on all three themes was handled face to face by all the participants (rather than individually and in written form).

We can note two possible conclusions from this concluding phase and how the group handled it. First, the fact that the group members all contributed to the plenary evaluation was an indication that the levels of trust and mutuality had evolved enough to make a reflection of this nature possible. Members did not retreat from one another when the group reached the stages of closure. Rather, they expressed a desire to handle it in that way—the consensus on this was clearly stated. Second, the manner of sharing evaluation in this way was consistent with the intention that we might enable one another in an appropriate way to see the task through, adopting a holistic method. In this sense we all became both educators and learners as equal participants in one another's learning.

This, then, is something of a story and, like many stories, inevitably it will gather elaboration and embellishments in the course of its telling.

## POWER

The response sheets that were used in the course of the week gave a clear indication that, for all the participants, there was a level of awareness that power was on the move. There were shifts, rhythms and patterns that permeated the whole event. This is hardly surprising, since all those in attendance were people who carried some level of influence in their own sphere and were bound to bring something of that to this particular event. What we perhaps began to see in ourselves was a heightened consciousness of how we were making use of this power and the growing capacity as a group to be able to talk about it. D. R. Forsyth writes, "Power, to a group dynamicist, is the capacity to influence others, even when those others try to resist this [1] Forsyth indicates that power in a group context involves several forces that come into play. There is the capacity to influence, the capacity to resist such influence and the processes by which each capacity is exercised.

In the first few sessions the organizers, planners and sponsors were perceived to hold the most significant information about what was hoped for in the week. As each day unfolded and information was disseminated—different cases were heard and group members became familiar with one another and their environment—power too became a more shared dynamic. In the first meetings a consciousness of the time constraints, the desire to put our material into book form and the fact that members of the group had not yet had the opportunity to form relationships of trust all meant that power was expressed in the manner described by Forsyth.

There are other more sophisticated and integrated understandings of power, however, and these probably relate more closely to where we hoped we might be by the end of the consultation. Paolo Freire, a Brazilian educationalist, has challenged our assumptions about power, education and community development. Freire reminds us of what makes the difference between a learning experience that plays out the power expressed by others over us and that which enables us, in the process of learning, to be empowered. He starts from the premise that education can be for either domestication or liberation. Both start from the same concrete reality. But the process of domestication leads to preset goals, known beforehand. The process of liberation relies upon the praxis of collaboration and communication.[2]

Herein lay our early dilemmas about how we would experience and express power in our consultation. We were to satisfy some preset goals and yet, at the same time, work collaboratively and communicate well. This, according to Freire's thinking, would appear to be something of a compromise and somewhat doubtful as a liberating learning opportunity. To the extent that both preset goals and collaborative styles of working were very present in the process, there has to be some acknowledgment that elements of both "domestication" and "liberation" were to be found. Rather than regarding this as inherently suspect, the view could be taken that this too reflects the experiences of those engaged in community development/organizing in the urban context. It would be doubtful if any learning setting is ever fully one or the other. While Freire's thinking helps to clarify and to distinguish between the more harmful and helpful approaches to learning, reality is never simply bipolar in its manifestation.

Nevertheless, it is heartening to those who struggle with and engage the "powers-that-be" to read and hear about Freire, his work, and the reminder that power cannot be contained by those who assume authority over others, which then results in further oppression of the powerless. That process of empowerment means exercising the liberty to question who sets the parameters and why.

We did this as a group. We negotiated, consulted, questioned, doubted, affirmed, encouraged, made alterations and became increasingly self-determining as time progressed. We discovered, through our strong desire to apply the principles of holistic ministry to our consultation, that

> the power of the individual is enhanced when the web of relationships is benevolent and encourages the most creativity. This gives the person the potential ability to participate fully in the relational web, to allow ones being to absorb as much experience as possible and to have such an effect on self and others that the whole relational aspect of life is enhanced and enlarged.[3]

Power was not and cannot be understood solely in terms of influence over another (cf. Forsyth). Rather, it is much more expansive than that. It is an ability also to *empower and liberate* (cf. Freire). But, even more than Freire's view, power is not simply a political activity that brings transformation of one's context and environment, it cannot be fully appreciated and expressed if the *web of relationships* (cf. Newton-Poling) is inadequate to the task.

In Franklin Joseph's case study he notes, "We wanted the community to set the agenda." This concisely expressed desire of the urban community-organizer as a principle of working with people every day in the process of empowerment also sums up the discovered and uncovered way in which power emerged through the consultation we attended in Manila. We could see the parallels between our own experience together and that of the much-needed power shift necessary if communities truly are to be given the freedom to set the agenda for themselves. This is not easy and requires that power itself be perceived not as a possession to be held onto but rather as a source of energy that can either be enhanced through mutual sharing in community or limited through remaining within the realm of the individual.

By the end of the week we had tested out the boundaries of where our collective power was to be found, and we discovered the benefits of allowing mutual sharing in community to really happen. We had choices all along the way. There were points at which any one of us could have fragmented the collectivity that we were discovering by insisting that our individual needs be met first. Our choice turned out not to be that pattern. In this we were true to the essence of the work in which we are each engaged in the urban context.

## EXPECTATIONS

From the start we were fairly clear that our goals included the search for approaches to holistic ministry with the urban poor that centered "primarily around the need to establish a credible witness for the gospel" (Dan and Kathleen Sheffield, chapter 2 above). There has always been a debate about the extent to which goals and expectations should be prescriptive, descriptive or postscripted. There is no ready or simple answer to what forms an appropriate pattern. What can be observed is that, where power becomes a shared, collective expression of a group's source of energy, the goals and expectations can be revisited and altered according to how the group progresses toward facing its tasks together. Timing is everything. To state goals too soon can stultify the process. To fail to name them at the appropriate moment can result in directionless busyness. All this begs the question of who has the responsibility or the right to name the goal.

In the setting of a week-long consultation with the hope of producing a book, it would appear, on the face of it, that the goals were so obvious that they almost did not need to be stated at all.

From the response sheets returned by participants each day, a slightly different picture was drawn. There was an even mixture of those who looked above all to the completion of a piece of written work in the form of a book as the main aim of the week, and others for whom there was a priority focus—that of developing networks of friendship and collegial relationships. While most participants included both as expectations, there was an apparent difference in priority among them. By the end of the week all the group members acknowledged that their expectations had been met, whether by accident or design. As questions of power and authority shifted, it became more possible for the broader spectrum of expectations to be addressed.

This is a recognized pattern for groups that have participants with backgrounds as diverse as ours. Speaking of Practitioner Inquiry Communities, Drennon and Foucar-Szocki note:

> Characteristically, decision-making power in inquiry groups is shared among the participants. . . . As the group carries out its work, hierarchical relationships . . . are diminished in varying degrees. This happens as group members pool their diverse knowledge, perspectives and skills in the effort to understand more deeply issues of

shared concern. . . . Authority shifts from experts outside the program to practitioners inside the program who come to develop and
articulate theories grounded in their real-world experience.[4]

We experienced firsthand that, having the opportunity to share encounters and to negotiate with one another about how both our individual and collective goals might be reached, the level of satisfaction
and sense of achievement endowed the consultation process with
worth.

The detailed ways in which this happened cannot be provided in
the space available here, nor would they necessarily be of relevance to
a wider audience, but the fact that this did happen gives rise to some
observations that could be useful elsewhere.

The combination of sponsors, practitioners and reflectors from mark-
edly different backgrounds and fields of expertise as participants provided a pool of resources essential to dynamic group learning. This
may have happened with some design, but it serves to reinforce further the point that the provision of such opportunities on a more frequent basis could effect more transformation than previously we have
been prepared to recognize. Policies and practice in community development and organizing could break into a whole new phase should
such learning be actively encouraged and financed as a clear strategy
for future holistic ministry with the urban poor. Practitioners and
policy-makers need to experience for themselves what transformation
means for them. Liberation for all starts with the poor becoming more
self-determining and being empowered—Paolo Freire, Leonardo Boff,
Jon Sobrino, Gustavo Gutiérrez and many others have been telling us
so for years.[5] Fr. Ben Beltran also enabled us to meet with this reality
by bringing us face to face with some of the women at Smokey Mountain. The meeting of theories, policies and practice in the melting-pot of
a consultation for one week in Manila urges us to allow such encounters
to become the driving force of our learning and decision-making. Only
then will our expectations, hopes and dreams for holistic ministry with
the urban poor have the chance of becoming even more real.

## MOTIVATION

Group motivation operates according to the same principles that apply to individual motivation. Factors that optimize group motivation

include having a goal to attain; feeling efficacious about performing well; holding positive outcome expectations; attributing success to such factors as ability, effort and strategy use; and receiving feedback indicating goal progress.[6]

When participation is spontaneous and not coerced, motivation to further the purposes of a group is usually high. In a situation where the purpose of the group has perhaps been lost or is incongruent with some of the views of its members, motivation can be strong but at the same time be working to subvert practice and understanding. For motivation to continue to be in keeping with the expectations of the group, the purposes themselves have to be both clear to and agreed upon by the participants. For adults to learn together effectively, the motivation to make the learning happen and to enable one another to be included has to be evident. It is a source of strength on which each group member can draw. Where it is found in a group, its members both derive energy from and energize one another. A. Rogers writes, "Motivation in education is that compulsion which keeps a person within a learning situation and encourages him or her to learn."[7]

Our consultation group members demonstrated commitment to shared goals, committed themselves to engagement with one another and the issues of holistic ministry with the urban poor and became a source of energy for each member. In this, the motivation was to be found. It would be inaccurate to suggest, however, that this was the pattern throughout the week. Just as levels of trust increased, power was distributed and expectations began to be met, the level of motivation heightened and accelerated as the week progressed. At the conclusion of the consultation the group was buoyant and confident that the task would be completed (not something that can be assumed to be the automatic outcome of such a venture!).

Fr. Ben Beltran reminded us of the necessity to address matters of power and purpose, because then motivation will take care of itself. He said, "Once the people have grasped the 'why' of what they are doing, the 'how' is not a problem." We saw this at Smokey Mountain, we discovered it in our own process and we now write of this in our collection of work and reflections on holistic ministry with the urban poor. To allow this further to permeate our learning together and from one another would be to release the power and motivation within us all to transform our local and global communities alike.

145

In short, motivation can be found through processes of empowerment and shared purpose. While we would appear to have endorsed
this in many ways through a variety of community development and
organization projects, there is still scope for exploration with regard to
what this means for fund-holders, sponsors, theoreticians and practitioners when confronted with one another. We can testify to the fact
that, with the opportunity we had in Manila in January 1998, we found
that these processes can transform and motivate people to venture into
new ways of envisioning their world.

ADDITIONAL REFLECTIONS

The value of our shared learning is to be measured in our capacity
to acknowledge what did happen for us, while at the same time recognizing that there are areas that remained untouched or inadequately
addressed in the context of our process. To name them is to indicate
that learning must go on. The struggle toward the development of
holistic ministry involves honesty and the will to work at issues that
remain unresolved. Our summary list here is noted with such honesty
in mind in the hope that, rather than courting sharp criticism from our
audience, it will encourage more determination on all our parts to redress shortcomings that are to be found in all aspects of work with the
urban poor—not just our own.

First, we noticed ourselves a contrast in the way we received and
processed material from those who were present among us and those
who were unable to attend but who had sent material for us to consider. We tended to be more critical of those who were not with us,
even though we placed a high value on their work. This raised questions for us regarding our own self-awareness. Do we tend to assume
liberties when we don't have to face the people concerned? Are we
being just in our responses? To what extent do we tend to do the same
when we formulate policies and projects that affect the urban poor?
Do we tend to "take liberties" if we do not have to actually face them?
If so, how can this information about ourselves transform us?

Second, it became apparent that the Western notions of security and
certainty as basic assumptions for life do not feature as central to the
experiences of the urban poor. We were confronted with people who
experience relentless insecurity and uncertainty, and we were reminded
of the fact that Jesus' teaching about the kingdom of God resonates

with the experiences of the urban poor rather than with the Western obsessions of security and certainty. This is a sharp challenge to those who operate according to Western value systems, particularly when it comes to determining how money should be allocated in work with the urban poor. This is not a new reflection, but we became aware of it once again in our consultation.

Third, women were very present in the consultation, but they were not often speaking for themselves. They were represented, they responded and they supported the whole process, but we were very conscious that, at points, we were still at a loss as to how to explain our inability to enable them to have a more central role. We were deeply touched and affected by their amazing strength, which we witnessed through the case studies, at Smokey Mountain, in administrative backup and ability to reflect in a meaningful way, but we could not help but feel we had failed them to some degree. This is a source of resolve for the future. In our commitment to holistic ministry with the urban poor we acknowledged our need to ensure that this does not continue without correction.

## CONCLUSIONS

It was said at the beginning of this chapter that this is something of a story. It is certainly something of a continuing narrative. Like all good stories, it does not really end here; nor does it pretend that everything will turn out "happily ever after" for all those concerned. Each of us has returned to our commitment to ministry with the urban poor, and with that in mind we grapple with the harsher realities of power, expectations and motivation. Our reflection on this event, which was an opportunity to develop through learning as a group, is offered as a contribution to the ongoing dialogue, which includes sponsors, theoreticians and practitioners in the very processes we experienced during one week.

Two concluding remarks which we hope could further enable this vision for holistic ministry with the urban poor to develop into the future are:

1. Groupings of sponsors, theoreticians and practitioners with a clear intention to engage in mutual integrated learning could enable new forms of urban ministry and mission to emerge. In order to create the space for this to happen, fund-holders and policy-makers need to incorporate this into their strategic plans.

147

2. By finding ways of being less fearful of our diversity, we will discover an energy and an honesty that can only further enhance holistic ministry with the urban poor. To energize and be energized by one another can be a wider liberating experience of the issues of power and powerlessness, wealth and poverty, male and female and East and West, not as an external observation exercise, but as personal engagement is the way into integrated, holistic understanding. It is also the measure by which the urban poor will evaluate our credibility.

## NOTES

[1] D. R. Forsyth, *Group Dynamics* (New Jersey: Brooks/Cole, 1990), p. 209.

[2] P. Freire, *Education for Liberation* (Bangalore Ecumenical Christian Centre Publication, 1975), p. 44.

[3] J. Newton-Poling, *The Abuse of Power* (Nashville, Tenn.: Abingdon, 1991), p. 25.

[4] C. Drennon and D. L. Foucar-Szocki, "Transforming Groups Developing Practitioner Inquiry Groups," in *Learning in Groups Exploring Fundamental Principles, New Uses, and Emerging Opportunities*, ed. S. Imel (San Francisco: Jossey-Bass, 1996), p. 72.

[5] P. Freire, *Pedagogy of the Oppressed* (London: Penguin, 1972); L. Boff, *Church, Charism and Power* (London: SCM, 1985); J. Sobrino, *Spirituality and Liberation* (Maryknoll, N.Y.: Orbis Books, 1988); G. Gutiérrez, *The Power of the Poor in History* (Maryknoll, N.Y.: Orbis Books, 1983).

[6] P. R. Pintich and D. H. Schunk, *Motivation in Education* (New Jersey: Prentice-Hall,1996), p. 189.

[7] A. Rogers, *Teaching Adults* (Milton Keynes Open University, 1986), p. 6.

# 10

# Promoting urban economic transformation at the grassroots

*Grant and Nancy Power*

### TRANSFORMING URBAN ECONOMIES FROM BELOW

The cases of holistic ministry in urban poor communities presented at the Manila consultation resound with three themes regarding community economic development. First, mission and development workers today are engaged in an unprecedented opportunity to partner with the urban poor to address their economic challenges as a witness to the gospel. Economic development cannot replace other types of urban ministry such as church formation and Christian discipleship. But it is inseparably bound up with them in the *missio Dei*. We live in an era of unrestrained global trade and investment, and its accompanying effects of widening inequality of wealth and incomes and lack of local control give a special sense of urgency for God's people to address the concrete economic circumstances in which the urban poor live. Far from irrelevant to urban mission, transforming the economics of urban poverty reflects God's special concern for the poor—and God's intention to liberate them from poverty.

Second, community economic development *as ministry* does not bring economic solutions to the urban poor but releases the capacities already present in the people so they can find their own economic solutions. We define community economic development as stimulating and supporting the emergence and expansion of viable, business activities initiated, owned and sustained by the urban poor. This process is most likely to occur whenever the poor shift away from seeing themselves as objects of other people's decisions or actions and toward authoring their own (economic) future. The challenge is to partner with the poor so they are able to create a stable, growing store of wealth as the foundation of their economic advancement. Though helpful, it is not enough for the poor just to find jobs. They also should become owners of local economically productive assets such as land, equipment and capital for investment. This is difficult to do in practice. It requires that missionaries bring to the field a sound understanding and integration of business, mission strategy and development principles. While results of missionary economic development work to date are mixed, we are seeing some breakthroughs in situations where the poor are organized so they can work collectively to launch or expand their own economic ventures. These locally owned and controlled enterprises use a "double bottom line" of building both business viability and community cohesion at the same time.

Third, the urban poor are, by and large, very innovative and industrious, yet few options are available to them in the marketplace to create enough wealth to overcome the economic forces that create or perpetuate their poverty. Because of these relentless marketplace pressures, missionaries need to negotiate a fine line between what "works" in traditional business and what truly empowers communities economically. Organizing poor communities to create wealth and employment "from below" actually stands in tension with a worldwide bias in urban economic policy toward conventional "top down" modernization strategies. These modernization strategies generally aim to attract and retain investment in mainstream economic "growth sectors," such as large-scale export and industrial goods, on the premise that the benefits of growth at the top will in time accrue to everyone's benefit. But the benefits of growth usually stay where they start. In this situation missionaries and development workers may need to follow a dual track of helping to launch viable enterprises in distressed communities and also struggling with the urban poor more broadly to create an economic order that is more just, humane and participatory.

In this chapter we will take a closer look at each of these themes in connection with the ministry cases described in earlier chapters and explore some of the practical implications of these themes for churches and mission and development agencies.

## The Rise of Community Economic Development
## on the Urban Mission Agenda

For all their diversity culturally and geographically, the urban poor across the world are distinguished mainly by their socioeconomic status. In Northern cities they are often excluded from the labor force and concentrated in neighborhoods where their separate status is maintained through confinement (based largely on employment connections and housing affordability) to isolated, blighted areas, out of view from their more affluent neighbors. In the developing world many of the urban poor were recently rural poor. Pressed by increasing poverty in the rural areas and pulled by the perception of increasing opportunities for employment and income, they migrated to the cities in search of a better life. Now they generally live in squatter settlements close to their places of work. They are predominantly members of the informal sector—that part of the urban economy that is "under the table," even though the poor "illegally" provide services that are critical to the dominant (formal sector) work force at very low cost.[1]

Economic development has attracted and sustained the interest of a growing number of missionary and church-affiliated development agencies working in cities during the last decade. The reasons for this growing interest are many. Chief among them is that these agencies are reckoning now with how fast and how much the world is urbanizing, and those who have witnessed firsthand the plight of the urban poor have found their own responses to that plight inadequate. Increasingly, they have seen the need for an urgent response that balances personal sensitivity, hardheaded practical creativity, and lasting community impact.

The broad movement of missions into urban community economic development is clearly seen in the case studies presented at the Manila consultation. As a rule these cases describe how community workers have set out to provide employment, job skills, production equipment and financing to run a business so the poor can survive—and thrive—economically. The association in Madras started a credit union for small businesses; the street people in Zimbabwe attended vocational-training programs and organized to produce and market various items such as vegetables, furniture and crocheting; and the Smokey Mountain residents also developed vocational training and started cooperatives.

Economics was one of the three main priorities of the Basic Christian Communities at Smokey Mountain. In the Hollywood-Wilshire Cluster in Los Angeles an economic-development corporation enables residents to start small businesses, and the youth are encouraged in academic pursuits after school. Similarly, in other cities around the world, missionaries have launched livelihood programs (such as vocational skills training) alongside evangelization ministries, while Christian development agencies have cut their teeth in "niche" programs such as microenterprise lending.

Not only has evangelical economic-development work represented a new effort to broaden its approach to urban mission, but it also has reflected a shift of strategy. Whereas earlier mission work had focused on meeting the immediate needs of the poor (relief), now they help the poor acquire skills and tools needed to meet their own needs (development). Among other things, churches in the North suffered from "donor fatigue," partly brought on by the recurrence of famines in parts of Africa and by a "rice Christian" syndrome in which people were seen as making confessions of faith as a means of accessing charity. These factors motivated them to reexamine their strategies and seek a longer-lasting response to poverty. The rise of evangelical agencies focused on microenterprise development, such as Chicago-based Opportunity International, and of denominational mission programs emphasizing economic development, such as Christian Reformed World Relief Committee, are clear evidence of this strategic turn.

Urban community economic-development ministries reinforce the notion that religion is a "whole-life thing" not confined to traditional church activities (such as worship) and traditional mission activities (evangelization). This social concern has been the basis of the churches' ministries in health, education and agriculture for generations. However, beginning in the 1970s and 1980s, the social teaching of Christian faith had come under fire from churches in the West, which, as mission sponsors, were unfortunately becoming captivated by an individualistic, one-sided understanding of Christianity that downplayed development work as "unspiritual." This reductionism echoed the backlash against Christian social concern one hundred years earlier in Western countries. So the rise of economic development programs can be seen as an important corrective to an otherwise one-sided bias in contemporary evangelical missions.

In other words, the shift among evangelical missions toward urban community economic development reflects a parallel, and profound, shift among evangelical churches on *theological* grounds. For example, the Oxford Conference in 1990 established a benchmark validation among evangelicals of the importance of economics in Christian faith. Among other things it affirmed that everyone has the right to earn a living, with enough time left over to rest and worship. It condemns poverty and protectionist policies that are detrimental to developing nations. It also notes that Scripture repeatedly expresses God's concern for justice and the poor.

In practice, evangelical economic development in the cities at its best is a rousing declaration that the Good News of Jesus Christ means that "the kingdom of God is at hand." As with the concept of *shalom* in the Old Testament, God intends that economic power be spread widely among the people and that everyone enjoy the fruits of his or her own labor (see, for example, Lev. 25 and Isa. 65:17–25). The Creator intends that people live in harmony with God, with the land and with each other. Thus the gospel is not just a verbal message but one that is made tangible by the missionaries' lives and even by economic structures that give everyone a fair opportunity to live a life of dignity, rather than enhancing the rich at the expense of the poor. Thus for the poor families of Smokey Mountain, one expression of the Good News is their transition from 90 percent earning a living by scavenging in the 1980s to 80 percent earning a living from work outside the dump by 1998. These new jobs are in more dignifying trades such as computer systems, auto repair and building tricycle motor taxis.

In summary, urban community economic development is becoming recognized as a dignifying and empowering way for the church to respond to the aspiration of the poor to create a better future for themselves in an unfriendly urban environment. In the giant urban economies that characterize the world at the beginning of the twenty-first century, community economic development can help people move beyond mere survival for those who are among the first generation of urban poor families as they strive to stake out a life for themselves. Properly executed, it can then provide a basis of *hope* and *a sense of purpose* for subsequent generations of the urban poor, who are otherwise vulnerable to unrequited frustration and exploitation. A dominant motive for Christian economic development comes from the conviction that God is concerned about every aspect of human life and blesses us so that we might be a blessing, particularly to those considered "the least" in our society. As in the Madras case study, empowering the poor can draw them by love into a genuine, enthusiastic faith in God, rather than manipulating or bribing them into a less genuine proclamation of faith.

The implications of this emerging emphasis on faith-based community economic development for the future of urban mission as a whole will comprise the remainder of this chapter.

### From Paternalism to Partnership

Having started the shift toward community economic development, Christians in the city have had a hard time getting it right. This has been in part because community economic development is inherently difficult. The time and effort required to launch a business in favorable circumstances—let alone in very challenging situations—can be substantial, and the results fragile and uncertain. An additional problem is that economic development is not just a single creature. There are many ways to do it. As we will see below, how this inherently difficult work is done can make or break the credibility and distinctiveness of Christian mission among the poor in the city. A third hurdle is the challenge of the city itself—in particular, its rapid pace, congestion and complexity.

To be successful, practitioners must integrate business skills, an unmistakable commitment to empowerment, and a thorough understanding of the cultural and institutional context in which the urban poor live. We contend that urban economic developers have brought to their task great business skills but have been lacking both in their experience with empowerment processes and in their appreciation and grasp of the complexities of the urban environment. This discrepancy between the expertise of workers and the demands and complexity of their work has caused mixed results among the urban poor, and discouragement for workers accustomed to success in business. Therefore, we want to explore specifically how these shortcomings play out in practice and consider some ways to overcome them. In so doing, we hope to chart a pathway for practitioners from the role of provider to that of partner.

First—especially in the developing world—urban economic development missionaries have failed to understand the profound clash of values between rural or minority or refugee families and the modern city. The face-to-face value systems imported by migrant families into the city are corroded and weakened over time by the exposure of the rural poor to urban secular/modern values and perspectives, and by time and distance from their traditional cultural moorings.

Such modern values may include saving resources to use as capital rather than giving them to needy friends or family members; valuing nature only for what it can produce for humans; and valuing humans only for what they contribute to the economy, rather than vice versa. These values are often not familiar to urban migrants and are very hard to adjust to. Their long-term effect in the lives of urban poor households can be stress, isolation and alienation—in short, a breeding ground for hopelessness, misery and violence. At the same time, as we have noted, the poor in the city are very resourceful and extremely deft at managing the pressures of the urban environment. However, missionaries, often blind to the significance of this clash of values, at times have unwittingly undermined the resilience of the poor as they try to adapt to the city by implicitly assuming that modern values are correct, unaware of their own acculturation to the West. In practice, *missionaries have imbibed uncritically the same secular modernist values that the city thrusts on the poor.*

Specifically, urban economic-development missionaries have tended to follow the lead of business managers and traditional economic development agencies in a bid to find what "works," without reflecting deeply about the value implications or impacts of these activities. These programs have been institution-led and agency-controlled, and have tended to focus on packaging services such as job training, technical assistance, finance and skill-building for the poor. The goal is to help working poor families in the city "fit in" or "make it" in the urban economy by taking advantage of the resources and services of an agency's development program. This goal is reasonable in principle, and its result is compelling: there have been many positive changes in the lives of urban poor entrepreneurs and their families, particularly women.

Yet, these development projects tend to be based on outsiders' perceptions and definitions of the needs of poor communities. Programs are designed based on an assumption that "one size fits all" in terms of program design and delivery, and on what is perceived to be realistic in light of the political context and the demands of funders. Programs usually are not checked carefully with members of those communities. Even if projects achieve their intended *output*, attention to long-range *outcomes* is sacrificed. The outward physical or technical improvements that go with these kinds of projects can mask a dependency or lack of initiative or substantive participation by stakeholders in the community. The mainstreaming ideology, delivered to the poor in the form of support services and loans, actually can undermine the poor by not nurturing their capacity to meet their own needs and become self-sustaining. Rather than giving the poor more control over their own lives, economy and future, these types of projects may actually take away control.

In addition, the mainstreaming approach glosses over the need of families to build (or protect or strengthen) their internal bonds of community and cultural values. By treating economic problems as a technical challenge isolated from other aspects of families' lives, the mainstreaming strategy is blind to the forces of social isolation and alienation created by the city's modernizing culture. For example, many low-income households bring with them a tradition of localized, small-scale enterprise to meet their own basic needs. Poorer communities tend to be more relationally focused and process-oriented but are confronted by severely overcrowded markets in the urban economy and an imperative always to increase productivity and be concerned about the bottom line.

Urban community economic development practitioners and the agencies that send them out have only dimly begun to see the depth of their unwitting collusion with secular capitalism. The broad historical impact of unrestrained capitalism has been that money tends to colonize the rest of life, whereas the agenda of the kingdom of God is to set people free from any and all forces that would bind and oppress them spiritually and socially. Thus the imperative of the gospel is to do the opposite of what the modern industrial economy demands. This does not mean that the gospel is anti-urban, but rather that it clashes with many values that are products of modernity. We do not argue that the modern industrial city must therefore be obliterated. But it must be transformed.

The second major shortcoming of many Christian community economic-development practitioners in urban missions is their grasp of the need for empowerment, or letting the poor take the lead in realizing their potential through economic change. Translated into practical terms, empowerment lends itself to a "people-centered" kind of economic development based on production by the masses. This is distinguished from the modern industrial mainstream approach to economic development that depends on industrial mass production. This is where the case studies from Manila, Madras and Harare are instructive. Rather than beginning with economic tools, missionaries and development workers cultivated leadership within poor communities through organizing. Out of this process local stakeholders come together (based on the advantages of collective action) to define and reflect on their situation, develop a vision for the future, identify key challenges, and harness resources inside and outside the community to meet those challenges. This approach concentrates on mobilizing the community to develop as it sees fit. The people in the community define the goals of economic development and participate in development projects from the beginning, seeking to overcome the tangible causes of their shared pain and frustration.

The people-centered strategy builds community rather than delivering a package of services. It mobilizes the assets, skills and capacities of residents, squatter associations and people's organizations, rather than focusing on their needs, problems and deficiencies. By seeking to understand and appreciate what the poor have rather than what they lack, the missionary can become a partner rather than a controller of the process and product. In addition, the emphasis on community building seeks to preserve and strengthen positive cultural values and relational cohesion. In short, people-centered development aims to strengthen the poor so they can build economic structures of production that are organic to them and that put them in control (or greater control) of their own productive assets and capacities.

The result is a dynamic economy with varied and fast-changing patterns of organization, rooted in local cultures and communities but intersecting at appropriate points with the structures of finance and exchange in the modern urban economy.

The cases in this book do not reveal directly the discrepancy we posit here between worker skill profiles and the challenges of the work

needed in urban community economic development. They are excep-
tional in that the development workers appear to bring special sensitivity to the urban context and the empowerment process. For this
reason the cases are particularly instructive. Some examples of enterprises or activities that have successfully emerged from people-centered economic development among the urban poor are worker-owned
producer cooperatives (e.g., bicycle repair business, Smokey Mountain); microenterprises spawned through solidarity loans (Harare, Zimbabwe); joint purchasing agreements; and major construction contracts
(Smokey Mountain). Though not presented in the case studies, another
important example is fair trade, which establishes linkages to international markets between Northern and Southern trading markets while
preserving a livable and fair return to small producers. For example,
Ten Thousand Villages is an organization that markets handcrafts from
several different countries. On the whole, these activities seek to increase local control of productive assets such as finance, real estate and
access to suppliers and markets so that communities can be stable, viable and self-sustaining. They seek to create an economic base from
which to trade on a level playing field with other communities and
corporations rather than being exploited and depleted by them.

Among the practical implications of the foregoing comments for
faith-based urban community economic development are the following:

❖ Rather than bringing economic solutions to the poor, emphasis is
  placed on unleashing the economic potential of the poor by facilitating their efforts to develop their own enterprises, or perhaps
  even to restore the economies that worked for them before the
  incursion of Western culture. In some cases, such as the Zapatista
  revolution in Chiapas, Mexico, and PRATEC (Andean Project for
  Peasant Technology) in Peru, the people's chief desire is to not
  have to participate in the global market economy. They do not
  consider themselves "poor" and they don't want to be "developed." The term *development,* coined by U.S. President Truman in
  1949, is often a one-way perception by Westerners that "others
  need to be like us."

❖ Rather than trying to make the poor conform to the survival demands of the wider economy, emphasis is placed on honoring the
  cultural values and preferences of poorer communities by enabling
  them to organize production in ways that reflect those values. Often

this requires taking small, simple, slow steps forward within the local people's frame of reference, bringing early recognizable results, and relying on the knowledge and creativity of the people so they can repeat and sustain the activity on their own later.[2]

❖ Often locally driven organizations take forms such as producer cooperatives or savings groups that would not be compatible with the individualistic character of businesses in metropolitan countries, particularly in the cities that dominate these countries. Development workers should become very familiar with how to organize and operate successful cooperatives and other group-oriented enterprises in the midst of a competitive market environment.[3]

### From Mainstreaming to Solidarity

Partnership with the poor requires not only a willingness to learn from them but also to suffer with them. In practice this suffering entails taking seriously God's prophetic summons to join with the poor in their struggle against powerful institutions for the sake of economic justice.

The call to compassion (in the biblical sense) has been appropriated by some evangelicals to mean moving in and living among the urban poor, sharing their pain and bonding with them where they live as a starting point for sharing the love of Jesus Christ. Various expressions of incarnational ministry have been undertaken by groups such as Servants to Asia's Urban Poor and International Teams. All of this is good and right. It is one thing for Christians to seek to relieve the suffering of the poor through charitable programs. It is quite another to become like them in their suffering so they might see God's kingdom demonstrated in their relationships on a daily basis.

However, as a poverty-eradication strategy, local incarnational ministry is only one piece of the puzzle. It tends to target communities as isolated entities, and as such does not even begin to address the broader economic causes of poverty such as widening inequality, lack of housing affordability, employment discrimination, poverty wages and patterns of disinvestment in distressed communities. We would argue that to suffer with the poor for the sake of economic justice requires taking a prophetic stance of resistance and transformation of the institutions and policies that control the urban economy.

159

According to the Bible, God calls his people not only to share the suffering of the poor and seek its alleviation, but also to strive to change the structural position of the poor by overcoming sources of their oppression and alienation (e.g., Isa. 58:6; 65:20–23). In practice, many evangelicals have been loathe to even touch this notion for fear of appearing communist, following the way of liberationist theology and (dare we suggest?) losing the financial support of the churches that support them from the West. So intent are we to distance ourselves from liberationism that we have neglected the part of liberation theology that the church most needs to hear: God's call to his people to advocate for a fairer world in solidarity with those who have been treated unjustly.

In neglecting this part of God's calling on the church in our time we risk discrediting our own confession as Christians. For example, Tony Campolo tells of an attempt in Haiti to market handmade purses for which the manufacturers received a living wage (still far below U.S. standards). He explained to some Christian women visiting from the U.S. that they could buy similar, mass-produced purses for less money, but by buying these particular ones they would support women trying to earn a decent living. In spite of his plea the visiting "Christians" ignored the just-wage purses and purchased the cheaper ones in town.

At the heart of evangelical reluctance to acknowledge the need for more just economic policies is a pattern of mass self-deception in the churches that an unrestrained global market economy is benign, or that it cannot be changed or that God is not in the business of changing systems. Yet there are serious problems in today's market economies because of the very unbiblical ways in which they operate. The current catechism adopted by most nations of the world regarding economic development is that jobs and income are best created by implementing a program or policy of export-led economic growth. Growth is stimulated when private markets flourish. An unrestrained market, in turn, will flourish if countries adopt a trade-oriented strategy of attracting foreign investment and building industries that will meet world demand for goods and services through exports.

This "export platform" approach to economic development is not only adopted, but led, by major cities. In fact, cities have increasingly become the "control nodes" (or finance capitals) of the global economy. Decisions about finance made in places like São Paolo, London, New York and New Delhi increasingly determine employment and earnings prospects for masses of people, both rural and urban, in countries on the other side of the world. Even if we see an explosion of new jobs and production factories in poorer nations, the basic decisions underlying the creation of these jobs are almost completely outside the control of the people who live and work in those production sites. An increasing proportion of international finance is made up of speculative trading in global currency and commodity markets—a practice that brings quick returns to cash-rich institutional investors but does not add value to the underlying production of the economy. Lastly, the ever-increasing mobility of capital has led to a corporate "race to the bottom," in which companies quickly move to whichever location has the lowest wages and lowest environmental standards.

Economists argue that the benefits of growth will be widely shared across the population of any country that embarks on a growth-centered economic program. What is good for the market is assumed to be good for people in the market, including the poor. But an increasing number of empirical studies suggest that what is good for the market actually harms people, especially the poor. In today's economy half of the world is left with virtually no capital. Workers increasingly are seen as pawns to be shed without recourse by their employers based solely on whether their activities reward shareholders, while governments are pushed to dismantle regulations that protect workers' rights to organize. Hard work and loyalty to one's employer often do not pay off. Capital is invested in (or withdrawn from) national economies based on investor profits, not development outcomes.

Finally, the wealth from rural farm-based areas is extracted and invested in urban areas, rather than reinvested in the rural areas, analogous to how a cancerous tumor depletes the rest of the body. This historical "urban bias" is arguably a leading force behind urban migration and its corollary, urban poverty. Self-interested economic rationality among global investors is exacerbated by frequent instances of government corruption and inefficiency in countries seeking investment. In either case the poor are left completely off the radar screen in the order of development priorities. For example, researchers at the National Autonomous University in Mexico estimate that as many as 15 million people have been driven out of rural agriculture and into urban poverty in the four years since the North American Free Trade Agreement (NAFTA) was passed in 1994. This occurred as farmers were forced to sell their land to large agribusinesses.[4]

In short, the unfettered global market system is designed primarily to serve the interests of investors, and its operations are based increasingly on the demand for short-term gains by these investors. As corporations and investment firms increasingly determine the scope and direction of economic activity they begin to amass the same centralized power economically that Marxist governments do politically. Along the way, huge inequities are created in wealth distribution. This tendency toward more centralized decision-making and rising social inequality is opposed to the biblical principle of Jubilee, which suggests that everybody should have the resources, opportunity and education with which to build healthy and flourishing lives, and that power should be decentralized.

The adherence of churches to the free-market paradigm is a capitulation to secular doctrine (in this case, economic neoclassicism) that dictates its own self-contained set of rules about what the world should be and do. From the perspective of the poor it appears as though we do not want to draw attention to the real social impact of today's economy, since we benefit from it the way it is. In this situation our ministries of compassion and economic development appear to be mere *palliatives*: far from bringing positive change, they create an illusion that change is happening in order to keep real change from taking place.[5] This is indeed the verdict that many developing-world leaders have reached regarding development. There is now an urgent need to reverse the strategy of development so that it fits the needs of the poor, rather than forcing the poor to fit into the needs of a development program that benefits governments and investors. The cases of urban ministry in this book point to three strategies for Christians in response to this situation.

❖ The development worker may be able to assist the people in understanding the choices they have and the implications of those choices. Perhaps the biggest decision is the extent to which they wish to engage in the global economy. The choice to not join the global economy is shrinking as global business reaches its tentacles into all corners of the globe to take land and resources by market forces or by violence. For example, some Habitat for Humanity workers in Zambia in the early 1990s facilitated communities to build better houses on land the people had occupied for hundreds of years, only to have the new government of Zambia sell the land to foreign investors. The people suddenly became squatters on their own land! Yet to fully accept the global economy requires a change in traditional values and can result in a lack of economic control in the local community. A CEO thousands of miles away can make a decision that causes hundreds of people to lose their jobs, with no accountability to those people. On the other hand, in order to resist the global economy, communities need not only to produce their own goods but to purchase them as well. Fr. Ben Beltran in the Philippines was not sure that small-scale production, or "cottage industries," could flourish, because consumers often prefer to buy slick, prestigious and sometimes cheaper multinational products. Resistant communities would also probably need to get official legal rights to their land and to network with other resistant communities and with sympathetic Westerners.

❖ If a community decides not to exit the global economy, the development worker may be able to advocate with the poor for changes at the level of macro-policy in coordination with changes at the micro (community) level. Especially critical are public protections for workers and communities such as livable wages, organizing rights, access to and control of land and capital for investment, and participation in metropolitan and international economic planning decisions. The goal is to change the current economy so it is more inclusive, more distributionally sensitive, more humane. The cases of urban ministry illustrate the power of collective action through community organizing. The Madras case study is an especially dramatic example of God working to bring justice through prayerful community organizing. Conventional economists are likely to resist these measures as inefficient and anti-competitive, but historically, social protections enacted through urban public policy have always been the one thing that has kept working classes from staging revolution. If the race to the bottom is to be reversed globally, urban workers and communities will need to organize across borders to raise the floor worldwide so they, as a whole, can live with dignity and hope.

❖ The development worker may be able to partner with the poor in creating the seeds of an alternative economy. In the words of Denis Goulet, the urban informal sector can sow seeds of change through "creative incrementalism." These deeds are small steps taken in specific communities that appear small and harmless in the wider economy but in practice spark a movement which multiplies their impact and can fundamentally change the way the economy is organized. On a global scale, creative incrementalism has spawned innovations in business that build community and turn a profit to sustain socially oriented enterprise. At the Manila consultation Fr. Ben Beltran stressed that as links are created between these innovations within and between cities, a kind of alternative global urban economy is being born based on kingdom principles of equity, sustainability and compassion. Structures and provisions have been designed in support of fair trade, livable wages and equity for all stakeholders in the interest of promoting sustainable livelihoods.

## FINDING GOD IN THE LIVES OF THE POOR: TOWARD A TRANSFORMING SPIRITUALITY

In closing this reflection we wish to highlight a hidden but very powerful lesson in Christian spirituality that is being learned by a growing cadre of urban community economic-development practitioners of an evangelical persuasion.

Increasingly, community economic-development practitioners are experiencing a kind of "reverse mission," where they find themselves on an unexpected journey in which the Spirit of Christ jolts their understanding of God and causes them to move to deeper faith through a face-to-face encounter with the poor. As the case studies demonstrate, many of the urban poor are people of extraordinary faith, courage, hope, strength, resilience and imagination—people who trust that God can and will do the impossible through them. Getting to know these people has taught missionaries much about living by faith. As Fr. Ben Beltran says about the women leaders of Smokey Mountain, "They have more faith than I do, as far as asking God for things and seeing them happen."

This discovery has been no occasion for romanticizing the poor. The poor, like the rest of us, are prone to conflict, despondency and fear. But seasoned workers speak of a blessing-in-reverse that has resulted as they have been humbled by the example of urban poor families coping with suffering, primarily in the fight to survive in the harsh environment of the modern mega-city. At times urban poor families have endured greater hardship—and stored up greater hope—than the missionaries themselves have ever known. They have given pause to missionaries who talked glibly about the call to suffer with the poor, yet balked in the face of the life conditions of the poor during their terms of service. Having come to the urban poor to offer inspiration and courage, instead they came away the recipients.

This increasingly common and baffling experience among evangelical missionaries in economic development has had the effect of deepening and enriching their theology of mission. They have found God already present in the poor communities of the city when they arrive there. They have seen God at work in the lives of poor families through their raw struggles with life and death. And they have been blessed by God through the testimony of God's work in the lives of the poor, who, while dealing with traumatizing hardships, maintain a sense of humor and respond to life's emergencies with extraordinary courage and creativity. In a sense, the quiet witness of God's Spirit in the lives of many poor families in the city preceded and superseded the open witness of God's people. The budding awareness of God's mystical presence among the poor and of the power of God to teach the rest of us about the character of God through the poor is a long-standing aspect of Catholic social teaching.

It may seem a paradox that God chooses to use the unreached to reach the reached, but it is not the first time (reread the book of Habakkuk; see also Luke 4:25–27; 14:15–24). Who is really reached and who unreached? That shades of both categories are in missionary and missionized alike has caused evangelicals to focus more on appreciating and learning from other cultures than on looking only for what needs to be changed in them. Evangelicals who seek to apprehend the fullness of God's work in the city today should not be surprised, therefore, to find themselves moving from proclamation to conversation, from spiritual resource to recipient of grace, from messenger to the one who needs hope and healing. In that new, humble place they may find their most powerful and relevant role in urban mission.

## NOTES

[1] See Saskia Sassen, *The Global City* (Princeton, N.J.: Princeton University Press, 1991), pp. 333–35.

[2] See Roland Bunch, *Two Ears of Corn: A People Centered Guide to Agricultural Improvement* (Oklahoma City, Okla.: World Neighbors, 1982).

165

[3] See, for example, Woodstock Institute's *Best Practices for Cooperative Development: Defining, Communicating and Replicating Success.*

[4] S. Timmons, "NAFTA Refugees," in *The Big Issue,* April 1998, pp. 4–5.

[5] See Denis Goulet, "Beyond Moralism: Ethical Strategies in Global Development," in *Theology Confronts a Changing World,* ed. Thomas M. McFadden (West Mystic, Conn.: Twenty-Third Publications, 1977), p. 23.

# 11

# Ecumenicity, gender and ethics

## With a biblical vision

*Althea Spencer-Miller*

In common parlance *urban* is a term used with a loose reference to non-agrarian communities of residence, commerce and seats of governance located within clearly demarcated geographical parameters. It connotes centers of restless activity. Urban people live with multicentric social contacts, and community is defined by shared interests rather than the wholeness of shared lives. Sophistry, alienation, rootlessness, isolation and intense privacy are some of the characteristics of urban life. The urban is a place of many polarities. There are polarities of values, virtues, economies and class that create an urban potpourri. Infrastructural organization, sophisticated architecture, easily accessed utilities and the technological cutting edge are common expectations of the urban. This descriptive definition evokes images of Paris, New York, London, Los Angeles, Mexico City, but not necessarily of the urban mission sites described in most of the case studies in this book. But these case studies are from urban settings.

The case studies represent and are missions to the underside of city life. The urban missionary operates in locations where the stench of the city's failure rises unabated. There where the urban missionary works you find the lie of the city's promise. The relationship between this underside and the phenomenon outlined above may hinge on the recognition that the city also encapsulates conflictual cultures of expectations and moral orders and bodies of customs. All these are loosely defined and often only loosely related. They lack the nexus of the small town and the village.

The sustained and courageous efforts of women and men of faith and hope to conquer the urban wilderness contained in these case studies must be met by encouragement and respect. Two factors require that these efforts undergo constant assessment analysis and description. One is the fast-changing, multiple faces of urban reality, which require constant and basic adaptations. Thus the pace of effective ministry to the urban citizenry should not unduly slacken. Assessment, analysis and description, done in a timely manner, help to sustain the pace. The other factor consists of the very urgency and importance of this work, as well as the magnitude of the efforts and sacrifices of community-development practitioners. This second factor evokes the sense that the practitioners' product should at least approximate maximal effectiveness. Urban mission and ministry may be approached with the restiveness that hope and promise produce in the face of tendentious chaos, seething systemic injustices and the paradox that today's solution may be tomorrow's problem. The manner and the success of the case studies is highly commendable. The chipping away at social problems is a perpetual task. The process repeatedly encounters new situations that raise new questions. Analysis should answer questions of the efficacy and relevance of the urban mission in the local and national contexts. There are three broad categories that formed the matrix within which I read the case studies: ecumenicity, gender and ethics.

The series of books of which this is the last is symbolic of the Western world reaching out to the peoples of Asia, Africa and Latin America, and making a difference. As a Jamaican woman these places are strange to me. Therefore the issues that I attach to the categories would not necessarily emerge from these cultures. I believe that there is some relevance in the issues I raise, and that they will at least help to identify some critical points of consciousness-raising for the practitioners of urban mission. In other words, the urban mission is not only accountable to biblical, evangelical or ecclesiastical imperatives. It ought also to be regarded as responsive and accountable to macro-contextual issues that help to define the forward thrust of a people as citizens of a nation with a particular economic, political and cultural history.

The prophetic concept of justice provides a plumb line. This contrasts with and also complements the evangelical and missionary concepts that informed the thrust of the urban mission. The biblical concept of justice pushes beyond satisfaction with the goals of projects accomplished and effective personal evangelism. It is important to see the material difference that missionary intervention has made to the people's living standard and to their empowerment in confronting their afflictions and the powers-that-be and their hopes for future generations. The end of each project must be justice realized. What is this justice?

Justice is substantially related to terms of parity, equity and equality. Justice requires the recognition of imbalances in the distribution of power and dominance based on economic and social locations in relation to the prevailing status quo. Justice also calls for discernment of the relationship among acclaimed values, legal systems and the maintenance of the status quo, especially where these relationships have a negative impact upon those whose lives do not influence the definition of the status quo. Justice does not permit the status quo to remain without challenge. Justice, therefore, employs paradigms for evaluation that differ from those developed and affirmed by an exclusion-tending status quo.

Where justice is the paramount evaluative criterion, it is insufficient that communities are empowered for income generation or for sufficient numbers of persons affected by development projections. Justice pushes through to questions about the criteria that determine how wealth is distributed in a nation; about the systemic forces that perpetuate and cultivate cultures of poverty; about the ethics of economics that govern the emergence of a community from abject poverty to marginal sustainable income-generating activity. The critical and analytical consciousness of a community ought to be engaged in reflection upon their condition and environment. This critical engagement is what liberation theologians name *praxis*. A theology of conversion can lead to an understanding that praxis is also the will of God in Christ Jesus concerning us.

## ECUMENICITY

Ecumenicity is the spirit of ecumenism. *Ecumenism* may be regarded as a succinct term for that sense of stewardship for the entire inhabited order. Ecumenism invites a holistic sensitivity to the interrelatedness of all life. Within the Christian religion it represents a sense of and

169

commitment to that total interrelatedness which compels an acknowledgment of a fundamental Christian unity. The foundation of this unity
is Christ Jesus himself. In the priestly prayer in the Gospel According
to John, Jesus prays for the oneness of his followers (John 17:20). The
reason given for the importance, indeed the necessity, of that oneness
is that the world may believe (John 17:21). Ecumenicity, which involves
mutual acknowledgment, cooperation, common caring and working,
is requisite for the optimal success of Christian witness. There are two
ultimate goals for urban mission. One is that the effective mission might
contribute to the manifestation of the characteristics of the kingdom of
God, for example, justice and peace, as a consequence of the saving
love of God in Christ Jesus. The other is that the mission might result
in the conversion to Christianity or of a renewed commitment to this
faith on the part of those persons who experience the urban mission as
a testimony to the saving love of God in Christ Jesus.

Most of the case studies are located in third-world countries. In one
form or another third-world countries have experienced various kinds
of colonialism. Christianity has played a significant role in that colonialism. In any one of these countries a colonial history can be taken as
a sign of a fractional present. During the period of European colonization up to the present, different Christian denominations arrived and
established themselves within these countries. In too many instances
the presence of a multiplicity of Christian denominations was characterized by fractious relationships.

That Christian social witness can result in church and congregational
growth through individual conversion is very encouraging. It dispels
the fallacies that social action and word evangelism are incompatible
and that social action is a self-sufficient form of evangelism. Fractious
relationships among Christian denominations result in a fractious witness. In the Third World such an observation raises questions about
the obvious correctness and requisite nature of church or congregation planting. That urban mission leads to church planting is indeed
welcome news and ought not to be automatically discouraged. A fractious witness is, however, a mitigating factor against an unevaluated
planting of churches and congregations. Put positively, the undesir-
ability of a fractious witness is a strong argument for working through
and with Christian groups that are already present in a mission lo-
cale.

The history of the church is a story of doctrinal and ecclesial schisms and the establishment of competing expressions of Christian faith and dogma. The residue of these divisions includes a legacy of distrust and alienation among broad categories of Christian groupings. The three most inclusive categories of demarcation are the Roman Catholic Church, the Orthodox churches and the Protestant churches. The Protestant churches are the most schismatic in tendency, and Protestantism has experienced within itself, broadly defined, the emergence of the Evangelicals, the Pentecostals and the Neo-Pentecostals (Charismatics). In many instances the issues that led to these divisions, though hairsplitting, inspired deep convictions that are sternly held. The issues themselves became identity markers within the various categories. It is, therefore, neither natural nor easy for churches or Christian groups to work together across the divisions. This is the challenge that also faces the urban mission. If the urban environment manifests a centrifugal tendency, and a tendency to fragment, it is clearly very important that the Christian witness countermands those tendencies. To this end the Hollywood-Wilshire Cluster encourages a model of ecumenical cooperation that contains many aspects. It is ecumenical cooperation across social, ethnic and cultural groupings, across congregations and across mission agencies. Where the will exists, it can be a stimulant for ecumenical cooperation among different denominations. Its reported success and the nuance in the criterion for success bespeak the value of ecumenicity.

The persons and nations that are beneficiaries of missionary benevolence stand in a bipolar relation to that benevolence. On the one hand, there is awareness of the tremendously constructive impact of the missionary enterprise. For this there is much gratitude. Yet there are negative and schizoid effects from the meeting of cultures in the Christian arena and an impact upon the receiving cultures that is partly deleterious. The history of Christianity as a tool of European inculturation from the fifteenth to the nineteenth centuries and in the twentieth century of North American-generated missionary activity raises concerns about the negative effects of a fractious witness. These concerns may not be expressed by communities that are receiving the urban mission. However, it might be useful for urban-missions practitioners and developers to be aware of these concerns, which affect upon the overall picture of community building and nation building.

## GENDER

Gender in a broad sense refers to the social roles of men and women that have been defined along the lines of maleness and femaleness. It means not only that women and men are delegated certain tasks, but also that some tasks are in and of themselves regarded as being either male or female with concomitant values attached to them. For example, nurturing roles are gendered female; roles requiring the exercise of physical strength and exertion are gendered male. In the economic arena female gendered tasks tend to receive a lower scale of remuneration. So, nurses who are nurturers and caregivers receive a lower salary than doctors who perform the manly decision-making and strategizing tasks. Accompanying these roles are conservationist or preservationist tendencies that enforce predetermined and discriminatory roles for both men and women. The diversities of gifts that men and women experience within their respective gender groupings are not recognized by role enforcers.

The pattern in development work is to direct women to female-gendered work. Many of the case studies reflect women's stories. This, I believe, reveals a consciousness that there is something correct and necessary about focusing on women in the field. It is a truism that female-gendered work tends to attract the lowest wages. Must our development projects always offer the tasks that are either oriented toward women or gendered female to women? Does this not keep women in a specifically ordered status, where marginalization now simply comes with a remuneration package but is still heinous? It is important that the practitioner and the developer of urban-mission concepts go beyond guidance for income-generating and other kinds of activities for women.

The justice imperative points to an adjudicating of the hierarchies of gender and economic power. Some leading questions may be: Are the women's projects restricting women to all their traditional roles, which usually attract low incomes? Would the women welcome an alternative? Is there a need to advocate for an improvement in the financial returns for female-gendered work? What are the systemic conditions that perpetuate and cultivate the conditions for the ongoing marginalization and impoverishment of women? What happens to the relational roles of men and women when women claim empowerment? How can male-gendered development keep apace with women's?

Errol Miller, a Jamaican educator, in his latest book on gender issues, *Men at Risk*, makes a persuasive case for the rescue of men. He
observes that women now outnumber men as students in tertiary levels. He argues that patriarchy marginalizes certain men as well as
women. He is concerned that men will soon disappear from the corridors of leadership in the Caribbean. The underdeveloped male must
become a burden to the developed female. This complete reversal of
the present situation is also untenable.

Concurrently the powers that hold patriarchy in place have a strong-
hold on the glass ceiling that prevents women from rising above it in
large numbers. Patriarchal systems will not permit the advance of either women or men to become a threat to its entrenched beneficiaries
and leaders. It is not apparent from his book that Miller intends to
establish an additional basis for competition between men and women
for scarce resources and space. But his position is too often in terms of
quotas and allocations. He argues at the end for andrarchy. Such is his
alternate vision.

But that is not the point. The point is that women and men might
need to struggle together in a world that is dominated by a common
enemy, the protected males. If this does not happen, the women might
find themselves even more vulnerable to the wrath of those protected
males. Men also need alternatives to drunkenness, unemployment, issues of low self-esteem, alternatives that lead to a new understanding
of themselves as men and the constitution of manhood. If not, the developed woman is doomed to be forever the servant of men, no matter
how well she does for herself as a woman. This should not detract
from the need to do women's work and to ensure the economic viability of women and the vitality of their self-esteem. It does point out the
need that ways be found to bring more men in as beneficiaries of development work. This way the development of women will not become another chain in their subordination and subservience to men. A
new consciousness is needed about the urgency of working with men
in development work. This consciousness must be attended by the conviction that women's work must continue unabated.

## ETHICS

The urban mission within the politico-economic matrix of
postcolonial and neocolonial history can experience some of the moral

tensions that polar realities create in those settings. Hence, there is admiration for the Ubunye Church and Community Ministries. The Ubunye Church and Community Ministries raises some ethical and doctrinal issues. One doctrinal issue is the permissibility of divorce. Should a church-related ministry encourage divorce? Ubunye offers a radical response to this question. It presents divorce as a sign of victory in a situation of abuse. Should the response to this be condemnation or some form of tolerance? This doctrinal issue segues into an ethical issue. From a biblical perspective the church is not comfortable with divorce, this ubiquitous reality of contemporary experience. Church responses range from total condemnation and intolerance of divorce to conditional acceptance of it as a necessary evil. The question of rightness in this situation then becomes both appropriately moot and undue.

Divorce as an ethical issue is moot in Ubunye because we start with the presupposition that the Bible either does not uphold divorce or, at least, it restricts the grounds for divorce. Yet when confronted with a situation of tremendous cruelty in which the *imago Dei* is destroyed in a woman and her children, the need for an escape is paramount. A permanent avenue of escape is a severing of the bonds of love, co-responsibility, and legal and spiritual ties through divorce. Very few rationalizations by the churches that abhor divorce seem to work in this situation. For example, it cannot be suggested that the woman in the example was not truly married. She was truly married. Now she is truly divorced. So the issue becomes moot. On the other hand, to discuss the rightness of divorce in this situation is undue because a true appreciation of the horror of the woman's situation leaves no alternative.

I believe that the context of the situation of the urban poor in its stark harshness reduces many clear ethical issues into paradox. It reveals that many ethical certitudes are sure only in situations where certain dynamics obtain. It seems that where those standards never existed or are eroded, ethical choices are no longer obvious because the situation requires choices between evil and the lesser evil. Such situations transform lesser evils into requisite cures. In such a situation the presumed evil is indeed the herald of the kingdom of God. Should such observations not affect our approach to moral and ethical proclamations?

## A Biblical Vision: Revelation 7:9

Revelation 7:9 reads:

> After this I looked, and there was a great multitude that no one could count, from every nation, from all tribes and peoples and languages, standing before the throne and before the Lamb, robed in white, with palm branches in their hands.

The throne is the great gathering place of the people of God. It is clear that the constituents of verse 9 are the subjects of the discussion in verses 13–17 in the same chapter. These verses identify them as the ones who have come through great suffering. They are cleansed by the blood of the Lamb and so are legitimately before the throne of God. This section of the vision concerns the rewards of faithfulness and perseverance. The book of Revelation, written at a time of persecution for Christians, provides Christians with a reason to endure to the end. After the trial comes the glory.

It is not altogether certain that the constituents of verse 9 are the ones who are to have the seal of God on their foreheads. The relationship between the 144,000 and the multitude is not clarified. Does the one displace the other? Do they stand as two separate groupings before the throne? Are the 144,000 even included in the universal multitude from every nation? Is there a group that receives a seal but does not stand before the throne? Was the multitude not sealed? Or was the great ordeal their seal? Is there a way to settle these relational issues? I offer the following.

As a reader of this passage, verse 9 always comes as a moment of relief. Verses 4–8 are excluding verses. They also establish a picture of perfection by the depiction of the perfect number, 144,000. Those who receive the seal are enveloped in a matrix of perfection. Every one of them is a Jew. The 144,000 constitute an elite and pure group. If they are the same group as the 144, 000 of Revelation 14, then their purity is further defined. They are the ones who have not defiled themselves with women. As a Gentile woman, I feel doubly excluded by this passage. I am not a Jew, and if the logic of Revelation 14:4–5 is followed, then as a woman I am necessarily unclean. On two grounds I cannot participate in this elite group. What then can be the fate of those who share a similar sense of exclusion when reading Revelation 7:4–8?

Revelation 7:9 and 14:6 use the demarcations that separate the peoples of the world. Not only do these demarcations separate into nations, in our contemporary understanding, they also identify the worthy and the unworthy, the valued and the non-valued. These are the demarcations that have supported the excluding tendencies of humankind. In verse 9 there is a governing every and a governing all. These are including terms. As a Gentile, I receive a new vision of possibility for myself. As a woman, I am free to believe that there may be a space for me. The vision of verse 9 bears a universal outlook. There is no nation, no tribe, no peoples, no language that will be excluded from that throne by dint of what they are. In the twinkling of an eye, the exclusiveness of verses 5–8 is transformed into a picture of universal inclusiveness, a picture of ecumenical congregation, a depiction of common humankind emerging in shared triumph. In Revelation 14:6, every nation and tribe and language and people receives a chance. In Revelation 21, the new heaven and the new earth see the nations walking by their light, and the people will bring into it the glory and the honor of the nations.

It is a vision of a just world, of a world at peace. It is a world in which the weapons of faithfulness and the will to endure challenge the status quo and conquer. In the end there is not a 144,000, but all are present in this perfect place. Their presence contributes to its glory and its perfection. One could say that Revelation 7:9 overthrows Revelation 7:5–8 to become the verse that endures to the end. This, I believe, is the objective of the urban mission: that those who were excluded become included, that God's kingdom will come on earth and the earth never be the same again. This verse provides a vision of the way the world can be when God's kingdom is present. It is a place of justice and peace.

The issues raised in this chapter provide a prism for the analysis of the work of the urban mission. They are a nudge toward addressing the macro-contextual issues of economy, politics and history that form the matrix of the urban mission. It may not be just to burden further an already-burdened worker or thinker. However, the urban mission continues to be relevant because the just city does not yet exist.

# 12

# Toward a theology of holistic ministry

*Benigno Beltran*

Thought precedes action. Every form of ministry reflects an underlying theology. A dualistic mentality cannot come to terms with a holistic ministry. Fragmented thinking will not elicit an integral service for the coming of the kingdom of God.

Various dichotomies in the symbolic universe of the Western mind have influenced theology in the West. Belief in the fundamental opposition of the immaterial human soul and the material physical body, for instance, has in the past resulted in forms of ministry that ignored issues of justice such as the marginalization of the poor, racism, gender discrimination and environmental degradation. This dualistic understanding equates ministry with saving souls, and sin with unbelief alone; it looks down on ministries seeking to answer earthly needs. Justice—a fundamental issue in our relation with God (Mic. 6:8)—is not viewed as constitutive of the proclamation of the kingdom of God, the kingdom of peace, justice and the integrity of creation.

## THE HOLISTIC WORLDVIEW OF ANCIENT FILIPINOS

Let us reflect on the biblical way of thinking and compare this with the Filipino worldview. The ancient Filipinos had a holistic understanding of reality. They organized life around a highly refined awareness of oneness with the cosmos. They looked at the universe in terms of interconnectedness, interrelatedness and interdependence. More weight was given to intuitive wisdom, synthetic thinking and ecological awareness. They did not have any word for "religion" because there was no need to bind the sacred and the profane together. They straddled a dream-crossed twilight between birth and dying, between the transcendent and the immanent.

This type of worldview can still be seen today in those tribes who went higher up the mountains or deeper into the forests to escape colonization by foreign powers. These tribes still maintain the principle of maximum human well-being in community with an optimal pattern of consumption. They still do not have a concept of private ownership. Two things stand out in their collective symbolic universe: first, the interconnectedness and interdependence of everything in the world (every aspect of the universe being a well-defined part of a dynamically patterned whole, an interconnected web of dynamic relations); and second, the intrinsically dynamic and relational nature of the human being.

The core of being human was defined not by what a living body is in itself, but by its relationship to others—"to be" is "to be in relation." Among pre-Spanish Filipinos the system of alliances for mutual support was of paramount significance in society. *Pakikisama* (smooth interpersonal relationships) and *bayanihan* (communal effort) have been important features in Filipino society, which is communal, person-oriented and interactive. There is no division between the spiritual and immaterial dimensions in the human being.

In these tribal societies, with their pre-reflective bond with nature, kinship-ordered cosmologies define the identity of the individual. Modernity introduces progressive differentiation of the individual from nature and from society. This jump from mystic consciousness to modernity, which started with the colonization of the archipelago by Europeans in 1521, has had profound implications for the way Filipinos today construct their identities and the way they relate to the Supreme Being and to the world.

With the coming of the Spaniards, the natives were organized by the sword and the cross from tribal societies, with their pre-reflective bond with nature and their kinship-ordered cosmologies, into a society with economic, political and cultural structures based on the European model. The coming of Westerners marked the coming of modernism, exalting reason and emphasizing a more critical commitment to human experience as a guide for human knowledge. This new stress on reason and experience brought with it a heightened consciousness of human beings as autonomous individuals, not simply subject to the past and to traditions of the community. Tribal ways of life were colonized by the world empire. The human being became separated from the cosmos and from others.

## DUALISTIC TENDENCIES IN THE FILIPINO COLONIAL HERITAGE

The symbolic universe of the Greeks, with its sharp distinction between unchanging, necessary being and changing appearances of the things of earth, gave rise to an understanding of the world that envisaged a deep split in the cosmos between two independent and mutually irreducible substances, a dichotomy between the intelligible realm of heavenly realities and the sensible realm of earthly phenomena. A radical dualism positing the existence of two fundamental causal principles underlying the existence of the world was built into the very fabric of Greek philosophy and culture.

Greek thought started with the mythologies of the Orphic cults and the works of Hesiod and Homer, then became systematized in the philosophies of Plato and Aristotle, ending with the Epicureans, Stoics and Neo-Platonists during the time of the early church. The Orphic system dealt with the origin of the gods and the world from a primeval chaos and darkness. Its theology and cosmology presented a special view of the nature and destiny of the human being. The soul, the divine or Dionysiac element, was sharply distinguished from the Titanic element, the body, which was the prison or the tomb of the soul. The human being's task in life was to nurture the divine element and keep the body pure till the soul was finally set free. Once the soul was set free as a reward for faithful observance, it attained everlasting happiness.

Alfred North Whitehead said that all of Western philosophy is footnotes to Plato, who understood matter to be eternal and conceived God to be a demiurge. The human being is a spirit tied down in the cave of the world of sense experience, from which he or she has to be liberated and led up to the world of Ideas or permanent values. In a person's experience with material things he or she encounters only shadows of reality, for the real is the Ideal. Plato taught that the soul existed before one is born into the world. The body is the prison of the soul, and matter is considered evil. To find the true self, a person has to be guided by eternal values of the spirit so he or she may return to the pure contemplation of Ideas.

179

This dualism heavily influenced Western thinking in general, with Plato's division between the sensible World of the senses and intelligible World of Ideas sowing the seeds for Descartes' dichotomy between the *res cogitans* and *res extensa*, between thinking and extended substances, Leibnitz's separation of actual and possible worlds, and Kant's severing the *noumena* from the *phenomena*. Hegel, Nietzsche, Marx and Freud are descendants of this kind of thinking, resulting in a dichotomy that opens up between an inert God, who cannot be known in himself, and the world of phenomena, conceived as a closed continuum of cause and effect.

In the endeavor to inculturate Christian faith into the prevailing culture, the early church was influenced by this dualism, an influence that continues to this day. The anti-cosmic and anti-somatic teachings of the Greek mystery religions found their way into Gnosticism and Arianism, docetism and adoptionism, to be embraced by the Bogomils, the Catharii and the Albigensians. These hybrid forms of religion understood God as eternally and immutably detached, a God who does not really interact with the world. This dualistic outlook conceived of an absolute chasm separating an immutable, impassible Deity from contingent, temporal existence.

These religious movements were also pervaded by belief in the fundamental opposition of the immaterial human soul and the material physical body. Their beliefs were grounded in an understanding of the human being as an ahistorical and individualistic monad in a static universe. Their religious writings and teachings were filled with hatred of matter. Christ was an angelic spirit whose body only had a corporeal appearance. He did not really die or rise again because he did not have a real body. The Bogomils, for example, taught that Satan, the rebellious creature of God, created the human body. The Albigensians in the twelfth century taught that the human soul, created good, had rebelled against God and was expelled from heaven. The devil at once imprisoned it in matter. Salvation for the soul consists in the liberation of the soul from matter and return to the heavenly state. This salvation is attainable only by ceaseless struggle against material allurements.

The Christianity brought into the Philippines by the Spaniards was heavily influenced by this dualistic way of thinking in its theology and piety.

### OLD TESTAMENT UNDERSTANDING

In contrast to dualistic ways of thinking, the Old Testament sees the human being holistically within a historico-eschatological horizon. Its view is synthetic, for there is no strict division between the "parts" of the human being and there exists no clear dichotomy of his or her functions. The human being is primarily considered a unity of vital powers by which he or she stands continually in relation to God and the world. This is made clear by the fact that whenever a statement is made about particular aspects of the human being, very often the statement could also be predicated of the whole being. In Hebrew thought the immaterial functions of the human being are not separated from the material functions, and the human being is not separated from the world and from others.

It might be helpful at this point to analyze the more important Hebrew anthropological terms.

*Nephesh*—This word appears 755 times in the Old Testament, and in 600 cases it is rendered by the Greek Septuagint as "psyche." The fact that it is translated into the Greek equivalent of "soul" in every case shows the difference between the Hellenic and Hebrew understanding. The Yahwist account of creation uses the term in Genesis 2:7, "Then the LORD God formed man from the dust of the ground, and breathed into his nostrils the breath of life; and the man became a *nephesh* [living individual]." The term also stands for life, or it could mean desire and yearning. It is interesting to note that when the Israelites speak of the displeasure of Yahweh (21 times in the Old Testament), *nephesh* is used. Proverbs 6:16 says, "There are six things that the *nephesh* of the LORD hates." In general, therefore, *nephesh* signifies life in connection with the individual. The human being does not *have* a *nephesh*; he or she *is* a *nephesh*.

*Basar*—This word is used 273 times in the Old Testament, and in 104 cases refers to the heart. Its primary meaning is "flesh" as opposed to bones. It could also mean the whole person, signifying creatureliness. It is used mostly in the sense of body as in Psalm 102:5, "My bones cling to my *basar*." It also connotes kinship, as in Genesis 37:27, "He is our brother, our own *basar*." The Hebrew sees the human being in his or her bodiliness as "flesh with others." Hence, *basar* signifies the human being in his or her weakness, as in Psalm 56:4, " . . . in God I trust; I am not afraid; what can *basar* do to me?" *Pol basar* is a circumlocution for the whole of humankind in its creaturely dependence on God. The priestly tradition sees in *basar* the moral corruption of all humanity. Thus, for Hebrew thought, *basar* expresses the intersocial, the political existence of the human being in opposition to every individualistic view.

*Ruah*—Although its meaning coincides with *nephesh* at times, *ruah* differs from *basar* and *nephesh* because it is considered an extension of a force of nature, namely, the wind (referred to in this manner 113 times out of 389). *Ruah* refers to God 3 percent of the time; *basar*, never. In Genesis 1:2 the *ruah elohim* was moving over the waters. Aside from the spirit, *ruah* could also mean "breath," as in Psalm 146:4, "When their *ruah* departs, they return to the earth." *Ruah* also means the force of life, as in Psalm 33:6, "By the word of the LORD the heavens were made, and all their host by the *ruah* of his mouth." Sometimes *ruah* is used to signify a driving charism that enables a person to do extraordinary deeds for God in the history of salvation. It could also mean force of the will.

Linguistically, the fundamental theme is the human being's wholeness as a person. A human being is a living, personal whole. No dualistic divisions exist. *Nephesh* is the human being striving for something. *Basar* is the human being facing God in the community. *Ruah* is the human being living under the divine promises. The basic presupposition of the Old Testament is a person's relationship with God as covenant partner and member of the community. The human being is constantly summoned to decision and response. Concern is not so much for the human being in himself or herself, but the person as a creature, a being before God, in all his or her weakness and mortality.

The Old Testament is conscious of humanity's sinfulness and aware of the ground of hope for future participation in God's kingdom. Death was seen as separation from vital community with Yahweh and entrance into the reign of darkness and impurity. Sin was understood to be the activity of the whole person, rooted in the heart of the human being, in what is most intimate in the person. Salvation was communitarian, understood as participation in the future lordship of Yahweh over the whole earth.

## New Testament Understanding

Writers of the first three Gospels follow the Old Testament understanding of the human being but view the anthropological problem concomitant with the question of redemption in Jesus Christ. Although the dualistic anthropology of Greek philosophy already exerted an influence on Late Judaic literature, the Synoptics do not diverge from the Old Testament understanding. Even if writing in Greek, "psyche" for these authors still meant the whole human being. They also differ from the Greeks in that they do not think of the body as hindrance to the soul or as the cause of sin. They do not consider human perfection as closed or static. The human being's future-oriented history overrides all considerations of a person as a microcosmos perfect in himself or herself. For the Synoptics, persons are open to the future, to God, and to the world precisely in their bodily life. The claim of God summoning people to a decision for authentic existence reaches each person in and through the concrete demand represented by the continuous presence of his or her neighbors in the world.

Like the other New Testament writers, Paul sees humanity in the perspective of the death and resurrection of Christ. In the light of the gospel of grace, a person is convicted as standing over against God, refusing to acknowledge God. The human being is one whose real vocation of service to God is opposed to the human's actual slavery to principalities and powers. Three terms are particularly prominent in Paul's understanding of human beings. For Paul, there exists an opposition between *sarx* or "psyche" (1 Cor. 2:13, 15:44 ff.) on one side and *pneuma* on the other. *Sarx* means the earthly, limited temporary sphere, humanity in its perishableness. There is no suggestion of sinfulness, only of human limitation and weakness. It means the whole human who faces the Holy One.

*Pneuma* is a mode of existence opposed to *sarx*. It means the whole person as affected and permeated by the power of the spirit of God. It should be noted, however, that even if Paul contrasts *sarx* with *pneuma*, he is talking about a basic contradiction within humanity, similar to the distinction between matter and spirit. What Paul wants to express is the contradiction between the weakness of the human being and the power of God's spirit. Thus, for Paul, the contradiction is *not* between psyche and the individual's corporal being (*soma*, the third term Paul uses), but *sarx* and psyche on the one hand and *pneuma* on the other.

Paul's use of *soma* is unique. It designates the organized totality of the person insofar as he or she is in communication with others. Thus the idea leans more toward corporality and not to the meaning of *body* in classical Greek anthropology as that which receives its limitations and its individuality through the form that is the immaterial principle. For Paul, the human being as body is oriented toward others, united with the world, under the Creator's sovereignty, hoping for resurrection through the possibility of obedience and giving of the self.

The meaning Paul gives to *soma* shows that he views a person's bodily nature positively even in the opposition of *sarx* to *pneuma*. There is no dualism at all that devaluates the body. Nor does Paul attribute a higher value to the soul. He does not consider the flesh as source of sin, although when he is considering the person as alienated from himself or herself and in opposition to God, Paul calls that person a sinner. Flesh will rise imperishable even if sowed in perishableness (1 Cor. 15:42). In their corporeity, human beings are open for the eschatological future made possible by Christ, but if they rely solely on their own strength, they will fall into sin.

### A New Paradigm for Ministry

Influenced by Greek thinking, modernism's paramount figure is that of the static and abstract model separated from the dynamic ebb and flow of reality like the Cartesian ego. This conception of being human fostered the individualism in modernism. Modernization detaches individual selves from their immersion in networks of kinship and locality (*Gemeinschaft*), fostering greater differentation between the individual and society (*Gesellschaft*). The universe is still generally viewed as a machine with elementary building blocks (atoms) based on the Cartesian belief that all aspects of the world can be understood by reducing them to constituent parts. Life in society is thought to be ruled by the principle of survival of the fittest, and unlimited progress alleged to be possible by means of technological and economic growth.

Various scholars have already distinguished pre-modern from modern society in terms of the shift from *Gemeinschaft* or communal to *Gesellschaft* or associative structures. In the urbanization and globalization process, the tension in this shift happens not only endogenously but also across contemporary societies. This double tension affects the way individuals identify themselves and how societies respond to the process of individuation among members and to intersocietal change.

This is the situation that inhabitants of urban centers find themselves in.

In Roland Robertson's theory of globalization, modern society has two poles of identity: the realm of societal-systemic functionality, and the realm of individual and relational being. Globalization repeats the tension between *Gemeinschaft* and *Gesellschaft* across contemporary societies and not just within them. In a globalized context both societies and individuated selves are revitalized. Both individuals and nation-states act in the context of relativizing world societies whose unity or identity express themselves in the encompassing notion of humanity.

Beyond a person's own bipolar individual-society nexus, there are now different possibilities for life in society, leading to the relativized construction of personal identities, which in turn further intensify the relativized constitution of national identities. The *Gemeinschaft-Gesellschaft* tension has been globalized—first with respect to images as to how societies should be patterned, and second, with respect to how the world as a whole should be structured. Thus more alienation and fragmentation of identities occur.

In a globally interconnected world, bringing in its wake transformations of unprecedented proportions, a new paradigm is needed—a coherent conceptual framework, a new vision of reality, a fundamental change in our thoughts, perceptions and values. The mounting social and environmental costs of economic development should make us aware that ethical choices are at the heart of economics. Economic theorists can no longer evade the ethical question of equal distribution of the earth's goods. Science can no longer look at the world only in the light of the Newtonian worldview; they must use the analogies of quantum physics. Ministers and pastors can no longer solve problems using the Ptolemaic and Newtonian symbolic universes.

In order not to fall prey to naive cosmopolitanism or narrow ethnocentrism, the proclamation of the gospel in the Philippines must be based on universal values shared by the rest of the inhabitants of Spaceship Earth. *Nasa daigdig ang utak, sa Pilipinas nakatapak* (While the mind is on the globe, the feet are firmly planted in the Philippines). This is what becomes clear from the voyage out of our colonial history and into the future at the compression of time and space in a globalized world. One must steer between the impersonal rationality of high modernism and the irrationalist anti-ethics of postmodernism, while leaving behind all dualistic ways of thinking in finding ways to engage in holistic ministry.

Contemporary Filipino thinkers are concentrating their reflections on the human being as an *etre incarnee*. Leonardo Mercado has attempted to follow this line of thought from many angles and perspectives. Dionisio Miranda has done pioneering studies on the *loob* (the inner self), and Jaime Belita has done studies on *diwa* and *logos* and has attempted to ground Filipino root paradigms in the mythos of a Greater Self. Alberto Alejo has followed the same line of thinking. Virgilio Enriquez has proposed the idea of *kapwa* as the core concept of Filipino social psychology; he takes it to mean a recognition of shared identity, for it encompasses the self and others. *Pakikipagkapwa* embraces both *paninindigan* as convictions, commitments and value, the regard for the being and dignity of others. The dynamism of identity lies in relating with others: *Kung mahirap maging tao, lalong mahirap ang makipagkapwa-tao* (If it is difficult to be a human being, it is more difficult to become a human being with other human beings).

Today the multiplication of identity tasks leads to anxiety and the experience of alienation in the modern individual, burdened with unfinished self-description. The human being will always be a question to itself: Where did I come from? Where am I going? Where do I belong? What can I trust? To answer these questions in a global system (where everything has changed except our way of thinking, according to Einstein), Filipinos have to burrow deep into the wisdom of the ancestors to discover the innate dynamism of the human self in its unfolding relationality, its rootedness in the universe, and the dependence of the sense of human meaning and value on the ultimate mystery. Filipino identity, for example, is necessarily a fruit of what has gone before. And from within themselves, and from the culture that embodies their meanings and values, new energies and new directions must emerge.

We are each a self in the process of becoming, an identity achieved in going beyond itself in relation to the all, the whole, the other, the ultimate. To be a human being is to be immersed in a universal process of becoming and communion. If we are to forge a holistic ministry and anticipate the *shalom* of the kingdom of God amid the threats and challenges of modernity and globalization, our consciousness has to become cosmic and integral, similar to the consciousness of the Scriptures and the ancient Filipinos. The story of the cosmos and the story of humankind is a single story. Every atom in our bodies was once inside a star. We ignore the summons into a universe of meaning, value and ultimate grace at the peril of denying our true identity if we engage in ministry with a fragmented understanding of the truth.

# Part three

# Conclusion

# 13

# Where cross the crowded streams of life

## Toward a new ecology of urban mission

*Kenneth L. Luscombe*

This chapter represents a synthesis and interpretation of the work of the consultation. Common themes and issues are woven into a treatment of holistic urban mission that seeks to capture the synergy of the dialogue. The author's assumption is that the notion of holistic mission undergoes a significant expansion in content and practical application when it is subjected to the systemic complexity of the city and the rich diversity of urban experience as narrated in the case studies. Drawing on the recent treatment of holism in "new paradigm" thinking, the author argues that a new ecology of urban mission is needed for cities in the twenty-first century.

### CONTROLLING TRAFFIC, CONTROLLING MISSION

The taxicab comes to a standstill. The long crawl begins. Ahead in the distance is the culprit, a congested intersection with four streams of traffic converging on one contested space. Jeepneys jostle for advantage. But the contest, like the progress achieved, is merely symbolic. There is no easy way to circumvent this dilemma. The logic of diametrically opposing straight lines rules, setting up yet one more contradiction in the chaos that is life in a growing, bustling third-world city. I am on my way to an international consultation on holistic urban mission, and my head is full of details. Despite the effects of a long night flight across the Pacific, I am exhilarated to be back in Manila. Glad I'm not a taxi-driver though!

Eventually we nose up to the intersection. That's when I first see him, occupying ground zero, confronted on every hand by converging, competing traffic, grime covered and grim-eyed with concentration, gesticulating profusely and sweating even more so, a solitary uniformed traffic officer.

What a job! The officer is a study in managing fragments. Charged with traffic control at a critical junction, he is reduced to regulating an absurdity, having the power to affect the progress of each, but without the power to solve the problem for all. Yet he is wholly immersed in the task. Only from the perspective of one passing through (with time on his hands) does this center-stage drama seem absurd, a mismatch of time and space, motion and meaning, parts and wholes. The officer has probably been working for hours straight without once seeing a traffic break in any direction. Each time he lets one stream through it immediately fills up at the tail end. With no possible way to be both fair and sort out the problem, the officer is reduced to adjudicating this spatial conundrum in increments of time until his shift is over.

The traffic officer reminds me of many leaders I know: dedicated people who are busy trying to manage the outcomes of complex systems beyond their grasp or control. Fully engaged in the part they have to play, they often mistake the part for the whole. As life becomes more and more complex, and as the turbulence of change rattles the whole system, they appear harried, dissociated and hemmed in. Learning is suspended and work becomes routinized. Being powerless to change the dynamics of the whole, they intensify their efforts in managing the immediate, working their piece of turf—their intersection—with ever greater intensity until their physical, mental, emotional and spiritual energy ebbs. Counseled to "thrive on chaos," they prefer to succumb to panic and entrench to survive the chaos.

We pass through the intersection and are on our way. The scene recedes but the image lingers. I am left wondering about where we are at today in urban mission, and if our many frenetic mission activities in the city appear similar—fragments of highly controlled space in a sea of flux and creative chaos. I wonder, too, if the intense particularity of much mission work does not promote a leadership that is incredibly focused but also limited, and more than likely to micromanage into virtual extinction the wild, exotic, unpredictable and unmanageable offerings of a fertile urban environment—all for fear of losing control. The need to control and dominate is so ingrained in the way of leadership under the (patriarchal) tutelage of the old and passing paradigm of technical rationality, industrial modernization and enlightened scientific progress that losing control is tantamount to madness.

But "losing" control, I would suggest, is a challenging but necessary paradox for mission leaders. Anyone who has experienced the bitter disappointment of being led down a predetermined road of mission ideology—where the line is drawn, straight and unyielding—will be wary of any attempt to constrain urban mission into a static and rationalistic formula. Likewise, anyone who has experienced the disillusionment of falling among "single issue" advocates only to be abandoned—beaten, bruised and bereft—along the way will be very wary of any attempt to reduce the dynamism and diversity of urban mission to a singular form. Particularity, singularity and control—these elements dominate the image of life at the intersection and are the very antithesis of a holistic urban mission.

## DEFINING "HOLISTIC URBAN MISSION"

But what do we mean by *holistic urban mission*? Recognized leaders in urban mission from around the world have been gathered to present and reflect critically on a variety of case studies of best practices in the field. Case studies have been chosen for their variety of approaches, their transparent success in achieving the outcomes sought and their explicitly holistic intent. Around the table is arrayed a formidable quality of leadership experience, representing a number of levels of complexity and a wide range of technical capacities in urban mission.

We are not the first such group to attempt a description of holistic mission; this is the fourth consultation dedicated to this theme. However, we are the first in the series to deal directly with urban mission. Each of the previous consultations employed the concept of holism as a heuristic device to explore ways in which evangelism and action for social justice are related yet discrete mission activities. It would seem that mission is considered "holistic" when it integrates evangelism and social action. But is this all, and is it enough?

Before proceeding any further, it is appropriate to note that the quest for a mission understanding that integrates evangelism and social action is timely. There is no question that the ideological rift at the evangelical end of modern Christianity, in which advocates for the primacy of evangelism or social action as the purest focus of mission vie vigorously for ascendancy, is a scandal. This rift presents a serious practical dilemma for those working diligently at the community level for the full and transformational development of the poor in their personal and communal struggles. Emphasizing the holistic nature of mission is a much-needed attempt to address this needless and fruitless dichotomy. But the question remains: Is this understanding of *holistic* enough?

When mission is composed in the vernacular of the urban it emerges as a narrative with a character of holism that includes but transcends the evangelism and/or social-action debate. Viewing contemporary urban reality in dynamic, comprehensive and relational terms—as distinct from the mechanistic rationality that drove the modern industrial urban era—provides new metaphors for the task of modeling in mission. These new metaphors help us to imagine and appreciate the intricate web-like nature of the connections between all things and to move beyond the limiting logic of simple binaries held in tension.

As commonplace as it may sound today, what we are dealing with here is no less than a paradigm shift in the thinking that lies behind the way we understand both the world and the role of mission within it. Urbanism—the way of life that is dominated by urban values—is all-pervasive, driven by dynamic local and global forces working simultaneously over time. Mission—a way of life dominated by the Christian vision—stakes out no less than all of reality and the (salvation) history of all reality as its domain. As the mission vision intersects with the urban world a bold holographic image of a transformed reality emerges. All the data that is needed to reproduce the whole image is already enfolded in the encounter. So, too, as a mission theology informed by the sciences regarding the unbreakable connection of all reality and an urban theology replete with the stories of those who have firsthand experience of the liberating power of belonging to the One who transforms reality, coalesce, a portrait of holistic urban mission emerges.

The selection of urban mission to climax the current consultation series on holistic mission gives us a good indication of the importance that mission leaders ascribe to this movement. Urban mission is a diverse and largely undifferentiated field, comprised of several rich seams, each with its own distinctive experience, historical development, geographic concentration, key problematic and cluster of associated issues, strategic focus, formative players, preferred methodologies and primary literature.

It is this diversity of approaches and levels that we endeavored to portray in the working matrix that was prepared for the consultation. The matrix identified four different but interrelated seams, each with several levels of complexity ranging from the local to the global. The case studies—with which you are now quite familiar—were chosen to represent a cross-section of interests from the matrix. They represent only a fraction of the possibilities. As you will appreciate, there are limitations to any boxlike rendering of what is essentially a holistic, circulatory and dynamic reality, and there will inevitably be overlooked, hidden or emerging activities in a process-driven and boundaryless phenomenon.

Delegates stepped into the conversation having already given consideration to the way in which they understand the term *urban* in relation to their mission in the city and why it is a good thing for urban mission to be holistic. Before presenting an integrated account of the discussion, let me provide a brief statement of the way in which I understand the words *holistic, urban,* and *mission,* given that what we observe depends on how we look at it.

First, I take *urban* to refer to the whole reality of the city, with its complex circuitry (people, places, products) its internal dynamics (plans, processes, politics), and its myriad manifestations (spatial forms, social processes, sacred sites, spirituality). Second, I understand the word *holistic* to refer to a deep ecological awareness of the way all things are essentially interconnected. According to the holistic paradigm, the dynamics of the whole influences the properties and patterns of the various parts, forming an inseparable network of relationships. Parts are individuated but not isolated entities, inseparable from the whole within which they are integrated. Third, I hold *mission* to refer to the self-revealed divine prerogative in creating, re-creating and bringing all things to their true fulfillment in the fullness of time. *Mission* refers also to our personal and collective response to this divine initiative of effecting salvation for all creation—in our interest, the urban world— by relating deeply, fully, creatively, critically and compassionately with

195

the city, in the city and for the city. These understandings are, I believe, the starting point for looking at holistic urban mission.

### Defining "urban"

It became very evident in the consultation discussions that there are almost as many definitions of *urban* as there are creative approaches to mission, and that the context plays a large role in determining the mission response. Furthermore, constant change in the urban context throws up creative new mission models and approaches. This is surely a sign of the vitality of urban mission today.

Before identifying the range of urban contexts, we should note the significance of accepting diversity and change as a creative part of mission today. The Christian heritage has for long been steeped in the modality of rural life. As a consequence, the traditional approach to mission has drawn deeply from the stability and predictability of the village structure for its form and style. By contrast, the city has been vilified as a place of instability, uncertainty, difference, indifference and danger. The unredeemed city is certainly this, but it is also much more.

Valuing the "otherness" and diversity that are part of life in the city is to step in the direction of accepting a form of mission awareness more appropriate to an urban world than the traditional, static wholesomeness of the rural idyll. But this does not yet go far enough. The next step, which is more like a conversion experience than a casual decision, is to accept responsibility for the welfare of the city as an intrinsic part of mission and to embrace the opportunity to experience in its welfare one's own well-being. In other words, we are to "tend and keep" the city like a garden, to be at home in the city rather than to fear it, misuse it or withdraw from it. And we are to do this as a free response to the unconditional grace given to us in our day-to-day urban experience through the city's true maker and keeper, whom we call God.

As it happened, the conference delegates' use of the term *urban* ranged across a wide spectrum of meaning from the local and specific to the global and universal. Urban mission, it seems, can be anything from a specialized approach to working with a particular people in a particular place, for example, the urban poor in an inner-city slum or outer-city shanty town, to the generalized approach deemed incumbent on all mission work today of addressing the signs and spirit of our times—our essentially urban times!

Let's consider this diversity in the meaning of *urban* a little closer. On the one side of the urban mission spectrum, *urban* refers to the local and the particular. For those who prefer working with a universal understanding of *urban* at the other end of the spectrum, this way of thinking appears excessively parochial and particularly exclusionary. To truly belong at this end of the urban-mission spectrum one must be "incarnated" in the everyday lives and living conditions of the urban poor, whether in program delivery, community organizing or the like.

Who, then, are the urban poor and where are they found? We know the familiar categories! Generically, they are the economically disadvantaged, the politically downtrodden, the socially disenfranchised, the culturally despised, the historically dispossessed and so forth. In more concrete terms, however, they are those who live, love and die on the streets. They are the ones who sort and sell trash, and who call the garbage tip home. They are the women who need personal and political protection from violent and abusive overlords. They are the children who play in toxic wastelands. They are the workers who provide menial services and receive meaner wages, who scrape together a meager existence on a daily basis with low expectation of living a long and healthy life. The urban poor are found in the nooks and crannies of the city, camping along the rivers, railway lines and ravines. They scrounge and sleep on downtown streets. They huddle together in the slums and tenement houses of the inner city or the depressed suburb and in the shanty towns and squatter camps that skirt the city limits. They are the forgotten ones who inhabit the institutions that house the socially unacceptable or impaired. And the urban poor are more besides!

Local urban mission is dedicated to "presence" with the urban poor. While it may be true that one finds a varying degree of "incarnational" proximity in practice, nevertheless the conviction holds—to earn a legitimate role in shaping the future of individuals or a community one must first be prepared to live with the people of the community. Urban mission in this style calls on the community of faith to be present and accounted for in the midst of the socioeconomic suffering and political struggles of the urban poor. Only in this way will the transforming values of the city of God be discovered, embraced and celebrated by

all, for all. The scandal in this mission is its call to a reversal in fortunes, as fortunes are wont to be counted in fortunate societies. With
this transforming inversion of social values the journey to a real down-
ward mobility is begun. In companionship with the urban poor the
unlimited and life-giving value of relationships is found—and therein
an upward mobility in the things that matter most.

The incarnational approach is considered by many to be the heart
and soul of urban mission, its essential and irreducible core. Be this as
it may, it is surely its conscience. The incarnational lifestyle is tough
because it is counter-cultural, especially in Western cities. Committing
your whole life—including the place you call your home—to be fully
present with the urban poor is costly and takes courage. For many it is
full of adventure. Critics of this approach are not hard to find. Before
becoming too dismissive we ought to pay close attention to the cri-
tique they bring to the wider urban-mission movement and to the wider
Christian community in view of the pervasive class, race and cultural
bias (if not downright captivity) of the mainstream majority church in
the city.

On the other side of the urban-mission spectrum are the approaches
that take a global or universal perspective on the meaning of urban.
The key factor is inclusiveness. Urban reality touches us all. The logic
goes something like this: we are all embedded in a web of life that
includes and interconnects all things. An ecological notion, the web of
life comes to greatest visibility in the city, where the natural, social and
built environments interact in space and time to form an inclusive environment. As people wholly embedded and inseparable from the complex ecology of the city, we ask questions about the fundamental
meaning(s), value(s) and purpose in life. We are not mere objects, essentially separated from all other objects. We gain our subjectivity and
personhood in relationships, not in isolation. Likewise, we cannot claim
a private realm of objectivity in the city from which we can make value-
free or disengaged observations about the urban process. We are in the
city, and the city is in us.

When specialists speak of the impact of the city on human life, individually and collectively, or explore the ontological meaning of the
city, or try to describe the urban dimensions to common human experience, they are usually taking the city in its complex totality as the
given reality. The lexicon of the behavioral sciences is replete with terms
that describe the negative psychological impact of living at risk in large,

198

crowded modern cities—anonymity, alienation, anomie, depression, fragmentation, loneliness, depersonalization and so on. Theologians have been divided on the ontological significance of the city for the life of faith or the content of the theological vision. For some, the city is the harbinger of all that is evil, idolatrous and opposed to the divine—the domain of the principalities and powers that vie with God for human allegiance. For others, the city is the prime metaphor for the eschatological city of God, and the context in which we are to create faithful analogies to the values of this city kingdom today.

Urban-mission leaders know firsthand the impact of the negative side of urban existence on the inhabitants of the city, especially those at the extremity. We experienced this impact powerfully in the consultation. Time was dedicated to processing—in plenary and in private—the psychological, physical, emotional and vocational distress that each of us was carrying to some degree. Incidentally, a full one-quarter of those who had accepted an invitation to the consultation could not attend because of personal illness or illness of their spouse. The stress and strain of the urban context contributes directly to the distress and pain of mission personnel. The fiery crucible of the city tests the metal of urban-mission leaders, from the street worker who sits with the vulnerable and the violent, to the advocate who works for change in the structures. Fueled by rapid change and high levels of stress, and without the necessary human and material resources to take the heat out of the situation, many urban leaders are in meltdown.

Cities are intense, concentrated, exciting environments. People in the full pursuit of life add vigor and energy to the ever-changing vistas of interesting shapes, sizes and color. But if one hesitates to look through the shimmering surface of activity in the city, peering into the faces, or down the hidden cracks and crevices between the towering buildings, one becomes aware of the brokenness of body, soul and spirit that is everywhere evident despite sustained efforts to keep it hidden or disguised. At base, the urban problem is distorted communications that speak of broken relationships and forfeited dreams.

A countervailing force of negativity flows through the very same connective arteries that sustain the intricate web of urban life. In theological terms we speak of this negation as "sin," an outmoded word that is outlandish to the ear of those who shape the dominant global ethos today. The popular mythology emanating from the media, the market and the aggressive advertising of multinational corporations urges a lifestyle of selfish acquisition, self-aggrandizement and instant personal gratification. The symbols that indicate the fulfillment of one's dreams are reduced to this type of drink or that brand of shoes. Little regard is given to the dramatic human price paid to support this materialist mythology, especially by those who are unable to "make it" in such a lopsided competitive environment. In cities around the world the poor labor in sweatshops to produce the brand-name items that others take for granted. Many of these workers are children who should be at school or at play.

Faith names the sinful presence of distortion in personal and social experience as "the Lie," in that it both distorts perception of the grace and truth of God that came to light in human experience through Jesus and disguises its distortion as the voice of reason and common sense. Evil in the urban system is the diabolic rendering—literally "throwing apart"—of the togetherness and belonging that is symbolic of the relational matrix through which life and identity are communicated.

Sin is such a part of the social structures into which we were born and raised that it is difficult for us to grasp fully the pathological distortion that is perpetuated when social opinion baptizes the current shape of reality as normal. Sin is inescapable. We are indelibly marked by the broken structures of social sin long before we consciously perpetuate this sin in the choices that we make. We bear the guilt of acquiescing in the injustice of a situation that serves us so well. The myth of presumed innocence is not strong enough to consistently contain our deep consciousness of complicity in the way things are in the world or the fleeting moments of awareness of the ways in which we silence the guilt through strategies of denial or distraction.

A holistic approach to urban mission will insist that it is insufficient to simply deal with the sinfulness of others (cf. evangelists), or the injustice of others (cf. social activists), and not to deal with our own complicity in the sins of our society. Once we name our need we can seek the divine forgiveness that sets us free—free to respond differently within our own time and circumstances as we move in hope toward the eschatological transformation, healing and integration of all things in the city of God.

To recap, the *urban* in urban mission can mean variously a geographical place (inner city, shanty town), a particular people (urban poor), special welfare-based programs (city missions), the process of socioeconomic change (urbanization, urbanism), the psychological impact of city life (alienation), urban planning and policy-making (built environment, politics) and a paradigm for theological reflection (metaphor, ethics, culture). Usually more than one meaning is implied in any approach, and the way *urban* is understood will be closely related to the choice of a particular style, focus and context of mission.

## Defining "mission"

This leads to the question of what the consultation discussion revealed about the meaning of *mission* in holistic urban mission. First, there was an implicit consensus on a common underlying theme—mission begins with God's immediate and ultimate concern for the welfare of the city and its inhabitants. God's eternal urban concern was given historic affirmation and the distinctive stamp of authenticity in the life, mission and destiny of Jesus of Nazareth. Embodying the "presence" of Christ, in the power of the divine Spirit, as the incarnation of God's eternal compassion for the city and its inhabitants is the response that gives the Christian community its distinctive mission identity. Second, the discussions made evident the sheer diversity of actions and outcomes by which the one mission identity is given its particular relevance in the city. When *mission* is defined inductively from the diversity of concrete activities employed to embody the passionate concern of God for the whole city, urban mission reveals its fullness and beauty in its fractal patterning and creativity.

Within this holistic pattern we can begin our theological conversations on the meaning of mission in any part of the interweaving process—with the actions of God on the one hand, or with our response to these actions on the other. The action of God in our cities precedes our present awareness and our often narrow sphere of theological and historical appreciation. God was in the city long before us! We step into a historical process that is not Godless, even if the presence of God is hidden, denied or not yet discerned. The narrative witness to God's transforming activity in human affairs and individual lives has been told, heard, repeated, recorded and amplified throughout the ages. It surrounds us today.

When the surrounding grace of God reaches and awakens us, awareness and response arise together. We respond in many ways, but primarily we want to talk about it. Finding the words to express the experience of God's saving and freeing grace is an intrinsic part of the

201

response of faith. However, being connected with the deep center of all things—the heart of God—is an experience of fullness and more. There is a surplus, an overflow of meaning and intensity to the experience of grace. With the apostle Paul we are under compulsion to express the joy that is inexpressible, even unutterable. We cannot stay silent.

Doing theology in the city is a communal activity. Urban theology attempts to bring the experiences of the grace of God in the city into a coherent framework. The impetus lies in the sheer richness of images and initiatives by which the people express their experience of the presence (or perceived absence) of God in their lives. It also lies in our desire to gain a clarified sense of just what is happening, how this relates to the insights of the wider church over time, and how this can be celebrated and communicated in our various activities in the community. We are aware that ultimate reality is far greater than any or all of the stories, metaphors, analogies, parables, rituals, liturgies and dramas by which we attempt to translate our intimations of it. And we are aware that even our best expressions are mere approximations. Yet there is a discernible network of connections that gives coherence and credence to our attempts at a nascent urban theology. What emerges in concrete human experience in the city today, in particular the experience of the urban poor, can be correlated with the theological corpus of the Christian community and with the implicit theological horizons in other fields of knowledge. All of this is theological grist for the mission mill.

If a theology of urban mission is shaped from the plurality of revelatory meanings that are gleaned inductively from the experiences of people in the city, especially the urban poor, what sort of experiences are we talking about, and what are the theological realities they disclose? This is where the case studies provided the consultation with a rich platter of possibilities. Where racism and ethnic conflict tear the city, there the motif is to work and pray for the peace of the city. Where injustices abound and dominating power quells the voice of protest and dulls the ache for change, there the passion of God is sought to inspire a transformation. Where the dignity of the people is marred, and the pain of broken promises and relationships wither the spirit, there the healing, forgiving and life-restoring presence of Jesus as the risen Christ is cherished. Acts of healing, empowering, advocating, protesting, comforting, accompanying, challenging, feeding, leading, praying, worshiping, housing, protecting, witnessing and so much more are all a part of the manifold mission of the people of God in the city.

Urban theology is a process of construction, as dynamic and unfinished as the human project called "the city" and the divine project called "creation" are dynamic and unfinished. The unfinished nature of reality opens the door to hope: a hope that includes both the immanent project of reconstructing society along the lines of justice, equality, environmental integrity and peace, and the ultimate project of the consummation of creation in the eternal city whose maker and builder is God. As people know themselves to be a part of the divine drama, so mission is alive with potential and theology replete with material. Urban theology is the concrete imagination of the people for a universal holistic mission.

## Defining "holistic"

In this light, what are we to make of *holistic* mission? If *urban* can include a range of meanings from the local and particular to the global and inclusive, and *mission* the singular initiative of God and the multiple actions of the people of God, what can we say about holism in the light of pluralistic partners?

For urban mission to be holistic it needs to be seen in eschatological perspective. "City" is the biblical and theological metaphor for the completion of history—the New Jerusalem. Mission has its identity in the affirmation of faith that God is the Creator of heaven and earth and all within it. God creates in freedom and with purpose. Creation is imbued with freedom, choice and futurity. God never ceases to act creatively at the heart of reality, just as reality is creatively held at the heart of God. When, in the futility of a freedom turned wanton, humanity chooses against its Creator, in freedom God acts again. The divine mission—to secure a destiny for all time and creation, an Omega Point where all is brought to completion beyond the vicissitudes of history. Mission is the prerogative and initiative of God. Mission is a holistic notion emanating from the wholeness of God and directed toward the fulfillment of creation. Eschatological holism is the full measure of mission—mission completed—bringing to eternal fullness the beloved creation of God, so that all creation, delivered from its futility and finitude, can exult in response in the glory of God who is "all and in all."

203

Unless mission is seen in this eschatological perspective, from the fullness of the divine intent, it cannot really claim a strong sense of holism. If we set out to define mission from the limitation of our as-yet-incomplete history, then we must necessarily divide reality into an unresolved dualism—the missioners (us) and the missioned (them). Only when mission is seen as the sole initiative of God (fact), to which we respond in multiple ways (acts), can the wholeness of mission be maintained. The fact of mission belongs in the heart of God (*missio Dei*) and seeks historical analogies through our active response. The consequent acts of mission are specific in intention—to reflect the mission of God to redeem, release, restore and requite—and limited to the time of history and the history of time.

The consequence of this holistic view of mission is very important. I am asserting that the mission does not belong to us but to God. To put it in other words, we do not have the mission—the Mission has us! This is good news. We can forgo the urge to give our mission structures and strategies the illusion of absoluteness, and the requisite suspicion of those who are not in accord with our sanctioned agenda. We are free to explore where God is active in our urban community—to discern, decide and demonstrate the corporate decisions we make even though we suspect our experience as finite and fraught with ambiguity. Ironically, this means we are bound (or free) to be heretics, since we must choose, and every choice for is also a choice against. We choose freely because we have an absolute confidence in the capacity of God to hold us in the loving accountability of acceptance.

If, as I have suggested, the holistic dimension of urban mission is established by the theological notion of eschatological completeness, then it follows that the usual way of establishing the holistic relationship between evangelism and social action is inverted in direction. The struggle to establish this relationship from an immanent framework—from "below," so to speak—appears in a new light. Rather than trying to combine evangelism and social action by juxtaposing, absorbing, amalgamating, homogenizing or overlaying them so that a whole image emerges in the unification of the parts, we can begin instead with the unshakable ontology of their relationship. We can do this by affirming the insights of the new science that all reality is essentially interrelated, and the theological notion that the ultimate principle of holism is found in the origin, oversight and outcome of creation/mission in the heart of God. Evangelism and social concern are in fact inseparable. What God has joined together let no one put asunder! However, the ontological fact remains unimaginable if we do not include the historical acts by which the integration is made concrete. The eschatological unity of mission in God will lead us to demonstrate the essential relationship between evangelism and social action in our activities as an anticipation of the promised fulfillment. But we are also free to explore the distinctiveness of each area on its own terms, since the question of their essential relationship is not at stake!

Holistic urban mission flows from the eschatological fact of mission into the historical acts of particular missions, a flow that allows us to experience in the incompleteness of the present time an anticipation of the completeness at the end of time. Every act in urban mission receives its character and direction from the whole drama and pushes it closer to its denouement. The integrity of mission is in the plurality of divergent activities. We must lay aside the old paradigm of "unifying fragments" in order to create the full emergent picture, and embrace the new (holographic) way of "integrating individuated parts," in which the whole that is fully embedded in each part is brought to ever-greater clarity of disclosure.

This is more than semantics. Unification attempts in history have usually been around a single absolute principle or vision, articulated by leadership that is subject to the same finite limitations as others, resulting in a competitive struggle to define the core unifying principle and defend it. If we can trust that wholeness is embedded in each part, and that the intensification of each part benefits all in the common struggle for clarity, then we can invest time, capacity and energy appropriately, that is, toward cooperation rather than domination. In this light it is legitimate, even strategic, to differentiate evangelism and social concern. A firm connection in the holistic oneness of God's urban mission allows these separate activities to be fully individuated without competition and creatively integrated without diminishment.

## THE EMPOWERING PRESENCE OF GOD AND URBAN SPIRITUALITY

As has already been indicated, the dynamic connection between the eternal city of God and the immanent pluralism of urban mission must be continually, if not heretically, discerned. Discernment will lead to declaration, clarification and celebration. Therefore, holistic urban mission requires a robust spirituality and an open, functional community.

Spirituality lets meaning flow into our daily lives. Community allows us to appreciate, check, appropriate and celebrate the meanings gleaned by spiritual discernment.

Urban spirituality is about vision and values. Through our practice of spiritual formation we perceive the implicate presence of God in the city, evaluate the meaning of these perceptions for our lives through the community of faith, and then shape a lifestyle in keeping with our discoveries. Urban spirituality, therefore, is mostly about paying attention. A heightened spiritual attentiveness in urban communal experience will see through the surface shimmer of the city, notice the disgrace and pain, then look deeper still to discern where the divine has been active by the instances of grace and healing.

We have already touched upon the power of the negative in urban experience, but it bears reiterating. The power of the negative is real, pervasive and threatening to our very existence by its deceptive appeal and our default to complicity. For this reason we need evangelizing—hearing again and again the Good News—to find a sure identity beyond the threat addressed to the very core of our existence. The power of the negative in the city is manifest wherever life is diminished, damaged or denied through acts of violence, neglect or seduction. For this reason we need actions for social justice—stepping again and again into the struggle with abusive power—in order to discover our relevance in the demonstration of justice, peace and integrity. Both evangelism and social action are imperatives that operate out of the holistic mission initiative of God and are dependent upon the empowering presence of God in every way.

As Christians our identity and relevance is derived from Jesus Christ, manifest in the life and death of Jesus of Nazareth and confessed in the destiny of Jesus as the risen Christ. The biblical witness to the Creator's eternal Word, the theologically inspired stories of Jesus of Nazareth, and the presence of the risen Christ in the mission community shaped and inspired by the Spirit's flow through Pentecost to this day is the definitive center of Christian mission. As Christians we become aware of the eschatological fulfillment of all creation in the death and resurrection of Jesus Christ, made present to us through faith and sustained in the community of faith.

As Christians involved in urban mission we draw deeply on our identification with the life, death and resurrection of Jesus as the story that reaches us and gives definition to our commitments today. Centering our existence in Christ through faith matters, and holds. It matters because in this event we are able to discern the passion of the Creator for the full liberation and integration of all creation. Creation matters to God. The city matters to God. Through the resurrection of the crucified Jesus, put to death by the powers of a dying world, we can say that the world in all its created reality has taken on deep spiritual and eternal significance. Material existence has been vested with a spiritual dignity and destiny beyond the mere presence of "spirit-energy" in the physical world, as revealed by the quantum scientists. With the resurrection of Jesus as the Christ of God, humanity not only takes on divinity, but divinity is forever invested with humanity. Furthermore, in raising Christ as the firstfruits of the resurrection, God is forever glorified as "the one who raises the dead." Despite the ambiguity of history and the opaqueness of human knowing, Christian faith boldly confesses that the biblical God of creation, liberation, covenant and incarnation is also the God of resurrection life and new creation. The voices of the old and new join in their testament: "Death has been swallowed up in victory." Reality now has teleology: an ultimate purpose, direction and destiny.

The story of Jesus Christ is the definitive center of our existence as Christians. But Jesus of Nazareth, too, was a person steeped in a story-formed community—a faith history shaped by God's emancipating love and concern for all creation. The Hebrew Scriptures—in salvation history stories, wisdom sayings, cultic songs and litanies, royal injunctions, prophetic challenges, images of the poet and the seer—portray God as the one who is always on the way to meet us. God is portrayed as a mysterious but active presence, moving with awesome intent within the affairs of history, present but not accounted for. The story is replete with competing and often conflicting ways of depicting God's relationship with the people and the kind of behavior required. One element is common, however. God is ultimately beyond any words used to describe the divine. And that is as it must be.

Many metaphors are used to name God, yet none can fully disclose the divine persona. The wholly "otherness" of God is beyond the limits of human imagination and language. God-language can never claim the objectivity of scientific inquiry. God is not merely another object in a world of objects and subject to precise description through disinterested and value-free observation. We speak of God in the light of encounter. We confess in retrospect that the meeting was as "real as real can be." We are different. The encounter has brought a greater self- and other-awareness, and we feel closer to God and more at home in creation. Most important, we know that all creation, from the least to the greatest, including the teeming complexity of cities, is the object of God's intensive care.

Still, no one has ever seen God! No one, that is, except Jesus, says the writer of the Gospel of John, who adds that the eternal creative Word of God took on "flesh and blood" in Jesus, and that in him the grace and truth of God became visible in human experience. "From his fullness we have all received, grace upon grace" (John 1:16). In the light of this disclosure, the metaphor of God's presence as hiddenness must be qualified. God is present as grace and truth in human form, as suffering love in human history and as the source of life that over- comes death. We are still in the realm of meaning-making through metaphor however, but now we speak of our urban-mission disciple- ship as "following Jesus."

The present hiddenness of God in relationship with all creation is the hiddenness of intimacy—we are hidden in God! But that is not all. Holistic faith confesses through the metaphor of intimacy that our re- lationship "in Christ" is one of a "mutual indwelling." In Christ "all the fullness of God was pleased to dwell" (Col. 1:19). Being "in Christ," our lives are hidden in God. But the apostle Paul takes the metaphor further still. He tells the young Christians in the city of Colossae that the mystery of God that has been hidden through the ages is revealed in their urban discipleship. He names this mystery, "Christ in you, the hope of glory" (Col. 1:27). The hiddenness of God is intimately present in our present cities in the form of hope—a hope inspired by the Spirit of life as the one who gives and guarantees the fulfillment of the prom- ise of an eschatological completion for all creation's longing in the com- ing city of God.

Holistic urban mission seeks to make visible the gifts of life, grace and truth that the hidden God presents in the city. We search our ur- ban experience for signs of God's activity, and we ask what is the most appropriate response for us as co-creative partners in God's mission. When people respond to the appeal of God through us to be reconciled and find the joy of becoming a "new creation," we are renewed in our efforts to create faithful analogies to the life of Jesus in our city.

Holistic urban mission is empowered by the Spirit flowing through the relational ecology of the city, mediating the grace of God to those who seek liberation from anxiety and the loss of meaning that existential aloneness in the city evokes. Divine grace frees us from the urge to create God in our own image or to equate the reality of God with our words about God. In freedom we can let God be God for us in our urban mission. We can celebrate the availability of God's liberating and empowering grace in its infinite fullness, as grace upon grace, an abundant grace, a wildly profligate grace far exceeding our finite capacity to contain it and never exhausted by even our most liberal attempts to give it away. Sustained in our witness by the divine promise to keep us in grace, we can give ourselves fully and freely as agents of grace in the city. The naiveté of hope is never put to shame by the complexity of urban life or the perplexity of urban mission, because the One who loves the city is present as the mystery within which we live and move and have our being. This said, holism must never be the grounds for boasting that we "have it all, already," nor should holistic delight distract us from the unresolved pain in our cities or emotionally satiate us so that we are content to simply "be."

This last point is very important for the spiritual formation of those engaged in evangelism, on the one hand, and social activism, on the other. For those doing evangelism the danger is dissolving the temporal elements of the journey of faith into those deep moments of oneness with the divine, especially in proclamation, which is only a short step from equating one's own powers of persuasion with the presence of God. An urban spirituality that is community based will remind the evangelists to stay "on the road," and that "following Jesus" on the road to the city will lead to a cruciform existence. Can one remain Christian and bypass both the city and the cross on the way to resurrection? Moving into the poverty, pain and fear of the city is the only way, spiritually speaking, to move through it and beyond it. Jesus said as much when he talked about a seed needing to be buried in order to grow, and when he cautioned his disciples against self-serving behavior by saying that to find life one must be prepared to lose it in self-giving.

Likewise for those engaged in the furies of social activism, urban spirituality will lead to a place of respite and rest. The temptation for the social activist is to dissolve faith into intense personal engagement and to look on those who seem to dwell perpetually in God's unmediated presence as irrelevant quietists, if not a part of the problem. Whereas those engaged in evangelism need a constant reminder of the long-term aspects of "following Jesus on the road," social activists need

209

to stop long enough to become aware of the immediate presence of God and to dwell in the timeless space of existential "belonging." When Jesus' invitation to "take up your cross and follow me" doesn't sound like good news anymore because "my yoke is easy and my burden is light" hasn't exactly been our experience, then it is time to stop and check the baggage. What exactly is the "cross" we are carrying around? Is it perpetual tiredness or impatience? Is it the need to "have it done my way," or to "do it all myself so that it is done properly"? Jesus' invitation is to lay down our burdensome activity, to put our self-serving aside—not to go fashioning it into the cross that we grin and bear as we continue our frenetic activity. Perhaps the "yoke and burden" that Jesus is speaking about—which is "easy and light"—is nothing other than having to admit that we are constantly in need of healing and liberation from our taking ourselves too seriously. We need Jesus' constant reminder to us (through others I suspect) to let it go, and follow!

## The Empowering Presence of the Community and Urban Spirituality

The spirituality of urban mission is based in community but formed personally. The personal has at least two aspects. First, our spiritual discipline is a search for God, in person. In the peak experiences of our lives we know that something of profound significance has happened. We know it with an acute awareness in our whole being. Theologically, we describe this awareness as being "addressed" by God, who speaks to us as no other can—with an intense intimacy in the interior of our lives, in that deep place of self-knowing, self-doubting, even self-loathing; in the place of inner conversation and unvoiced dreams. God comes to us as the One who knows our most inward and intimate longing to belong and guides us into the wonderment and sheer joy of being integrated with the wellspring of our very existence. We find the meaning of life, no less.

Second, in our searching God meets us as a "personal" Other. God relates to us in our individuality and in so doing establishes our awareness of personhood—the knowledge of being a person who is seen, accepted and loved. We belong! From the deep existential awareness and joy of this belonging where it really counts we are free to give ourselves to others, and to all reality, in relationships of mutuality, solidarity and care. Our personhood is confirmed in relationships and constituted as a social reality. Furthermore, the logic of the incarnational approach to urban mission lies in this empowering aspect of personhood, in the deep relational integration that is at the heart of an urban spirituality. Since we are sustained by the deep structures of belonging, we are empowered to build community relations as neighbor with neighbors (and strangers), friend with friends (and enemies), and above all to be true to ourselves.

As an inner-city pastor I came to appreciate early in my ministry that finding authentic personhood in relationships made the difference between those who were able to make the journey into community with the urban poor and those who were not.

The model that informed our urban mission was the incarnation approach—to be fully embedded as a community in our neighborhood of the city so that we could embody the life of Christ for the life of the people in all our actions and attitudes. The road of understanding that leads to the maturity demanded of the incarnation approach—as reflected in our particular experience—is worth describing. I will describe it sequentially, although in fact the modalities of behavior were more overlapping and dynamic.

The learning process began with our arrival as newcomers and our initial insertion into the community. Since the church had all but died out as a presence in our neighborhood, it was a matter of mission necessity for people to move back into the city in the earliest stages of rebuilding the community of faith. Once inserted in the new situation, the next challenge was to begin the process of investment—settling in and putting down roots, learning how to negotiate the neighborhood, sensing its moods and its rhythms, finding out where the various services and groups were located, living into its special ethos. During this time we discovered the hidden delights and special surprises that our neighborhood had to offer, as well as the places where one should proceed with caution. We began to appreciate the qualities of the people we met as we accessed the schools, shops, services and so forth. The caution and tentativeness that marked us as newcomers in the neighborhood gradually subsided as we gently probed the relational networks of the community and became better acquainted with the local community dynamics.

The shadow side of the process of investment I will call the phase of imitation. Looking back, this shadow persona to our group of wildly enthusiastic, energetic, idealistic, highly educated, church-based, middle-class urban-mission activists still brings a wistful smile. As an aberrant distortion of the overwhelming desire to belong, to be inculturated in the neighborhood, we began to dress, speak and posture like the urban poor, especially the teenagers from the welfare housing estates with whom we were now in constant contact—our peculiar interpretation of them, that is. Now, I am a great believer in mimesis as an important early learning skill for children. But in our case the mimicry rarely rose above the ridiculous. Who appreciates being aped? As the youth grew in confidence and began to figure us out, they soon let us know that they would prefer to meet us as "real people." We had made a lot of progress in our relationships with the local youth by this time. So much so that despite our lapses into imitative behavior, for many we had become too close for comfort. These were young people who had suffered abandonment time and again from significant people in their lives. What was to say that we would be any different? As self-protection, one by one they began to create situations that gave them cause to withdraw.

Oftentimes the testing was accompanied by violence. In each case the person on the urban-mission team stood peacefully by his or her commitment to "be there" for the other person. The truth of the commitment was then tested by many of the young people by breaking off their contact. The waiting began, transforming the process of investment, with its shadow land of imitation, into a period of isolation. Rejection by the very people we had "given up so much to be with" began a wilderness sojourn from which some of our number did not emerge with their original commitment intact. A few returned to their suburban homes and churches, disillusioned by the overall lack of acceptance and appreciation for their efforts. The majority buried themselves deeper within the cocoon of our little church, where the poor were duly celebrated as the focus of God's concern and therefore of our urban mission, but where they also featured more as a linguistic presence in the liturgy than as a real presence in the pew. There is a yawning gap between the idealized poor and the actual poor in our largely middle-class and educated churches in the West, especially, dare I say it, the newly gentrified urban churches in the inner city, with their surplus of professional caregivers and social workers.

Fortunately, most emerged from the wilderness with few visible scars and a lot of valuable learning. The phase of integration had begun. Again, it was our relationships with the people of the neighborhood that made the critical difference in our learning, including renewed relationships with the youth, who eventually returned to see if we really were still there for them! Integration was invested with the hard currency of mutuality and respect. The turning point was quite simple. The loss of relationships hurt. In the experience of loss and hurt came the realization that the "other" had become a friend. Friendship is wholly different from treating someone as the fortunate object of benevolence. A friend receives my affection, not my affectation! Furthermore, we learned about the deep, hidden power of relationships, experienced sometimes in the powerlessness of rejection, and we came to realize that power exists in more forms than merely the socioeconomic and political. Relationships that rise above personal, class and ethnic differences, and which refuse falsity in any form, produce a whole new source of power—the power of solidarity and mutuality. It is the power of one through the empowering of oneness.

Belonging is a liberating aspect of community life, and freely available. Our small inner-city community grew immensely in the realization that the good news of the gospel is essentially embedded in the spirituality of belonging. God had worked deeply in our lives to bring about a new self-awareness in the hidden places, through transforming the generic "urban poor" into the characters we knew, individuals and families who had become our friends.

## HOLISTIC URBAN MISSION IS RELATIONAL AND ECOLOGICAL

This leads me to my reading of the central affirmation of the consultation—that holistic urban mission is essentially relational, and that the holistic relational vision is supported on inner theological grounds by current scientific reasoning and in the popular cultural appreciation of "the way things are" today. Listening to the urban-mission thinkers and practitioners at the consultation table, two things become clear: that urban mission has been defined in relationship with the urban poor from the outset, and that urban mission is holistic and ecologically aware in its approach to the city whenever it stays true to its core value of living incarnationally.

First, urban mission has always been premised on a radically relational vision. In solidarity with the urban poor the urban-mission community members have shared their conviction and experience of God's salvation, liberation and promised restitution with those for whom the message indeed came as "good news." This has been the case since the earliest times of mission activity in the city. It has been particularly true in the modern period of urban life ushered in with the Enlightenment and the urban Industrial Revolution it gave birth to.

The new age of the machine witnessed the rise of the human project, as scientific breakthroughs in all fields reinforced the dominant cultural ideology of unbounded confidence in the capacity and progress of the human spirit. The modern era was ushered in through rapid industrial expansion and urbanization, beginning in Europe and spreading to the New World and beyond. New technology made possible an aggressive global colonial expansion in the nineteenth century, bringing with it a proliferation of new urban centers of trade and commerce. While "foreign missions" accompanied the colonial expansion—sometimes leading, sometimes following—urban mission did not stray far from its primary relations with the urban poor. In rapidly expanding mercantile centers like Manchester and Sheffield, or industrial port cities like Newcastle and Glasgow, urban industrial missions worked in solidarity with factory workers caught up in the poverty-inducing conditions of rapid urbanization and the suffering of heinous work practices and conditions.

The rise of urban industrial mission in the United Kingdom was mirrored in the Worker Priest movement in France, with its radical concern for the working urban poor and its movement out of the Catholic parish in critical protest with the dominant ecclesiastical and priestly paradigm of faith. The genius of the Worker Priest movement, as with other special urban-mission ventures of the time, was its reliance on a relational connection with the urban working poor rather than with a formal ecclesiastical connection to the local parish with its legitimizing practices and protocols of ministry.

With the rise of the program-centered and welfare-oriented city missions, urban mission entered a new era of intervention on behalf of the urban poor. Pioneering work was carried out in the street level rehabilitation of the urban poor by the organized distribution of charitable donations and the provision of agency-based care through providing meals, accommodation, clothing and, in latter times, job-skill training. This was the era of social concern through feeding and housing, in combination with evangelistic gospel proclamation in the city-mission chapel—a required activity if you wish to be fed—which some have whimsically referred to since as "'Abide With Me,' and a cup of tea" holistic urban mission. City missions still flourish today in most of the major cities of the developed world.

The broad social changes that created an upheaval in Western culture during the sixties and into the seventies, and the rising concern over inner-city blight, poverty and endemic racism—the so-called urban crisis—saw urban mission in its heyday. Well-suited to the radical tenor of the times, urban mission was supported through the denominational judicatories and boasted a cadre of feisty operators and brilliant spokespersons.

In due time, however, urban mission's radical edge was blunted. The interest of the denominations turned away from the bleakness and violence of the inner city to the greenness of the fertile suburbs. Mission money no longer circulated through the city as it had, and urban mission was faced with diminishing resources to maintain expensive and aging facilities. The radical spirit burned low as the bills came in, and activists paid the price—with interest—physically, emotionally and spiritually. Not surprisingly, those still standing in the urban-mission wilderness began harnessing the rising interest in alternative communities, at that time very much a back-to-the-land counterculture movement, and adapted them for the inner city. Others moved out of the church and into the formal political structures or the academy.

Since the mid-seventies, especially through the eighties, urban mission was carried forward largely by a renewal of interest in inner-city congregational and parish life as the base from which to rebuild the faith community, in connection with the urban poor, following years of sociological indifference, ecclesiastical neglect and economic demise. At this time the ecumenical church worldwide was awakening to liberation theology and the gospel for the poor, an awakening that had already taken place within the inner-city parish, but without the fanfare. The rising emphasis on the geography of urban mission, whether the inner city or the working-class industrial suburb of the West, or the perimeter shanty town and disorganized city slums and squatter settlements of the developing world, the metaphor that motivated urban mission during this period was incarnation.

Second, urban mission is genuinely holistic when it takes into account the total environment in which it is embedded and does so by recognizing and fostering the health of its own ecology, its own household economy and ethos. Urban mission must take a radically ecological stance today to advocate for a livable and sustainable future for all

215

creation, starting with those who are most vulnerable and at risk of demise. Urban mission, therefore, brings to its concern for the urban poor a concern for the environment in this present crisis of ecological devastation.

The holistic challenge to urban mission is to discover the patterns that connect at a deep level to create a matrix of meaning in the complexity of the city. Sometimes the patterns are visible, as in the celebration of relationships. Many times the patterns are part of the mystery of the city, buried in the collective unconscious or hidden in the deep interconnections of life that are the domain of the spiritual and the subject of discernment.

An important connecting thread in the pattern of the consultation was, as you will recall from my earlier comments, the common conviction that the discerning eye of faith can point to traces of divine grace in the city—imprints left in the consciousness of the urban community in the wake of God's passing. I raise the issue again at this point to trace the pattern of connection between the intimations of grace and meaning in the city, the centrality of relationships as the connective tissue, and the language of stories as the best way to try and express the otherwise inexpressible depths of grace in the communication of life in and through relationships. Stories speak the language of relationships.

## Story and Grace

We experienced both story and grace time and again in the passionate renderings of the case presenters. Their storytelling had a gripping effect on us. The love for their community was so transparent that they were easily transported in their recollections to another time and place. They paraded before us a cast of urban characters—special people who had become so much a part of their lives that in sharing the stories of these people it became evident that they were sharing their own story. Long after the details of the characters and the plot of the story have been forgotten, we will still remember the power of the relationships that bound it all together. The stories, the storytelling and the storytellers were utterly compelling. They bound us into the life of the community and gave us a sense of connection in the common hearing of the stories.

On one memorable afternoon we had the opportunity to hear the story in situ, visiting the Parish of the Risen Christ on Smokey Mountain in Manila at the request of the parish priest, Fr. Ben Beltran. We sat and talked with several women leaders of the community, listening to their recounting of the way in which the people, who formerly made their home and living on the city garbage tip, are being transformed in every area of their common life—a demonstration of holistic urban mission the like of which is rare to find. There was an atmosphere of deep respect as the women told their story with a quiet dignity, all the while incorporating us into their story for all time. In this and many other moments of the consultation we sensed that we were on holy ground indeed.

Later we were taken to a building that stood on a new development site jutting out into Manila Bay. In the building was a model to scale of a new port that is in the process of being constructed. The land is new, having been built up in the bay by bringing in soil. The composted garbage of Smokey Mountain is being used to top the new foundation. Once the port facility is completed, it will include restaurants, hotels, office buildings and light industry. The former rag pickers of Smokey Mountain have been retrained to start new industries or staff the new development. They have been an integral part of the process of transformation, a holistic urban-mission approach that incorporates the full spectrum of *urban* that we identified earlier: place, people, process, projects, political advocacy, planning and paradigm-making.

At the heart of the process of community organizing on Smokey Mountain is the community of faith. The energy of the community has been organized to bring about the changes that are currently taking place at every level of their lives, from housing to health, from education to economic development. The deep Christian faith of the people has seen the mountain literally being removed and cast into the sea. And in its place has risen the first few of the multilevel housing complexes that will one day soon house the three thousand plus families of the community. The people are the builders, not only of the new housing but also of a whole new life. Working collectively, the urban poor have achieved a radical transformation in their part of the city.

Clearly, holistic mission imagination is alive and well in the experience of urban communities such as the Parish of the Risen Christ and the other case studies that were featured in the consultation. These communities have flourished despite the challenge of rapid change and the constant need to stretch limited resources. For a long time now, small, hardworking, robust urban-mission groups, congregations and parishes—the "Cinderellas" of the wider church—have been critically engaged with people in the midst of the city's pain and distress. The perseverance of these small mission communities, often under duress, points to a certain knowing, a certain shared source of sustainable meaning and value in their urban experience that is not immediately obvious or accessible to those who are merely passing by.

Deeply embedded in those parts of the city that always appear at the bottom end of socioeconomic or environmental scales of livability, these urban-mission communities demonstrate a measure of faith and hope that is infectious. No stranger to the ambiguity of the city, the spirituality that most characterizes the faith commitment of the urban-mission community is openness to the mystery of God's presence in the manifest incomprehensibility of urban existence. Confident that God is in their future as the ultimate destiny of all reality produces a lively hope that defies the outsider's ascription of depression and hopelessness to their part of the city. Living joyfully in the spirit of hope has an immediate impact in the community, creating the very conditions that are a necessary part of the coming fulfillment of their faith.

## THE EFFICACY OF COMMUNITY ORGANIZING

The considerable constraints under which urban mission operates due to the meager material and human resources at its disposal has given rise to a wide range of practical interventions. One particular approach surfaced repeatedly in the case studies and plenary discussion, because of the way in which it achieved lasting changes in the lives and living conditions of the urban poor. The approach is community organizing. As a grassroots and democratic approach to the self-empowerment of the urban poor through joint action on commonly held issues, the efficacy of community organizing lies in its philosophical and theological strength as well as its methodological power.

Community organizing begins with a longing for change that smolders in the belly of the people, like an untended fire that has burned itself down to coals and ashes. Once the dormant embers of diminished power and of lackluster dreams are stoked and fanned, awakening flames of restless hope in ready individuals, then the passion for change sweeps through the heart of the community, burning fiercely in the collective will and firing the corporate imagination. With an awakened longing for that which does not yet exist, the imagination begins to trace the outlines of what could be. The future begins to take shape in a way that was until now nothing more than an impossible dream. Parents imagine schools for their children. Mothers imagine being able to read and write. The family imagines running a business. Children imagine playing. Fathers imagine building a community with streets, lights, water, sewers and safe housing. Youth imagine adulthood.

At the heart of the organizing approach is the formation of small coalitions of people who are willing to work together to address a particular issue. The people share their hopes and imagine what the concrete outcome would look like. As the coalition gains clarity of the end goal, then the incremental process of acting and reflecting begins, always with the ultimate goal in view.

As further coalitions are formed around an ever-expanding range of issues, so the focused efforts of the community are multiplied. More and more community members are drawn into the process. In order to establish the democratic voice and participation of the people, and to ensure the coordinated development of the community, the emerging leadership forms a new "super coalition" or organizing of the people. A congress of the people creates a permanent and democratically elected organization. This organization becomes the vehicle for furthering the development of the community and serves as a way for the people to advocate for their own concerns as citizens participating fully in the life of the city.

To help people to imagine with a constructive longing is to set out on the path of empowerment. That is why it is more important for urban mission to work for the conditions that promote the self-empowerment of the poor through the creative use of their imagination than it is simply to give them things or to do things for them. Ironically, mere acts of charitable giving in place of empowerment end up giving more than they presume to give—they give a future, yes, but as a possibility greatly reduced. The future stays firmly in the hands of those who have the capacity to give from their present abundance and future security. On the other side of the transaction, a loaf of bread indeed gives the hungry person strength for another day. But the next day will see the need for more bread. Feeding the longing imagination of a person to be a breadwinner by building the capacity to act—through the power of collective action—will satisfy the hunger for food as well as the hunger for a different kind of future. The litmus test for our understanding of the transforming power of the gospel in our own lives is whether the urban poor can sit with the dignity of experience at the same table of opportunity as the non-poor and claim a future of their own making.

The good news that faith is under compulsion to communicate in words, actions and attitudes is that the future is open for all and moves toward its fulfillment in the intimacy of God. The divine Spirit, moving through the city and working in cooperative action with the discipleship community, inspires the imagination and communicates the energy of hope. The inspired imagination will simply refuse to let the future be closed. The divine Spirit woos it forward in the real anticipation of real achievements toward its completion. Community organizing in urban mission is premised on the unlimited capacity of even the poorest of the poor to achieve the potential of their humanity through collective effort. Because it is oriented toward community and seeks to incarnate the value of mutuality, it is a movement of love. Because it is oriented toward transformation and seeks to achieve this through organizing the people to discover their power to act, it is a movement of hope. Holistic urban mission as community organizing helps create the conditions for releasing hidden potential into concrete achievement.

Community organizing adds a decisive cutting edge to community development. Faced with only the cost of the organizers, usually few in number, community organizing can operate at very low cost. Mobilizing the potential for change that lies dormant in the community enables community organizing to achieve high impact. High impact at low cost is the calling card of organizing. Unlike many project- or program-based approaches, community organizing is not subject to preset limitations; it can work exponentially to include the whole community in both the process and the benefits, without sacrificing depth and quality. The community-organizing approach fosters the emergence and equipping of local leaders, thereby creating a trained cadre of future organizers to continue the expansion of the program. In this way the local approach to organizing can be replicated over and over again. Furthermore, community organizing is responsive and pragmatic in style; it has a healthy understanding of the use and abuse of power and how to work constructively with power, including the confrontations and conflicts that vested power interests frequently provoke. Ultimately, the community organizers aim to leave the community with the only fitting legacy of their efforts toward the empowerment of the people—a permanent organizational capacity whereby the people can oversee their own continued development.

Over the week of the consultation, discussions in the plenary sessions, as well as conversations in the corridors, over meals, and during after-dinner walks, repeatedly raised the conviction that for mission to be transparently holistic it must become much more inclusive of those who have traditionally been left without voice or power. An immediate in-house priority was identified—to address the persistent gender imbalance in urban-mission leadership. Closely related to the gender issue is the need for mission leaders to listen intently to the experiences of those who are building meaningful lives in the midst of adversity.

The time has long since passed when leadership could convincingly speak over the voice of the poor, as if talking about transformation could substitute for the experience of transformation. In our current prosaic world of leadership, where mission is likely to be clarified by pointing to "mission statements" and "core values" as propositions on paper, we need to hear afresh the poetic voice of the Spirit of transformation speaking through the emerging voices of experience in the community. I suspect that amplifying these voices will do more to re-source the human spirit than yet another seminar by the latest human-resource guru. Without the inclusion of those rendered voiceless and powerless, mission can never claim to be holistic. And I don't mean inclusion as mere benevolence, or with reluctance because down deep we know it is theologically and politically advisable, but with enthusiasm and gratitude that the grace of God is still liberating and transforming human life.

The challenge for urban mission as we approach the twenty-first century—the first truly urban century—is to make accessible through our full engagement in the city a holistic vision of the transforming grace of God that seeks to liberate, renew and perfect creation. All the ingredients necessary are available. To bring to light the image of a holistic new ecology of urban mission we will need to create a social holograph that depicts the profound interrelation and interdependence of reality. As Christians we hope and pray that our holographic existence will unfold with clarity the enfolded promise of God for the eschatological fulfillment of redeemed creation. We will seek to fore-shadow in living color the metaphor of the holy city, the New Jerusalem, prepared with the Creator's final touch—like the radiant perfection of a bride on her wedding day (Rev. 21:1–2). But the eschatological holograph of urban mission must be created in the midst of the city in our own time and place, investing current urban reality with the hope for justice, inclusion, equality, solidarity and peace.

## A Vision for a New Ecology of Holistic Urban Mission

So we come to the end of the chapter, the consultation, the book and the series! In this moment of completion I am quieted by the responsibility of penning the final words—final only in the linear logic of a book, of course. Indeed, if this chapter has been about anything, it has been about the multilateral connections and flows that belong to a dynamic and complex urban reality. In terms of the metaphor with which I began, I have tried not to be confined by the linear logic of straight roads, well-defined lanes, and contested intersections. Instead, I have played with the interconnecting architecture of roundabouts, flyovers and cloverleafs. I trust my contribution has been true to the task of integration and leaves you, the reader, in the roundabout of debate on holistic urban mission with your options intact—to head straight back without pause into the substance of the book, the consultation or the series as a whole; or to forge ahead unhindered in anticipation of new vistas opening up; or perhaps to take off on a lateral road in a whole new adventure of discovery and contribution.

With one last panoramic sweep from atop the flyover, let me summarize aspects of the vision of a new ecology of holistic urban mission. I see urban mission impelled by faith and sustained by the holistic vision of "fullness" in the coming of the city of God. Faith confesses that God is the Alpha and Omega of all creation. Within the space and time of creation all reality is interconnected and shares a common destiny in the eternity of God. Creation has a *telos* that gives purpose to life in the midst of time. As only God can perfect creation, so faith confesses God's mission prerogative for the liberation of creation from the entropy, death and decay of existence. This divine mission informs and impels our mission in a co-creative partnership. Therefore, faith leads us to the witness and service in the concrete reality of this as-yet-unfulfilled and still unjust world of cities.

I also see urban mission characterized by love and the joy of belonging. At the heart of love is belonging. As an integral part of created reality, blessed with consciousness, we are aware of our incompleteness and filled with a deep and insistent longing to belong, to be "at home" with God and the universe. Faith confesses that the creation is God's dwelling place. Within the ecology of creation as home we are joined as one people, one family, one household. We are fully at home when we share equitably and joyfully in the economy of the household, when we participate fully and freely in the common life, and when we experience the easy familiarity of knowing what is appropriate behavior. To foster the spirit of belonging is the goal of urban mission, starting in the places where the loneliness of alienation, rejection, exclusion and oppression are most keenly felt.

I also see urban mission being sustained by creative relationships built on trust. Relationships are the essential forces that build the web of life, allowing for both individuation without loss and integration without diminishment. Relationships are creative; they bring to community a synergy that creates a whole larger than the sum of the individual parts. Because our cities are crippled by the rending of relationships and distrust that is bred of distortion, so urban mission will seek to foster relationships of trust across the urban fault lines of race, color, ethnicity, creed, class and religious persuasion through the consistent demonstration of compassion, mutuality and solidarity. Urban mission will include wholesome relationships of care with all aspects of creation, including the natural and built environments. Because relationships are based on the vulnerability of trust, so urban mission will need to exercise and impart faith and courage.

Lastly, I see urban mission at its strongest where the church is at its weakest—in community with the urban poor and powerless, and in conversation with those who hold the balance of power in the city. Transformation is needed at all levels of urban life. Urban mission will stand in solidarity and companionship with the poor and powerless, nurturing movements for change that arise spontaneously when communities work together to shape their own lives and living environments. Likewise, urban mission will stand with the poor as partners to advocate changes in institutional policies and practices wherever the poor are left vulnerable to exploitation. Transformation involves a different way of viewing reality. New leadership will emerge from the experience of urban transformation. The role of urban mission will be to build leadership capacity, to encourage innovation and risk taking, to celebrate achievement and to amplify the emerging voices of experience while challenging the voices of contradiction that refuse to enter into a genuine dialogue for change. Urban mission will continue to be the voice of conscience and courage in the citadels of power, including the church.

The city of God is among us as an implicate dimension of our urban existence—present in potential and partial fulfillment, or should we say, present in the potential fulfillment of each part—but not yet fully explicated. We see now in part(s), as if looking at our reflected image in a murky mirror. But then, faith confesses, we shall see in full—a realized holism.

So it has been in our conversations around the table—revealing and concealing, with instances of transformation and intimations of potential not yet fully unfolded. As the consultation proceeded, case studies from vastly different cities in vastly different cultures around the world conspired to take us deeper and deeper in our awareness of the complexity of urban mission and the undisclosed richness of life enfolded in each community's story. And in our conversations we became more and more aware of the reasons for our being here. At times it came with vivid flashes of insight. At other times it unfolded with a steadily growing strength of clarity, not unlike that first stretch after a midday nap. Sometimes it involved a trance-like leave-taking as we journeyed back home in our thoughts to check in with those we love and missed, those who share most intimately our struggles and joys, those whose opinions we cherish even if only construed in an imaginary conversation.

Why had God brought us to this hour? To discover traces of the divine presence in the experiences of the urban poor through the case studies and site visit? Yes! To get a fuller understanding of the ways in which evangelism and social action can be integrated in practice and in theory? Certainly! To find encouragement for our ongoing journey of learning by meeting with colleagues—old and new—and by sharing with one another our insights and learning? Definitely! Or, was it to find refreshment for our spirit by drawing resources from the common well of spiritual wisdom? That too! We came because we care about the city. We came because we find our calling in serving with the urban poor. We came to discover more about the source and sustenance of urban mission in a spirituality of holism and a life of compassion—the kiss of peace and justice in the city!

## POSTSCRIPT

Back in my adopted city of Los Angeles after the long Pacific flight home, I am driving on the Interstate 10 freeway when we come to a complete standstill in traffic at the cloverleaf intersection with the 210 North and the 57 South freeways. Somewhere up ahead an accident has shut down the system. Urban life is indeed ironic! Nothing to do but wait, and ponder. The city has a way of reminding us that human life is lived under a "cloud of unknowing," and every attempt to speak meaningfully of God and the city is at best a "stuttering and stammering."

# Appendices

# Appendix A
# Consultation participants

| Name | Organization | Country |
|------|-------------|---------|
| Ben Beltran | Parish of the Risen Christ | Philippines |
| Grace Dyrness | Center for Religion and Civic Culture | U.S.A. |
| Steve Ferguson | Fieldstead Institute | U.S.A. |
| Franklin Joseph | Organizing People for Progress | India |
| LeRoy Lawson | Hope International University | U.S.A. |
| Ken Luscombe | World Vision International | U.S.A. |
| Toniel Marimba | The Urban Advance Project | Zimbabwe |
| Donald E. Miller | University of Southern California | U.S.A. |
| Grant Power | West Angeles Community Development | U.S.A. |
| Nancy Power | West Angeles Community Development | U.S.A. |
| Don Schmierer | Fieldstead Institute | U.S.A. |
| Jayne Scott | Community Learning Network | U.K. |
| Dan Sheffield | Free Methodist Mission | South Africa |
| Althea Spencer-Miller | Caribbean Conference of Churches | Jamaica |
| Edna Valdez | MARC Publications | U.S.A. |
| Tetsunao Yamamori | Food for the Hungry International | U.S.A. |

ADMINISTRATIVE STAFF:

| | | |
|------|-------------|---------|
| Susan Brigado | Development Foundation of the Philippines | Philippines |

| | | |
|---|---|---|
| Roy Capati | Development Foundation of the Philippines | Philippines |
| Marie Demafelis | Development Foundation of the Philippines | Philippines |
| Lisa May | Fieldstead Institute | U.S.A. |
| Jo Ann St. Don | Fieldstead Institute | U.S.A. |
| Marisol Velasco | Development Foundation of the Philippines | Philippines |

# Appendix B
# Case study guidelines

### 1. Acquaint yourself with the concept of holistic ministry.

Although reconciliation with man is not reconciliation with God, nor is social action the same as evangelism, nor is political liberation all there is to salvation, nevertheless we affirm that evangelism and sociopolitical involvement are both part of our Christian duty.

Both are necessary expressions of our doctrines of God and man, our love for our neighbor and our obedience to Jesus Christ (see section 5 of the Lausanne Covenant). Tetsunao Yamamori expresses this concept as follows:

> Ministering to physical needs and ministering to spiritual needs, though functionally separate, are relationally inseparable, and both are essential to the total ministry of Christ's church.

### 2. Describe the context of your case study.

Describe the people-group with whom you have done your work. What is its history as a people-group? In what material and spiritual ways were the people poor? What are the causes of their material poverty? Spiritual poverty? Social poverty?

### 3. Describe your holistic ministry program.

What type of development project did you implement (water, food production, health, microenterprise, integrated)? Describe it in some detail. How did it come into being? What kind of development process did you use? How were the church(es) involved? How was Christian witness to take place?

### 4. What were the results?

What kind of material or physical transformation has taken place? How have the lives of the poor improved? What evidence of spiritual transformation in people and in the community have you seen? What evidence of cultural or social transformation have you seen?

### 5. Describe the results of people deepening their relationship with or coming to know Christ.

What has happened in spiritual terms among the people? What evidence can you cite that demonstrates that evangelism or renewal is taking place? How was the local church involved? Is the spiritual change limited to individuals? A particular church? The community as a whole? Are churches growing? How are Christians becoming part of the social transformation in their communities?

### 6. Identify the factors that contributed to the emergence or growth of a Christ group (a growing church or a new group of believers).

How did the development project contribute to evangelism or renewal in the community? What role did the development agency staff play, if any? What training did the development agency staff have in terms of Christian witness?

### 7. Evaluate your case study.

Looking back on your history with this project, are there things you would have done differently? What obstacles prevented full success? What hindered the results of the spiritual ministry?

# Appendix C

### Master of Science in Management
### in International Development

# Hope International University

Hope International University

Hope International University exists to serve the church in its mission of discipling the nations by providing Christian higher education to help students develop for leadership in the church and society. Hope International University emphasizes education for church-related careers that have a high probability for Christian influence upon people and society.

## The Degree

The Graduate School of Hope International University offers a 36-unit Master of Science in Management (MSM) degree program in International Development through email-based distance learning. (Only 30 units may be required for those with 6 units of related undergraduate course work.)

## Objective

To increase the professional competencies of practicing or potential technical specialists and managers to build capacity and development through values-oriented course work and project-based learning, emphasizing skills that build community.

## Target Group

Current and aspiring leaders interested in applying broad management skills to build capacity in partnership with communities and local resources to empower community members to meet those needs.

### Relative Emphasis

Students are prepared to serve in community development by building local, national and international partnerships through integrated projects and management rather than enterprise and income generation.

### Program Distinctives

- ❖ Distance learning and global interaction
- ❖ Online access to international experts
- ❖ Values-centered
- ❖ Intensely practical
- ❖ International faculty
- ❖ Accredited by WASC

### Historical Background

From the beginning, Food for the Hungry International (FHI) has collaborated in the design of this program. FHI field country offices worldwide are used initially as contact points for program information and enrollment. Other organizations like World Vision, MAF and MAP International also cooperate in our programs.

**For further information contact:**

Hope International University
School of Graduate Studies
International Development Program
2500 E. Nutwood Ave.
Fullerton, CA 92831
Phone: (714)879-3903
Fax: (714)738-4564
Web: http://www.hiu.edu
Email: alanr@xc.org

# MARC

*Bringing you key resources on the world mission of the church*

The Mission Advanced Research and Communications center (MARC) is a publishing arm of World Vision, an international partnership of Christians whose mission is to follow our Lord and Savior Jesus Christ in working with the poor and oppressed to promote human transformation, seek justice and bear witness to the good news of the Kingdom of God.

Other titles in the Cases in Holistic Ministry series:

▶ *Serving With the Poor in Latin America*, Tetsunao Yamamori, Bryant L. Myers, C. René Padilla and Greg Rake, editors. Real cases are presented from throughout Latin America. In-depth analysis from leading mission thinkers will broaden your understanding of holism in action. $12.95

▶ *Serving With the Poor in Africa*, Tetsunao Yamamori, Bryant L. Myers, Kwame Bediako and Larry Reed, editors. Actual cases from different African countries contextualize holistic ministry. Commentary and analysis highlights such topics as holistic healing, AIDS, evangelism and more. $15.95

▶ *Serving With the Poor in Asia*, Tetsunao Yamamori, Bryant L. Myers & David Conner, editors. Cases and commentary from seven different Asian contexts reveal how holism impacts anthropology, theology and other disciplines. $15.95

Urban mission titles:

▶ *God So Loves the City: Seeking a Theology of Urban Mission*, Jude Tiersma and Charles Van Engen, editors. An international team of urban practitioners explore the most urgent issues facing those who minister in today's cities. Their unique new methodology reveals the first steps toward a theology for urban mission. $21.95

▶ *Signs of Hope in the City*, Robert C. Linthicum, editor. Christian leaders from around the world, including Ray Bakke, Viv Grigg and Robert Linthicum, discuss the critical factors that will surround urban mission into the 21st century. Their dynamic dialogue challenges you to reflect on many innovative urban ministry theories. $7.95

▶ *Costly Mission*, Michael Duncan. The author's candid personal story of ministry in the slums of the city reveals the tribulations of an urban missionary and reminds us that such a calling is costly—often at a  personal level. $9.95

Recent MARC titles:

▸ *Sexually Exploited Children*, Phyllis Kilbourn and Marjorie McDermid, editors. One million children are forced into child prostitution every year and an estimated 10 million children worldwide are victims of the sex industry. As difficult as it is to address, we can no longer avoid the problem. This volume is a hands-on, practical resource for people who are ready to respond. It is uniquely designed to help you become an effective instrument to facilitate Christ's healing and love to broken children.  $24.95

▸ *Together Again: Kinship of Word and Deed*, Roger S. Greenway. One of America's most respected missionary statesmen, Roger Greenway reunites evangelism and social action under the banner of evangelical missions in this concise but powerful presentation.
$5.95

▸ *Choosing a Future for U.S. Missions*, Paul McKaughan, Dellanna O'Brien and William O'Brien. Takes a hard look at current mission realities and offers you promising new possibilites for the future of your organization. Engaging dialogue between church leaders and mission agency leaders highlights current mission dilemmas and presents a new learning methodology to help you identify and choose a vision for the future of your organization.  $11.95

▸ *Mission Handbook 1998-2000*, John A. Siewert and Edna G. Valdez, editors. The premier mission networking resource. Listings for over 800 mission agencies bring you key information about U.S. and Canadian organizations, including names of CEOs, phone and fax numbers, e-mail addresses, Web site URLs and more. Also contains up-to-date information about today's paramount mission concerns, including trends and analysis.
$49.95

---

## Contact us toll free in the U.S.: 1-800-777-7752

Direct: (626) 301-7720 • Web: www.marcpublications.com

800 W. Chestnut Ave.
Monrovia, CA  91016-3198  USA

World Vision

MARC books
are published by
World Vision

---

*Ask for the MARC Newsletter and complete publications list*